Second Chances

Lisa Battalia

BATTLEWORKS PUBLISHING
Langley, WA

Battleworks Publishing

Langley, WA

Contact www.lisabattalia.com

ISBN Paperback 979-8-9866896-2-3

ISBN Hardcover 979-8-9866896-3-0

Contents

To Stephen, whose joy for living made him larger than life, whose struggles made him all too human. My dearest brother, oh, how we miss you.

Chapter One

It was almost like Brandon was in Lori's room, not three time zones and thousands of miles away. Lori only had to pat the duvet a few times to find her phone and read Brandon's text message one more time before bed, his comforting words like the last sip of buttery wine.

Baby, I miss you. Wish I was holding you. Sweet dreams.

Lori drifted off contentedly but by the predawn hours felt like she had chugged a pint of yearning with a chaser of doubt. Wide awake and restless, Lori ticked off her frustrations. She wanted Brandon there with her, not the lonely weight of his imagined arms. How could their relationship ever take root, each still tethered to the opposite coast by an entire life built during the decades apart? Once-a-month weekends, deferring responsibilities while they took turns to travel, crisscrossing the country so they could be together; they were managing, but how long could it be sustained? Especially as they had screwed things up before, with Lori's insecurities and Brandon's wanderlust, both of their missed cues and bad timing. Certainly they were older and wiser with age, but did the universe really dole out second chances, especially if you blew it more than once already? Lori could recall every twist and turn on a path she had started down as a teenager, a convoluted journey that somehow, miraculously, deposited her back in Brandon's arms in midlife. She still had no idea where the road would take them.

Brandon McManus was the rare New York City borough kid transplanted to Lori's picture-perfect village nestled on Long Island Sound. It could not have been easy for Brandon's mom, Joanne, a single mother at a time when divorce was nearly unheard of in their sleepy hometown, but Joanne wanted better schools and safer streets for Brandon and his sister, Sarah. Brandon fit in quickly at their high school because he made the varsity lacrosse and soccer teams. The girls, though, saw something more than that. Brandon was very cute. He was worldly-wise, a bit exotic for their small town. Lori's best friend, Sharon, grabbed him as her boyfriend. By graduation, Lori and Brandon were friends, two quiet kids who benefited from their position in the orbit of Sharon's popularity. When Sharon exited for a summer internship, though, Lori and Brandon were suddenly hanging out alone. Years later, ensconced in her tidy, suburban house in Maryland, Lori could still remember the thrill of hanging on to Brandon's every word, and his attention, discovering she had smarter things to say when the right guy was listening.

Lori lost her virginity to Brandon late that summer of their senior year. She would like to believe she felt guilty because of Sharon, but they were on the verge of a whole new stage of life. The warmth of Brandon's spotlight gave Lori courage, and she took her chance on a muggy, moonlit night. She led Brandon to the nearby woods and her favorite hiding place in the rocks. It was hardly wilderness, but there was always something enchanting about a forest, and the small-town girl believed she was showing off something a bit wild to the city-slicker boy. When the boy kissed the girl, there was no turning back, even though the girl admitted to her status as a virgin and the boy was momentarily reluctant. Lori insisted. Perhaps she was bored of her virtue, but Lori remembered it as more compelling. The push and pull she felt with Brandon, that she was someone interesting and could be…somehow more, demanded a physical expression. Brandon was kind and careful. Still, when he ejaculated, his deep-blue eyes filled with hunger and something like awe. Of course, Sharon returned from her summer with expectations of Brandon, and he didn't break up with Sharon immediately. Lori shut Brandon out, hurt, of course, but also afraid she would never be as desirable as a girl like Sharon or as smart as Brandon seemed to think she was.

It was a shock when Brandon showed up sophomore year at Lori's genteel liberal arts college as a transfer student. Lori was doing well academically but had yet to find her social footing. She was elated to have a best friend. Brandon was determined to make up for missed educational opportunities, and they spent evenings poring over class work and grappling with big ideas before they had the chutzpah to take over the school newspaper when the former staff got too cozy with the administration. What controversies could have been so important? Lori wondered, suspecting their self-righteousness would embarrass the affluent, middle-aged mother of two she had become. Those long nights with Brandon at the print shop, though, writing on the fly, anticipating the fuss they would cause on campus, the excitement was real. They weren't romantic partners. Lori still felt the shame of losing to Sharon and feared sex would ruin the

3

best friendship she ever had. That didn't stop her from longing for Brandon, even as he got serious with a girl named Jocelyn. Lori daydreamed that Brandon would find her alone in a hallway and pull her into a hidden corner, the need to be quick and secretive driving her fantasy. He would kiss her hard, immediately open her mouth with his tongue, and shove his hand down the front of her pants, curious fingers finding her wet. She could nearly cum to such thoughts, even in a room crowded with their friends.

Instead, they graduated college, and Brandon moved west with Jocelyn. It secretly stung, but Lori still had her best friend. She could not help thinking about life in anticipation of how she would describe it to Brandon and how that made her more curious and aware. They wrote each other long letters and occasionally came back to their hometown at the same time. Lori and Brandon would wander the tree-lined streets or meet up at the one bar and talk their way slowly through the places they had seen and how they planned to change the world. It was their own form of foreplay, and they would rush to find someplace barely private enough to satisfy the agonizing buildup and furtive sex that was intense and wild. Brandon seemed to want her as much as she needed him, but then he was gone, back to Jocelyn, leaving Lori confused and hurt.

By then, Lori was attending law school. She was bored by her first jobs and observed that women got the demeaning support roles unless they had a professional degree. Lori still had dreams of making a difference in the world. She met her soon-to-be-ex, Peter, at the prestigious Washington, DC law firm that hired her after graduation. He was the senior associate on Lori's first assignment. The hours were crazy long, but Peter helped Lori navigate her new role. She was surprised at how much she liked the work despite that the clients were corporations with plenty of resources. Lori had to be quick, tough, and

4

smart, and she thrived to be taken seriously, not to mention deemed a success. She shared that with Peter. Lori's Italian-American parents were impressed by Peter's Mayflower pedigree, a vulnerability, Lori suspected, of families that still described themselves by a qualifier. It was even better that Peter's grandparents removed themselves from the Social Register as a gesture of social enlightenment. Before Lori knew it, she and Peter were engaged. It seemed so logical to plan a grown-up life. They promised each other to leave the law firm and do "good" work once student loans were paid off and they bought a house.

Brandon and Jocelyn came to Lori's wedding. Lori also furiously made out with Brandon under the deck of Lori and Peter's townhouse not long before the celebration while Peter and Jocelyn chatted in the living room upstairs. Lori knew how cliché that sounded, but she didn't dump Peter at the altar. That only happened in the movies. Anyway, Brandon was unsure what he wanted to do for a living, still tagging along with Jocelyn on her quest to be a famous modern-dance artist. Lori was afraid that Brandon would always be a dreamer, uncompromising in his beliefs but unable to commit to a family or even pay his bills.

Lori's life seemed stuck on fast-forward once her children came along. She felt a ferocious love for Ben the moment he was born. Lori went back to work but quickly succumbed to the never-good-enough syndrome, missing important work deadlines and Ben's early milestones. When Catherine was born, Lori quit her job. They didn't need two incomes anymore. Lori felt a new and vital purpose—to safeguard and shepherd her most important creations—and her heart was full. Lori failed, however, to anticipate the effects on her marriage, that her and Peter's worlds would grow immeasurably distant and unequal. Peter never left the law firm; he worked even harder, if that was imaginable, and succeeded wildly. Lori often felt like Peter's secretary and the family administrator, utterly alone in both the joys and minutia of their children's lives. She stopped being interested in Peter's work. Their home practically vibrated with a simmering, unspoken resentment on Lori's part that Peter was never there when they needed him, and, on Peter's part, it seemed, anger that when he was there, nobody seemed to care.

It was still a body blow when Peter left on one day's notice with no arguments or discussion. It made no sense to Lori; the dysfunction of their lives seemed so normal, judged against the families all around them. Fathers all worked long hours to afford the luxuries of their entitled lives. The children were the mothers' primary responsibility because everyone agreed that the continuing ability to grab the brass ring was a family's highest priority. Half of all marriages end in divorce, but not in that competitive world, not with those ambitions. Lori felt isolated and ashamed when Peter left, emotions she bulldozed through to normalize her kids' lives as if she could ever really shield them from the pain of divorce. Not surprisingly, the shame lingered, that she failed her kids and the dream of a perfect family.

Lori was also coming to understand that her marriage was not simply a victim of divergent work/life priorities. Work pressures were Peter's means to justify his selfishness. Lori could still remember standing in a cold, pouring rain on a Cub Scouts camping trip, embarrassed by her difficulty in assembling the tent. They were the only fatherless family on the trip because Peter signed up at the last minute for a solo weekend to unwind at a sports-car driving school. What Lori struggled with only after Peter left her was how to forgive herself. When did she lose the courage to ask for what the family needed? Why did she stop believing she needed anything herself?

That was Lori's state of mind when Brandon stepped back

into her life. A brief meeting after losing touch for many years. It was Christmas in their same, sleepy hometown, of course. Lori was sitting with a cup of eggnog in Joanne's living room, still in shock at Peter's recent desertion and taking baby steps to re-engage socially. Brandon walked in with his lanky, pony-tailed teenage daughter, her nose in a book. Brandon was still so handsome, tall, and fit, his close-cropped hair thick and mostly dark. Lori forgot that middle-aged men did not have to fade to soft, balding, and gray. She felt awkward standing there gawk-ing, ignoring that her life was a train wreck so she could trade small talk with the man who was her elusive, idealistic first love. Lori bolted for the door. When Brandon followed Lori to her car, looked at her the way he always had, and asked how she was really doing, everything shifted. Lori finally could tell someone how scared she felt, how ashamed, how guilty, how hurt by Peter's betrayal. Brandon attentively listened before he kissed her. He certainly was not a teenager anymore. For the first time in ages, Lori felt seen and safe and...oh god, red-hot desire.

It was nine months before Lori accepted Brandon's invita-tion to come to see him in Seattle. She was afraid to destroy a fantasy employed to keep her afloat, like a Herculean ghost, as she sleepwalked through a marriage, tended Peter's ego and ambitions, juggled the children's demands; their busy life intent on swamping her. It was the dream of an alternate life with Brandon, one more equal, passionate, and meaningful. What if an actual relationship could not live up? When Lori found the courage to visit Brandon, she convinced herself it would be a fling to get Brandon out of her head and move on. Wrong again. There was still crazy chemistry and something deeper still. They had managed a few visits since that first; each one left Lori feeling steadier. Brandon's generous affection and his chal-lenge to Lori to embrace her sexual desires were enough to remind Lori she was once a dreamer and a fighter. She wanted to be those things again.

Lori was still wary, though, wobbling on the cusp between renewed strength and residual fears. Lori and Brandon had restarted a relationship, but they could never re-enter the bubble of intimacy existent when they were young and full of possibility, before mortgages, kids, and exes. They were doing a good job pretending, sure. They'd made a pact for once-monthly weekends as if it was just the two of them, resolutely ignoring all the complications pounding at the door. As if there was all the time in the world for purposeful conversations and intense pleasure; steep hikes with ever-shifting views of mountains and sea when it was Lori's turn to travel to Seattle; the leisure to daydream a new life where they could be together with their kids. Lori wanted that badly, but she knew she was still threading a dangerous needle. Lori wasn't ready to upset the reality that a majority of her days unfolded on a different coast, flat and decidedly unchanged, carefully tended around the needs of Ben and Catherine. Lori learned it was safer that way after she impulsively took her kids to Seattle for a visit with Brandon and Fiona. Lori's sister, Emily, and Lori's best friend, Jeanette, were imploring Lori to find someone closer to home and less complicated to fall in love with, but it seemed a fragile miracle to have Brandon back in her life. Lori could imagine even more happiness by embracing the complications. It was also entirely possible to lose him again, to the distance and the responsibilities that attached in middle age like greedy barnacles. Then where would she be?

Lori's phone chimed with a new text from Brandon as daylight began to brighten the sky beyond her window.

Morning Beautiful!

She smiled before texting back, noting it was four-thirty in the morning in Seattle.

You're up early!

Lori sat up in her king-size bed, rubbed the sleep out of her eyes, glanced to confirm she was indeed alone. Lori had barely mussed the covers on one small third.

I wanted to wish you good luck today.

Oh shit, Lori remembered, throwing her head back on the pillow. She needed a lot more than luck to get through the day ahead. Thankfully, Ben and Catherine were with Peter for a dad's weekend. That meant one less set of responsibilities, at least until school let out. Ben, nearly eighteen, Catherine, fifteen, were certainly old enough to fend for themselves, yet Lori still made them breakfast for a good start to the day and packed them lunch.

Wish you were here. No kids around this morning.

Damn! The things we could do. I'd make you be loud.

Ugh. Why aren't you here?

Sorry, baby. I had no idea Jocelyn planned to run off to New York.

Jocelyn had been Brandon's ex for many more years than Peter was Lori's, and like Peter, Jocelyn was mostly an absent parent. Lori had figured out it did not much matter. The co-parenting dance was inescapable, even if the partnering was infrequent and you mostly just stepped on each other's toes.

How can she do that?

It's her MO.

Can you still come east next weekend?

Don't worry. Jocelyn knows I'll kill her
if she's not back in time to take care of her daughter.

I'm glad. Thank you. How's Fiona?

She's good. No thanks necessary. I'm starving for you.

Lori grinned and felt the familiar, sharp stab of desire, releasing enough endorphins to loosen worry's hold. Brandon seemed to read her regardless of the distance.

Let me walk you through a quickie.
Climax is good before a fight,
raises the testosterone level.

Seriously? You remain a font of fascinating wisdom.

I studied warrior cultures for the defensive tactics
training I run at the FBI Academy. I'll let you in
on a secret. For all our techie brilliance, life still
revolves around basic needs and instincts.

LOL

An orgasm will be good for you today. Can't argue with that!

I guess not.

Lori's hand was already inching beneath the elastic band of her ratty pajama bottoms. She was thinking, wistfully, how she always slept luxuriously naked with Brandon.

I bet you're wet already!

Of course. From the moment I got your text.
I'll need both hands if I'm going to be quick about it.

LOL! Have at it.

Lori dropped her phone and closed her eyes, immediately conjuring Brandon's face between her legs. A wayward, dark curl falling on his forehead, eyelids hooded by translucent skin pulsing with the tenacity of his desire. Lori surrendered to her imagination. Her fingers became Brandon's tongue, searching, then locked on target, a weapon of sorts, honed by skill and previous gambits. Every one of Lori's muscles tensed happily, nerves swollen and buzzed as she brought herself to climax. She expelled a deep moan, welcoming the rout, confident that Brandon would chivalrously accept her surrender and send her off to win the real battle.

Thank you, baby. I feel better already!

Glad to hear it.

I better get ready for combat.

That's the spirit!

Lori dropped the phone again, stretched, and groaned, trying to muster the will to get out of bed. Mondays were always hard, but that Monday... She sighed and shook her head. Her phone chimed again.

You've got this!

Would she ever tire of that particular sound signaling a text from Brandon? It still gave her butterflies of excitement, like waking to a snow day. Another ping from her phone.

I've known you a long time, Lori. Remember back in college, how quick you were to pick an argument or take on a righteous cause? You're smart. You can be tough. You know what's what. Let everyone see that!

If only it was that easy, Lori thought, as she flung off the covers. She was still bemoaning how such a day could have happened as she brushed her teeth roughly. Coffee wasn't sitting well. Her stomach tightened again into a grouchy knot of nerves. They hadn't slept well either. None of it was in her control, Lori reminded the face in the mirror, steadying her hand to not make a mess of the mascara.

Lori was working toward that morning's job interview for almost two months. She heard about the opening from Jeanette. *That's what best friends are for...* Lori could hear Jeanette's jubilant croon, and Jeanette deserved the credit. Lori would never have discovered the opening if Jeanette hadn't known someone who knew someone who worked at the small, not-for-profit foundation that lobbied for the interests of kids with

12

learning differences. The salary was almost laughable compared to Lori's last paycheck from the law firm, but she didn't miss her power suits and impressive client roster. Lori could rely on Peter's promised alimony. As much as she hated the dependence and the begrudging gratitude it required of her, alimony gave Lori the freedom to work on issues and help people that she cared about. Catherine was diagnosed with dyslexia and ADHD early on. She had parents who could afford expensive educational testing, tutors, and an array of therapists. Lori had the time and energy to stay on top of the endless details of Catherine's educational plan. Not everyone was so lucky. It also was fortuitous that the foundation's offices were nearby and the hours somewhat part-time. Lori could still pick up Catherine at the bus stop and help her navigate homework struggles.

It had still taken all Lori's reluctant courage to apply, despite that she volunteered to run a million projects at the kids' schools and for local charities. In that work Lori aced, without formal training, project management, fundraising, recruitment, marketing, and publicity. None of it shut down the practiced voice in her head: Who would want to hire you after all these years? Then there was the application, pulling together a résumé, job references, pay requirements, things Lori had not thought about in years. Lori managed, but was still a bit shocked when the foundation called to schedule a phone interview. They seemed particularly interested that Lori had a law degree. Even if she was rusty, Lori could provide legal advice as needed. The foundation narrowed down the search to three finalists who the board of directors would meet in person.

Obviously, Lori couldn't say she was unavailable, even after she got the imposing summons in the mail. Her divorce proceedings, which Lori and Peter had been negotiating through their attorneys for over a year, were unexpectedly set for a formal court hearing on the exact day that the organization—

Lori hoped, desperately since she had made it that far, would be her new employer—set aside for final interviews. It was the one day when all the necessary staff could be in the office. Lori's interviews were scheduled for the morning. The hearing started at one in the afternoon. Thankfully, Lori could make it without asking the foundation to accommodate her schedule before she was even offered the job. Apparently, you don't say "no thanks, not convenient" in a court case, her divorce lawyer sternly informed her, not unless you absolutely could not make it.

"I didn't even know there was a court case." Lori tried hard not to scream at her attorney.

"Peter has changed things," her lawyer had answered nonchalantly.

Chapter Two

Lori dug deep to find an old work skirt and blazer, professional but not too much. Her silk blouse, she discovered, was a wrinkled mess, squished between sweaters and jackets she only recently unpacked into her tiny, cramped closet. She should have taken it to the cleaners. Lori made dry cleaning runs at least twice a week when she was responsible for Peter's impeccable wardrobe after the delivery service failed to return his favorite shirt on time. How did Peter manage? Lori wondered, searching to find the ironing board buried behind a basket of never-likely-to-be-ironed linen napkins and tablecloths. They were ridiculously expensive and used once, long ago, at a dinner party for Peter's clients. She should have donated them to Goodwill when she moved, Lori thought, as she struggled to set up the board without tripping over sets of shoes she had pulled out for consideration.

Cursing at obstacles cluttering the floor of her tiny bedroom, Lori reminded herself that her new home was cozy, not small—the consolation prize in the game called "Division of Marital Assets." Her book club friends were impressed by how fast Lori settled in, how warm and inviting she made her new place. "Exactly like you," they told her. Implying, since they were Peter's neighbors again and would know with a glance from the sidewalk that the "marital property," their large, lovely house Peter had moved back into, remained mostly dark and empty. Lori took one last look in the hall mirror, straightened her jacket collar, and gave herself a pep talk: Stop lamenting, get moving, and kick some butt!

Lori arrived at the foundation's offices a few minutes early. She fussed with lipstick in the visor mirror. She tried to fix her hair, caught in an awkward stage between the short, practical cut she'd worn for years and growing it out into something more… sexy? Lori slapped up the visor. "I am strong and smart," she mumbled, remembering Brandon's words, then took a deep breath, exited the car, and shut the door with a decisive slam.

The building entrance opened to the foundation's small reception area, neat and sparse if a bit rough around the edges. Probably money better spent on the work, Lori was thinking, when an expensively-dressed woman in her late fifties walked through the interior door, right hand extended.

"Ms. Brewster, I presume."

"Yes, and Lori is fine."

"Lori, then. We're ready for you. Come on back."

Lori followed, worried that she should have worn a suit, but the whole thing was over in a blur. Before Lori had time to be nervous, she was saying thank you and being shown towards the door to reception. Lori caught the eye of a young woman in a crisp pantsuit. She looked to be just out of graduate school. Her makeup was flawless; blond, shoulder-length hair parted and straightened with military precision. They grimly nodded to each other as Lori exited the parking lot. She drove straight to the courthouse, afraid to lose any momentum. It took some time to find a parking space, but she called Brandon.

"Hey there. Can you talk? I have a few minutes before court." Lori could hear Brandon grumbling under his breath, likely some insult about Peter. "I wanted to tell you the interview went well."

"I knew you'd do great," Brandon said.

"It was easier than I expected to explain away the 'mommy years.' Almost everyone who works there took time off to raise kids."

"Interesting."

"Turns out I knew more than I thought about the work they do from my battles to get Catherine the help she needs at school."

"What do you know!"

"I saw my competition. She was a lot younger, with way better grooming instincts. She looked ready to take over the world!"

"Superficial details!"

"She certainly looked the part."

"The world can't throw you over yet, Lori."

Lori laughed, but it was tentative. "I don't know… Midlife. Raising teenagers. A single mom for all intents and purposes. The foundation might prefer the younger competition's dress for success. And her lack of complications. Anyway, now I need to get through this f'ing court hearing."

"You can say it, Lori. It's a fucking crap move by Peter."

Lori unloaded her keys and phone as instructed by courthouse security. Stood to be searched for weapons while her legs trembled. She had eaten a few bites of a protein bar that she grabbed on her way out that morning. Despite, or because of, the suste-nance, all Lori's unspent nervousness from the morning's inter-views regrouped into a cement block lodged tightly in her belly. Where were Brandon's magic fingers when she needed them? The thought made her smile. Lori threw back her shoulders and stood a little taller before she checked the overhead monitor and headed to the courtroom of the judge that ordered her to appear. Lori found her lawyer, Naomi, waiting outside the door.

"We can go in when they're done with the hearing in progress," Naomi said.

"I'm nervous," Lori confessed.

"I expect it's a preliminary matter, and I will do the talking. Think of it as a business meeting. We're here to learn what Peter's got on his mind."

"That doesn't help. Peter's a trial attorney. This is his element, and he hates to lose."

"Lori, you're a smart, competent woman."

Lori suddenly wished people would stop saying that. It felt like nonsense considering the facts. She was standing outside a courtroom. The life she constructed around the well-being of her family was to be splayed before some judge, who, Lori suspected, would not have the time or patience to understand a family in its small and important details. Then Lori saw Peter and his attorney walking towards the courtroom. They were wearing business suits, of course, but somehow, the matching strut, the identical, tight smiles, they looked like Spartans girded for battle.

"Naomi," Peter's lawyer said to Lori's attorney, saccharine smooth.

"Hello, Paul," Naomi responded. "Good to see you. Shall we go in?"

Peter followed his attorney with a nod to Lori and a barely audible hello. Lori and Naomi led the rear. The clerk called

18

them up to the counsel's tables before they had a chance to take seats in the gallery. The judge jumped right in.

"I'm not sure why we're here today," she said, shifting her gaze from high on the bench, first at Lori, then Peter. "Your attorneys have submitted what looks like a comprehensive, signed agreement dividing the marital property and establishing joint legal and physical custody of the children, as well as an access schedule. I'm prepared to issue a final divorce decree. Actually, as I think you are both aware," she looked at the attorneys with raised eyebrows, "I would have done so by written order without the need for the parties to appear."

"Your Honor." Peter's attorney stood up. "We asked for a hearing today because my client has some concerns…."

"You're not, I hope," the judge interrupted, looking over at Peter's lawyer like a hawk surveying its mark, "rethinking alimony. The agreement is generous to your client's wife, but no more so than is appropriate for a woman who has sidelined her professional career to raise the children."

Naomi turned her head slightly and gave Lori a subtle smile.

"Actually, Your Honor, my client has some concerns about the welfare of the children."

"What!" Lori gasped. She stopped herself when Naomi shot her a look.

"Continue," the judge ordered.

"Ms. Brewster is engaged in a relationship with a man that lives in Seattle. She travels there frequently, and her boyfriend comes to Maryland as well. Mr. Brewster is concerned about what the children have been exposed to and that the relationship is causing them unnecessary anxiety."

Lori was reeling. The tone, if not the words…, Peter's lawyer made it sound so unseemly.

"Mr. Parker," the judge flipped through her files, "your

19

client has been separated from his wife for," she paused scanning, "approaching two years. New relationships for both parties are inevitable. I'm sure you would agree."

"Of course, but...,"

"I'm going to stop you for the moment," the judge interjected. "I would like to hear from Ms. White."

Naomi stood up and glanced at her notes.

"Good afternoon, Your Honor. Mr. Parker is correct that my client is involved with a gentleman in Seattle. She has been careful about managing the relationship relative to her children. Her friend visits when the children are with their father, Mr. Brewster."

"I have to interrupt," said Peter's attorney. "Ms. Brewster brought the children to Seattle some months ago."

"Is that true?" The judge turned to Naomi.

"Yes, Your honor. Mr. McManus, that is Ms. Brewster's friend, is also a father, and they spent a few days sightseeing with the children."

"Seems innocent enough," the judge said, and it seemed to Lori that the judge's face softened.

Naomi spoke again before Peter's attorney could respond. "My client will tell you that she regrets she may have introduced the children to Mr. McManus too quickly. However, the circumstances were such that she planned to travel to Seattle by herself during a time when Mr. Brewster was scheduled to take the children on vacation. Mr. Brewster canceled the trip at the last minute. Ms. Brewster was trying to salvage the children's spring break."

Peter's attorney jumped up aggressively. "Your Honor, during this alleged 'sightseeing' trip, the parties' son, Benjamin, saw Ms. Brewster kiss her so-called *friend*."

Lori noticed the attorney's use of air quotes and started seeing red. Naomi put a firm hand on Lori's shoulder.

20

"Really, Mr. Parker, is this worthy of the court's time?"

"There is also the matter that, more recently, Benjamin has seen some of his mother's texts with her boyfriend, sexually-charged texts."

Naomi's hand stayed tight, so Lori stared straight ahead. She was in shock, before anger kicked in at Peter and his lawyer, then humiliation, and, shit, when did Ben...? Why would he tell his father? Lori was having a hard time breathing. Her little boy... no, Ben was growing into a perceptive, young man. How could she have let that happen?

"Mr. Brewster," the judge spoke directly to Peter, "have you discussed the issue with your wife?"

"No, Your Honor, I thought it more appropriate to..."

"Let me stop you there. I am not diminishing the importance of what has been raised, but when you two," she looked at Peter and paused for a moment before turning to Lori, "became parents, you committed to your children's welfare, first and foremost, no matter what happens between you. In your papers, you have agreed to co-parent. It is my strong belief that the courtroom is not the place of first resort to handle the continuing, often difficult, issues you will face. Do you both understand what I am saying?"

Before they could answer, Peter's lawyer spoke. "With all due respect, my client feels that the court should prohibit the children from spending time with Ms. Brewster when she is with her lover."

Naomi interjected quickly. "I strenuously object to the..."

The judge put up her hand. "Does the submitted parenting agreement address how the parties will handle new relationships, overnights with new partners when the children are present, etc.?"

"It does, Your Honor," Naomi answered. "And I might note that the couple's older child, Ben, is nearly eighteen."

"Still…," Peter's lawyer tried again.

"Mr. Parker," the judge cut him off, "is there anything else the court needs to address today?"

"There is." Paul picked up a paper from the counsel's table and waved it towards the bench.

"My client seeks an order forbidding Ms. Brewster from moving out of state with the couples' children, at least not with their daughter Catherine who is still a minor. Ms. Brewster was unwilling to agree to that as part of the parenting plan."

"Is that correct?" The judge turned to Lori's attorney.

"Ms. Brewster has no current plans to move out of state," Naomi answered.

"Is your client willing to put that in writing?"

"She would prefer not to, in order that the parenting plan remains flexible. Ms. Brewster has family in New York, and her parents have health issues that could require her assistance to take care of them."

The judge shook her head, seeming a bit annoyed.

"Ms. Brewster, do you have plans to move out of Maryland?"

Naomi answered. "Your Honor, Ms. Brewster has no current plans. Just this morning, she interviewed for a job here in the county."

"That's encouraging, but I'd like to hear from your client." The judge directed her eagle eyes at Lori. "Do you foresee moving out of the state?"

Lori stood up; it seemed the right thing to do.

"I do not, at the moment, but my husband, I mean, Mr. Brewster, spends very little time with our children. It seems unfair …, I mean, if there is a better place for the three of us, or at least me and Catherine, to live, why we…" Lori paused, sensing her argument sounded weak, and she harnessed some rusty legal training and started again.

"Your Honor." It came out a little wobbly, so Lori took a deep breath before she continued. "In the past two years, there have been multiple occasions when, regardless of the shared custody agreement, Mr. Brewster has been unable, at the last minute, to take the children as scheduled. He has client trips that have taken him out of town for weeks, even a month at a time. He has made special plans with the children, and has promised to be at important events, then repeatedly canceled because of a client conflict." Lori was on a roll and paused long enough to notice it felt good. "We are here to determine what is best for our children, and I believe we can all agree that it is not best for them constantly to be reminded that they are not his priority, particularly if there are adults in their life that can be more consistent and supportive."

Naomi stood up next to Lori. "If I may…"

"No need, Ms. White." The judge looked again at Lori as if considering something.

"I understand your concerns, Ms. Brewster, but it will be difficult for Mr. Brewster to improve on his record if the children move out of the state." The judge scribbled something on the papers in front of her. Without looking up, she spoke to the assembled group. "I will sign the divorce decree and enter a separate order barring Ms. Brewster from moving out of Maryland with the minor child. Ms. White, if your client's plans change, or...," the judge's gaze shifted to Lori, "if you have additional concerns about the time Catherine is spending with her father, we can revisit the issue. Ms. Brewster, would you like me to grant you permission to change your name?"

Lori turned to Naomi, confused. "Do I need to do that?" She asked under her breath.

"If you want to legally go back to using your maiden name," Naomi whispered back.

Lori hadn't considered that. There was a time when the

WASPy gravitas of Peter's surname mattered, as much as she hated to admit that. It would also mean something to renounce it. In a courtroom of all places. Peter's playground. Lori squirmed in the chair. As empowering as it felt, changing her name might be a fatal blow to her children's hope that they were still, somehow, a family.

"Not at the current time, Your Honor."

"Fine. Is there anything else counsel?"

Both attorneys quickly answered no before Lori was ushered by Naomi towards the courtroom exit. Lori looked down at her shoes. She did not want to see the other faces in the gallery, fearing they might — at least before airing their own dirty laundry — be enjoying a sense of schadenfreude. She absolutely would not look at Peter. Naomi put out a hand and told Lori to stay put outside the courtroom while Naomi rushed ahead. Apparently, she needed to say something to Paul. When Naomi came back, she directed Lori to a small bench.

"Sit down. Take some deep breaths. This is why I work so hard to settle these cases without going to court."

"I thought we'd all agreed on that plan." Lori was shaking her head.

"The fact is," Naomi said, "we should have had a signed decree months ago. Paul kept finding reasons to delay. He ignored my requests for a sit-down so they could have a petty confrontation, I'm afraid. I'm sorry, Lori, I got played."

"It was awful."

"I'm guessing that was their plan, but look on the bright side."

Lori looked at Naomi, baffled.

"No, really. You won today, hands down. You're officially divorced. You've got a solid financial settlement as long as you're cautious with your money. We successfully front-loaded alimony, so you'll be okay even if you eventually remarry. Don't do that too soon."

Lori made a pained face.

"That's all in your control," Naomi continued. "The judge wasn't falling for any of Peter's bullshit. Go out tonight and celebrate."

"I can't," Lori grumbled. "I have the kids."

There was only enough time to head to Catherine's bus stop. The radio came on automatically when Lori started the car, the voices of the local public radio station that usually made her feel virtuous for listening and helped alleviate the humdrum of an ordinary day. She flipped off the audio. Nothing could distract Lori from her anger, not to mention that she was the parent in charge after that humiliation. She must greet the kids with a smile and follow the expert's advice: Never tell your children what a jerk their other parent could be.

"Siri," Lori growled, "call Emily."

"Hey, Sis. What's up?"

"Arrggghhhh." Lori sounded feral.

"Wait. You had your court date today, right?"

"Just left the courthouse. I'm officially divorced."

"So why do you sound like you want to kill someone?"

"Peter made the whole thing incredibly ugly."

"Of course he did. Did you get what you needed, though?"

"Mostly, I guess, moneywise yes, if I'm careful. I can't move away with the kids, not without going back to court."

"I told you Peter would never go for that."

"What if I want to move to New York, to be closer to you and Mom and Dad, so my kids can feel part of a real family?"

"Come on, Lori."

"It's not that far. Peter would see them as little as he does now."

"Lori, you're the best mom I know. You've given those kids every ounce of your love and attention. That's the definition of family. Period. Anyway, you don't want to move to New York. I see what's going on."

Lori paused for a moment. "Emmy, it's not like I'm gonna pack up the car, throw the kids in the back, and move to Seattle. It's not the right time. Ben's in his last year of high school. Catherine just got started, but…, dammit, I don't want to wait forever." Lori's sudden anger gave way to a pained laugh.

"What's so funny?"

Lori answered slowly, trying to put her thoughts into words. "All those years married to Peter… 'I,' 'you,' 'the children,' it was always a zero-sum game. Then I spend all of four days together with Brandon and our children." Lori's voice grew animated. "Peter pissed all over the trip, but by the end of the week, all three kids happily piled together into the back of the car. Ben acted like he made a new best friend after Brandon took him to the range. Catherine was practically giddy to be shown attention, even if it was from someone else's dad. The thing is, Em…I can see that with the right ingredients, love can multiply.

"Life is funny that way."

"Is that such a bad thing to want to show my kids?"

"It's gonna take a lot more than a few visits; you know that, right? Even then, your kids might never see it."

"Don't say that."

"Look, Sis, Thomas has been way more of a father to my kids than my ex-husband, but push comes to shove, their loyalties are still with the man they call Dad, no matter how many times he fails to show up."

"What should I do? I loved how it felt when we were all together. It makes me want more."

"Don't push it for now. You've got a lot happening on the home front. Plus, you still get weekends with Brandon, no dependents underfoot, and tons of fooling around, I assume." Emily chuckled. "Hell, do you know how many people would trade places with you for the uninterrupted sex?"

"It's not just that, Em."

"I know, but you need to keep your focus. For your kids."

"I will."

"For now, you move with caution because your ex is a prick and a hard-ass litigator."

"That's depressing."

"Not today. You're officially Lorraine Romano again. You should celebrate!"

"Actually, I didn't ask to change my name. I thought it would upset Ben and Catherine."

"There's plenty of time for that, but do something special."

"I'll have a glass of wine while I help Catherine with her homework."

"That will have to do." Emily gave a knowing laugh.

"I'll need the fortification before I talk to Ben," Lori added. "You won't believe what came up in court about... Shoot, the bus is here. I'll have to tell you later."

"Call me soon, and Lori..."

"Yes."

"Remember to breathe."

"What would I do without you, Em?"

∾

Before Lori even reached the bus stop, she caught a glimpse of Catherine letting down the armor she put on for school, her face relaxing from a scowl into its natural, trusting gaze and mischievous smile.

"Hi, Sweetie. How was your day?" Lori asked as Catherine threw her overloaded backpack onto the back seat.

"Okay, I guess." Catherine slipped into the front and shut the door. "Can we stop for frozen yogurt on the way home?"

"I don't think so. Mommy had a really long day."

"Please. Can we?" Catherine begged. "I've got so much homework tonight. I can't face it yet."

"All right," Lori said with a sigh, "but only if we find parking nearby. I cannot deal with fighting for a space right now."

Catherine finally looked over at Lori. "Are you okay, Mom? You don't look so good."

"I've had better days, but don't worry, sweetheart. I'll be fine."

Lori waited for Catherine to go to bed before talking to Ben. Her shock and anger were mostly dissipated, but Lori had no idea what she was going to say. Lori knocked on Ben's bedroom door disregarding the utter exhaustion she felt.

"Yeah," Ben said, protest infiltrating his meager response.

"It's Mom. Can I come in?"

"I was about to hit the sack."

"It's important."

"Can we talk in the morning?"

"No, Ben. I'm coming in."

She opened the door as Ben scrambled to close windows on his computer. Lori was sure she didn't want to know what he was looking at. Not then anyway.

"I heard from your dad today about something troubling."

"I'm not sure what you're…"

"You read my texts with Brandon?"

"What? No."

"Don't lie to me, Ben. When did you do this?"

"I don't know."

"Forget when. Why?"

Ben paused, closed his computer, and flipped his legs over the edge of his bed, so he was no longer reclining. It still startled Lori to see her son's body look so much like a grown man's. Ben took a deep breath and let it out.

"Do you remember that day you ran into the grocery store to get milk? You said, 'don't look at my phone.' I don't know. I thought that was, like, you inviting me to look."

"Really, Ben?"

"I don't know."

"I have a passcode on my phone."

"Mom," he made a disbelieving face, "you use the same password for everything."

"Why did you tell your dad instead of talking to me?"

"I don't know. It was disturbing." Ben's mouth curled like he was drinking sour milk. "Brandon was texting things about putting cuffs and a collar on you, and…"

"I get it," Lori interrupted. She sat down in Ben's desk chair, moving things around his desk while she tried to gather her thoughts. "First off, Ben, my phone is absolutely off-limits." She swiveled the chair, so she was looking at him directly. "Do you understand?"

"Yes."

"Yes, what?"

"I won't look at your phone."

It was Lori's turn to take a deep breath and let it out slowly. "You have to understand, Ben. Your generation seems to think sex is as inconsequential as ordering a cup of coffee, but it's the most intimate and exposed we can ever be." Lori grew animated. "That's why I'm always telling you, just because you're old enough to drive, you shouldn't be rushing into sex."

"Mom!"

"What? You're a good-looking kid, and girls always go for the athletes, right? Sex should be something more, though, and don't get me started on porn. Pornography has no reality to an actual sexual relationship."

"Mom, I'm not discussing porn with you."

Lori took another breath to refocus. "What I'm trying to say, Ben... The things that Brandon said to me, it's because we have an understanding." Lori got up and sat next to Ben on the bed. "Look at me, please," she asked him gently. "This is really important. Brandon and I are fully adult, and it's absolutely consensual. It takes a lot of maturity, honesty, and trust. When you have those things, sex can be, well, a lot of interesting things. But, buddy, you've got a long way to go."

"I'm almost eighteen, Mom. Teenagers grow up fast these days."

"Maybe. Anyway, I'm sorry you saw those texts."

"I'm sorry I looked."

"I'm still angry about that."

"You never cared before if we looked at your phone."

"What if I text things about your father or the divorce. Of course there are things now that I don't want you to see."

"You're right. I get it."

"Things have changed, Ben. For good or bad, they're gonna keep changing." Lori felt calmer, and her voice slowed down as she remembered something. "When you guys were little," Lori continued, "I tried so hard to figure out what made you tick, what it was that you needed from me. I swear every time I thought, 'I've got this,' you or Catherine would be at a brand new stage. I was flat on my ass again." Lori saw the hint of a smile on Ben's face.

"I guess that's just life," Lori said.

"What do you mean?"

"We have to keep moving with the changes, okay?"

"Okay."

"If it's something about me, or about us, you talk to me first. Promise?"

"I promise."

"Good." Lori nodded once as she pushed herself up from the bed and headed out of the room.

"Mom?"

"What?" Lori stopped halfway to closing the door.

"I think Dad has a girlfriend."

Lori squeezed hard on the handle. "That must be nice for him. Have you met her?"

"Not yet."

"Do you want to talk about it?"

"Not really."

"Are you sure?"

"Yeah."

"Then get some sleep."

Lori barely had the energy to respond to Brandon's text, but it was the fourth one he sent, and it wasn't fair to leave him hanging any longer. She pressed the call icon below Brandon's sleepy, smiling eyes staring out from the small circle on the top of her phone screen. It was a photo Lori snapped while they were drinking coffee one morning over Brandon's objections that he hadn't taken a shower. Lori felt a little spark every time she saw it, even the tiny version she uploaded to her phone contacts.

"Hey there," Lori said when Brandon picked up on the first ring.

"Lori, are you okay?"

"Yeah. I'm sorry I wasn't able to talk sooner. It's been a really long day."

"Tell me about it," Brandon said with a chuckle. "I felt bad that I couldn't check in with you earlier. I led back-to-back interviews and case meetings all day, and I was late getting Fiona from her friend's house."

"No worries. Catherine had the homework night from hell, and Ben, shit, I better wait and tell you about that when I see you next weekend."

"That's fine, but how was court? You haven't told me anything."

"It was humiliating and painful, but my lawyer tells me I should celebrate. I'm officially divorced."

"Really? Wow. You certainly buried the lede."

"You're right, so sorry." Lori laughed. "It's been a crazy day."

"How does it feel?"

"There hasn't been time for it to sink in. But good, it feels good."

"You don't sound convinced."

"No, no. It's not that. Peter pulled some ugly shit today. He's a terrible person, but I'm, literally, too tired to talk about it."

"That's okay. I understand."

"You sure?"

"Yeah. Get some sleep."

"I'm so glad you're coming. We're going to celebrate."

"If you say so."

Chapter Three

By then, they had a routine. Lori knew exactly where to pick up Brandon at the far end of the arrival zone. Lori would spy him scanning for her car, standing on the curb a head taller than anyone else. His strongly-built body, the set of his jaw, radiated restrained self-confidence. He was the stranger you would instinctually turn to for help if something bad just happened. Brandon spotted her and swung his bag over his shoulder. Lori put the car in park. Before she could hop out to greet him, Brandon threw his bag onto the back seat and slipped in next to her. He kissed her lightly on the cheek.

"Let's get out of here," he said.

"Everything okay?"

"Sure."

"Are you hungry?" Lori asked.

"Not really. I ate something on the plane."

"How was your flight?"

"Okay, a little too choppy over the Rockies."

"Sorry for that. Peter always told me I was silly to worry about turbulence; that I should think of it as bumps on the road."

Brandon was quiet.

"How's Fiona?" Lori asked finally.

"She's good. Ben and Catherine?"

"They grumbled about going to their dad's again. Peter's got a bunch of weekends to make up, but kids like nothing better than routine, right?"

"True."

There was another long pause.

"My god," Lori spat out, "we sound like an old, married couple. What's going on?" When Brandon didn't answer, she blurted out, "Talk to me."

Brandon answered after a pause. "Our last conversation worried me."

"I was so tired, but I promise to tell you all the gory details." Lori took her eyes from the road to show Brandon a quick smile, but he was staring straight ahead.

"Are you having second thoughts about your divorce?" Brandon asked tersely. "Be honest, please."

"God, no. Is that what you're worried about?" Lori's face scrunched in disbelief.

"Yes."

"Really? I had no idea."

"That's why I'm telling you."

"Do you want me to pull over? So we can talk?"

"Only if you need to."

Lori felt like she needed to, but maybe their topic of conversation was one of those it was better to have while driving. She took a deep breath. "Since you asked me to be honest, Brandon, there were times when I thought I should work things out with Peter, but only because of the pain the separation was causing Ben and Catherine."

"Kids feel the betrayal of their parents' divorce for a long time."

"I know that, but I'm learning my feelings count too. I don't have to sacrifice my happiness for their sake, do I?"

"Of course not."

"Why would I return to an empty shell of a marriage and all that resentment and loneliness?"

"In my line of work, I see women go back, sometimes again and again, to the men that hurt them most."

"Why?!" Lori gave Brandon a quick, quizzical glance.

"They may not believe they have other options. The men provide a kind of anchor and stability, however vicious, and women feel drawn back to their foothold on financial security."

"You're an FBI agent, Brandon. You protect abused women and victims of sex trafficking. That's hardly relevant to my situation."

"I'm talking about human nature, generally. I'm overexposed to it."

"Is this about money? That Peter makes more than you do?" Lori thought she saw Brandon wince; perhaps she phrased that too clumsily.

"I'm checking in, Lori. You sounded unsure when we spoke. I want to know where your head is at, determine if the situation is making me too vulnerable."

"Wow. You sound like a cop, not the man I thought loved me."

"Of course I love you, but maybe I can't separate those things. My job makes me careful."

"Okay…" Lori spoke haltingly. "I guess I can understand that."

"It's not only Peter," Brandon continued. "There must be other men who are interested in you. You're a beautiful woman."

Lori gave him a skeptical glance.

"You're not just a pretty face. There must be men that run in your same circles; divorced men that live close by and want to show off your intelligence at high-powered events, take you nice places, and yes, have more money."

Damn, she had spoken carelessly. They had exited the highway and were driving on surface roads near Lori's house, so she pulled over, put the car in park, touched Brandon's cheek, and turned his face towards her. "Brandon, I can't believe you are worrying about other men." Lori's head was shaking, eyes squinting with emphatic disbelief. "There's no one else. It makes me sick that you would think that."

"Lori, you asked what I was feeling. I'm not trying to hurt you."

"But it's so crazy. Do you know how many times a day I think about you? About the life we might build. When would I be making plans with other men?"

"I forgot, okay. Women don't think like men."

Lori looked at him, confused.

"Men are territorial by nature, and I haven't been around to defend my claim," Brandon added with half a smile.

"Are you serious?"

"No. Yes. Listen," Brandon said, taking hold of her hand, "forget I said anything."

"I'll try," Lori answered, fumbling to put the car back in gear, "but to be clear," she added with a touch of anger, "I don't run in any circles."

They parked in Lori's driveway. It was Brandon's first time actually seeing her new place, but he must have sensed her anger and didn't comment; he just grabbed his bag, held the front door open once Lori unlocked it, then stood just inside as if waiting for permission. Lori simply walked toward the kitchen. "I need a glass of wine," she said. "Do you want one?"

"Sure, or whiskey if you have it." He finally followed her in.

"I do, that brand you like. What's it called? Something with envy."

"Apropos."

"I bought it for you." Lori glanced pointedly at Brandon as she reached into the cabinet for a glass. He walked quickly towards Lori, took hold of her arm, and kissed her; finally a real kiss. Their tongues met, his like a stiff drink, melty and bracing, but Lori hesitated. Brandon pulled back and leaned in again to whisper, "Relax, Lori. You're one big knot of tension."

"It's just…, first Peter, then Ben," Lori's words were halting, "now you. Sometimes it feels like all the men in my life want to hurt me."

Brandon pulled her into a tight hug. "No, baby. I'm sorry, I needed to ask." He took her hand and led her to the kitchen table. "Tell me what happened in court."

"I really don't want to relive it. Peter had the nerve to argue that his kids shouldn't be *exposed to my lover*." Lori mimicked the lawyer's snide voice. "Then Ben tells me his father has a girlfriend. What a hypocrite."

"He's a prick."

"I guess men can be like that." Lori smirked, trying hard to shift her mood. "I suspect Peter picked a fight because of his suspicion that I never quite got over you."

"Male jealousy is not pretty; I'll give you that." Brandon reached out for Lori's hand. "Did the judge lecture you on female propriety? I'm guessing the esteemed title doesn't overcome the paternalism of the male brain."

"Actually, *she* didn't take the bait," Lori smirked as she emphasized the judge's gender.

"Wow. I'm really showing my unconscious bias in spite of all my Bureau training."

"It was certainly fun," Lori added, "to watch her cut off

Peter's lawyer and lecture Peter not to use the courtroom to handle our differences."

"She," Brandon said with emphasis, "sounds like a very wise judge."

"I didn't get off scot-free. There's nothing like having an entire courtroom hear about your sexting."

"What?!" Brandon's reaction pushed his body back in the chair.

"Peter's lawyer brought up that Ben read some of our more explicit texts."

"How the..."

"It's awful to think about, I know. I talked to Ben, and I tried my best to put what he saw in the context of grown-up sexuality."

"I think you're missing the point." Brandon pulled back his hand.

"No, really, the judge didn't fall for that either."

"What Ben did, Lori, is a huge violation of our privacy."

"Believe me; he's sorry he looked. He's just a big kid."

"He's not a kid, Lori."

She felt stopped in her tracks. It was such a sudden insight that in her anxiety for Ben, Lori failed entirely to consider how Ben's conduct would injure Brandon and the trust necessary for their relationship. Lori felt a terrible distance invade the space between where they sat on opposite sides of the snug table. "I'm so sorry, Brandon."

Brandon just stared silently at the ice cubes he was swirling in his glass.

"We're here. Together now. No need for phones."

Brandon still said nothing.

"I want to feel close to you." Lori grabbed his hand. "Please."

"I hear you, Lori. It just... changes things."

"Ben will never do it again. He promised. I've reset my passcode." Lori's tone grew pleading. "Can we go upstairs, please and cuddle?"

"Let me finish my drink."

There was a long silence before Lori got up and climbed into Brandon's lap. He was still fixated on his glass as if assessing a threat. Lori slid her fingers through his hair and kissed around his earlobe, hoping to find even the smallest softening of his mood. When she sensed it, Lori tipped back his head, found his mouth, and kissed him eagerly, her tongue searching for both lust and love. Brandon responded by grabbing Lori's head tightly. He dug his hands through Lori's hair. She leaned in and mumbled, "We'll get through this."

"Tell me you're mine." Brandon's sudden exclamation fell roughly against Lori's ear.

"I'm yours," she answered before Brandon tore at Lori's blouse, popping buttons.

Brandon buried his head in Lori's chest, but it felt more like he wanted to growl than to kiss her. Lori felt pain and relief in equal measure when Brandon grabbed a fistful of her breast. He kissed her mouth, lifted her by the buttocks, and sat her on the edge of the table before breaking off abruptly to grab at her pants and pull them down only to her knees. Brandon quickly stepped out of his own jeans and was inside Lori. Thrusting fast and furious as if to beat back interlopers, he did not kiss her. Brandon's eyes were somewhere else when he climaxed, his cum still burning inside when he pulled out, sat back down on the chair, and hung his head, breathing hard. Lori slumped her shoulders to hide her breasts. She pulled up her pants.

"What was that?"

"I don't know," Brandon answered, sounding chastened.

"Do you feel better?" Lori's tone betrayed her shock.

"A little."

"Is that another male behavior I can't understand?"

"Maybe."

Lori sat for a long moment, then reached out to stroke Brandon's face. She knew from her own frustrations how physical distance created space for serious doubts to creep in. "I think I do understand," Lori said, her voice softening despite Brandon's gruff behavior. "You needed to reclaim me?"

"Something like that."

"It was only in your imagination that there was any competition." Lori tipped his chin, so he was forced to look at her. "And Ben…, all I can say is that I'm sorry. I messed up. I'm glad you told me what you were feeling and didn't keep things bottled up."

Something heavy seemed to lift off Brandon's shoulders. He stood up and gently took Lori's hand. "Let's go upstairs and do things the right way."

They made love then, and Lori felt time stop. It seemed like Brandon needed to kiss and taste every inch of her body; her temples and earlobes, the triangles formed by her clavicles, the delicate skin on the insides of her arms, even her armpits, before anointing her breasts and belly. He moved down her legs to her toes, sucking each one, then glided back up to graze the soft flesh of her inner thighs. Lori attended to his every movement, noticing her muscles constrict and then loosen as Brandon's fingers, lips, and tongue moved across the planes and curves of her body. She tried to articulate her pleasure, but Brandon's attention unspooled any thoughts that tried to collect and be uttered until his lips finally brushed against her pussy, and Lori uttered a long, guttural moan. Her hips curled to contain the flood of sensations. Above her dark triangle, all she could see of Brandon's eyes were their crinkly corners holding a smile. Lori closed her own eyes to embrace the texture of Brandon's tongue moving in broad, wet arcs before its narrowed tip focused directly on her clit, teeth occasionally nipping. Brandon alternated places of focus and shifted pace as if constructing a tower of pleasure. When he finally tongued her deeply inside, Lori felt it like a boy thrilled to have found a puddle to play in. Her gratification spiked, an orgasm exploding in waves that spread to her fingers and toes and the roots of her hair. Her entire body shuddered and arched. Brandon lifted his head.

"I love you, Lori."

Lori raised herself from the bed and pulled Brandon towards her, their mouths a blur of her wetness, their saliva, heat. She broke apart to gulp for air. "Fuck me, Brandon, so there's not the tiniest space between us."

Brandon paused above her long enough for his eyes to sear her own, then he entered and filled her completely in one hard thrust that left Lori breathless. He scooped up her shoulders and shoved his arms beneath as Lori wrapped her legs to cinch her feet at the small of Brandon's back. Bound together, hips rocking in tandem, his cock teased her pussy until they both came, groaning through jealousy and anger to give voice to pent-up desire. Brandon collapsed his full weight on Lori with the relief of a drowning victim pulled onto the boat. Then he rolled onto his back. A few moments later, his breathing signaled unconsciousness but not before pulling Lori into a protective embrace.

❧

When Lori woke up thirsty, she dragged herself to the bathroom for some water. Returning to the bedroom, she was stopped in her tracks at the sight of Brandon's restless body. The sheets were wrapped in a wild mess around his legs. One arm was thrown back, crookedly framing his profile, while his breath escaped in an uneven stutter. Lori climbed back in next to Brandon, and his body jolted as if from a bad dream. Lori, too, had tossed and turned through the night as she tried to make peace with her feelings. It bothered her that Brandon imagined her with other men, that he could be worrying about that while she was thousands of miles away, behaving like a pathetic character in a Victorian novel uselessly pining away for him.

A tense phone call came to mind. It was late spring after Peter first got wind of Lori's trip with the kids to Seattle, and Lori was called into her attorney's office. Peter was using the alimony card to criticize her parenting decisions even though he was never around to help raise them. Lori blew a fuse. After sitting and yelling in her car, she forgot to attend an important school presentation by Catherine. A week later, driving around to organize the next school event, Lori spilled her coffee, averted her eyes from the road, and hit a telephone pole. Lori had called Brandon from the bed where she had been instructed to rest. Lori confessed that she felt overwhelmed. She probably griped that Brandon was too far away when she needed him. The shock was that he seemed so willing to concede victory to the competition (the distance, their kids, her ex, apparently the availability of richer men closer to home). After the call, Lori lay in bed agonized to imagine their breakup, but they survived the crisis. Brandon unexpectedly flew across the country to make sure Lori was okay, and when he left, they were on more solid ground. Still, the memory made Lori feel small, like a child confounded by how complicated adults could make their lives.

It seemed a better idea to tune into the noises of early morning, birdsong and dogs barking, cars ferrying kids to Saturday morning games. Familiar sounds that were muffled and comforting with Lori's ears pressed between Brandon's hand and his belly. Lori matched her breathing to Brandon's, focused on its rise and fall, slow and calm again after his earlier agitation. She cupped Brandon between his legs. He told her once how nice it felt to wake to her hand nestled there, and Brandon's soft, warm body gave Lori reassurance, like a favorite blanket. It wasn't long, of course, before his cock began to stir and stretch as if to test the day's possibilities. Lori smiled at its predictability before she traced around the sharply edged corona, her mood turning as playful as the bouncing of Brandon's member. Lori felt drawn down his abdomen. Flicking her tongue against a fully engorged cock, Lori tasted a drop of pre-cum that fed a frisky hunger, and she took him fully in her mouth. Brandon was suddenly awake, muscles tensed, but he didn't speak. Lori did not stop; she took him deeper, using lips to shield her teeth like the soft mouth of a hunting dog. When Brandon finally moaned aloud, Lori shifted to her knees. She hovered above him for a measured moment before again capturing his cock, absorbing the brief sense of gagging and taking more of him, hoping to signal that she would never betray him. She paused again to seal the message, then increased her bobbing pace to keep rhythm with Brandon's clenched ass and bucking hips.

"Fuuuuuuck, Lori." Brandon rose, then fell back as he came. "What was that?"

"You still seemed upset this morning. I wanted you to know that you have nothing to worry about."

He laughed. "I'll start worrying more if that's where it gets me. Come here." He pulled Lori down and kissed her. "I didn't realize I was bothered. You usually do enough worrying for the both of us."

"I have to confess, I am stressing over my to-do list." Lori realized that was probably background anxiety beneath her other worries.

"Oh, right. You've got home improvement projects for me. I didn't forget."

"I'm sorry. It's probably the last thing you want to do, but this house is old, and I don't know how to fix things." Lori made a face. "Peter liked to hire people, but I paid the bills. I know how much repairs cost, and I'm supposed to be cautious with my money."

"I don't mind. Go make some coffee," Brandon grinned at her, "unless you want me to make you cum first. It seems only fair."

"Tough call..." There was genuine hesitation. "I think I'll go with your handyman services," Lori said, climbing out of bed.

Brandon grabbed her ass, laughing, but she didn't turn back.

"Okay then," he said. "Tell me where to find the toolbox. I'm guessing we'll need at least one trip to the hardware store."

Chapter Four

Lori had started to love, if not everything about the old house, the simple fact that it was hers. She negotiated a good price, qualified for the mortgage, and, somewhat to her surprise, did not run from the title company offices when presented all those papers committing her alone to pay back the loan. With Brandon's visit and his handy skills, it began to feel like a home. Lori forgot how good, frustrating in spots to be sure, but how satisfying to gather supplies and repair what was broken, turn a worn item into something pretty. Lori's bedroom window could be opened more than two inches, and Brandon managed to get all the ceiling fans working. Lori admired the fans in each room when she first saw the house, disappointed that no matter how many times she alternated using the wall switch and the cords hanging from the fixtures, she could not get them moving to flush out the stale, air-conditioned air when crisp autumn arrived.

Brandon also replaced the rusted-out medicine cabinet in the bathroom Lori shared with Catherine and even added the matching set of lights. The new fixtures sat in a box for weeks. Every time Lori tried to read the installation instructions, her eyes glazed over. Brandon walked her through it slowly. Lori felt confident that, on her own, she could replace the cabinet and lights in Ben's bathroom as well. The ice dispenser worked again. That felt like a small miracle. They even scraped and spackled the wood trim and mantel around the fireplace and selected complementary colors from the paint wheel to bring out the details and add sophistication. That gave Lori ideas for painting each of the three bedrooms. The previous owners left the walls scarred with ungainly holes. Lori would take them on, one room at a time.

The projects required not one but three runs to various home supply stores. They stopped during one outing at a local deli to wolf down Rueben sandwiches, the real thing for Brandon, turkey instead of corned beef for Lori. They agreed the sandwiches were not quite as good as what you could get in New York City, but the big, melty messes were good enough. Brandon wiped some stray Russian dressing from Lori's cheek, laughing when he could not dislodge some spackle stuck there as well.

"You should see your hair," Lori told him. "You look like you've gone gray."

"I thought I had." Brandon made a face. "Got those genes from my dad, I guess, hard as I've tried not to inherit his traits."

"No! You only have a speckling of gray. It looks distinguished."

"I guess. If you like that sort of thing."

"I do," Lori said as she leaned across the table to kiss Brandon. When Lori sat back, she felt a hand on her shoulder.

"Lori, is that you?"

Lori turned. "Oh… Hi Wendy."

"I haven't seen you in a while," Wendy responded, "and I didn't recognize you. Your hair is so different, and not because it's covered in paint." Wendy was carrying a to-go bag and staring at Brandon.

"I thought I might grow it out," Lori said, flustered. "Um, Wendy, meet my friend Brandon. He's helping me with some projects on my new house."

"I heard you had to move," Wendy said.

Brandon stood up and offered his hand. "Hello Wendy, a pleasure."

"For me as well, Brandon. I don't think we've met before."

"Brandon's in town for the weekend," Lori interjected. "He lives in Seattle."

"That's quite a distance for a weekend. You must be enjoying our weather."

"I am," Brandon answered, "although it's quite nice this time of year in Seattle."

"I thought it always rained."

"A common misconception." Brandon smiled gentlemanly, though Lori could sense a sharpened edge in his response.

"So, how did you two meet?" Wendy asked.

"I don't remember. It seems like we've known each other forever," Brandon answered coyly.

"Really?" Wendy's eyebrows arched so high Lori thought they might break.

"We went to high school together and then the same college," Lori added quickly.

"How interesting." Wendy's gaze shifted from Brandon to Lori. "How is Catherine settling into high school? It must be a hard year for her."

"She's doing great. Thanks for asking."

"That's good to hear. Well, you two get back to your lunch. I've got to get these home to the hubby and crew." Wendy lifted the bag in her hand. "I'm sure we'll bump into each other soon,

Lori, and we can catch up," Wendy added before walking toward the cashier.

Brandon sat down, mumbling only slightly under his breath, "What a bitch."

"Brandon!" Lori was struggling not to laugh.

"What?! She was. That felt like a scene from one of those The Real Housewives of…."

"She's not really a friend."

"I hope not."

"We did, like, a thousand PTA projects together."

Brandon shook his head, saying, "She managed to impugn your daughter, your marital status, your longer hair—which I love, by the way— and, I think, me, in all of, what, forty-five seconds?"

"I guess that's the female version of *my dick is bigger.*"

"Women actually behave like that?"

"Not friends, well, not usually, but it's a very competitive place."

"I had no idea."

"At least she saved me the trouble of telling people I'm involved in a relationship." Lori shrugged.

"You like being the subject of gossip?"

Lori paused for a moment. "You know what. I don't care. I'm honored to be seen around town with a strong, sexy hunk in dirty work clothes." Lori smirked.

"I'm feeling uncomfortably objectified right now."

"Now you know how it feels to be a woman." Lori laughed, but her smile turned to a frown.

"It bothered me what she said about Catherine. She struggles in school, but kids get labeled in this town, and then people can't see anything else."

"Catherine's a great kid, Lori."

"I know that, and she really likes you. We need to all spend more time together." Lori looked at Brandon intently. "Honestly, I don't give a thousand fucks what Peter thinks about that. If he was trying to scare me, I think his little court charade backfired."

～

Lori and Brandon worked on house projects past the fading light and made an easy dinner with things pulled from the refrigerator. Afterward, cleaning up the pots and pans, their hands touched under the running water. Lori smiled to herself, thinking for what seemed like the thousandth time since Brandon came back into her life, how wonderful even the simplest moments are when they are shared.

"How about we go chill on the couch," Lori suggested. "I'm sore all over."

"You make a good apprentice." Brandon winked. "I bet you worked some new muscles today."

"It's good pain."

"Too sore to fool around?"

"Maybe. I'm a little bruised from last night."

"Are we okay about that?" As Brandon asked, his entire face softened.

"Yes," Lori said, "but please stop threatening to cut and run."

"I've heard you loud and clear."

Lori kissed Brandon with lips pressed hard in acknowledgment, but then she pulled away.

"What's wrong?" Brandon asked.

"I hate to go there." Lori paused. "I'm like a broken record."

"What?"

"Is this enough?"

"How do you mean?"

"There are some things the divorce hasn't changed."

"Like?" Brandon looked anxious.

"Nothing about my feelings for you." Lori squeezed Brandon's hand to reassure him. "But the judge agreed with Peter that I can't move out of Maryland, at least not with Catherine, or without asking the court's permission." She looked hard at Brandon. "I'm guessing you're not ready to move east."

"I didn't say that."

"Even if you were, we can't get married. I don't want to give up my alimony, not yet." Lori clenched her hands. "I still feel like I'm tied to a goddamn leash."

Brandon cupped her face and stroked her cheek. "It's okay, Lori. There's no rush. Anyway," he grinned, "a collar can be a lot of fun, and believe me, there are things Peter can't control."

Lori was still pouting.

"How many of your neighbors do you guess are watching porn right now?" Brandon asked.

"Um, exactly none."

"It's Saturday night; even stodgy folks fool around on Saturday night."

Lori laughed. "Around here, if anyone's watching, it's a husband, alone in his home office."

"That's sad," Brandon said, then his eyes crinkled with possibility. "Want to watch?"

"Porn?"

"Sure, and I'll understand if you fall asleep." He smirked. "You worked hard today."

"In that case..." Lori handed him the remote. "I have no idea where you find that kind of thing on TV."

It was Brandon's turn to laugh. He got up and brought back Lori's computer from the kitchen. "We'll have more luck on the internet," he said when Lori looked confused,

50

then he fiddled with the keyboard. "Prefer amateur or the real deal?"

Lori looked more befuddled. "What's amateur porn?"

"Real people filming themselves having sex."

"That's a thing?"

"It's quite popular."

"Are they attractive?"

"We can hope."

"I guess it sounds better than those ridiculous plots, like a woman who seduces the cop who just arrested her."

"Never happens to me."

Lori gave him a sidelong glance.

"I swear," Brandon said as he propped the computer on the coffee table. "Here, I found a good site."

They were seated on the couch, side by side, knees barely touching as they skimmed through a few clips. Lori's curiosity quickly overcame her reflexive qualms. The videos were in so many ways ordinary, with shaky footage like a bad home movie. The action was happening in messy bedrooms with passable furniture and clutter on bedside tables, jumbles of electrical cords, and yesterday's clothes still lying around. There was actual tummy flesh, on the women mostly; the men were all so skinny. Lori glimpsed dyed hair with roots that needed touching up, and one woman forgot to remove a band-aid from her finger. But still, no gimmicky setups. Just naked bodies and women apparently attached to spiky, high heels. And so many close-ups of vaginas! Everyone seemed to have shaved their pubic hair, women and men alike, which surprised Lori. Some of the shots were so tight you could see stray stubble. Lori could not fathom why anyone wanted to see their private parts in such detail, let alone share that image with the world. What struck her most, though, was the honesty. Lori assumed porn always required fantasy with a splash of dominance or degradation. These men were generously attentive, seeming to revel in their partners' bodies, and the women's faces expressed real sexual need as they were pleasured, genuine excitement as they tended to their men.

Lori felt suddenly compelled to kneel on the floor for a closer view. They were currently watching a naked, decidedly middle-aged couple. The man stood next to the bed, his partner lying down, legs bent open at the knees. Her hips arched towards the ceiling, clearly willing him to touch her while she reached out to fondle his balls. Lori touched the screen and traced the man's hand as he brought it to his mouth. He studiously sucked his middle finger until, with slow deliberation, he dragged it from the woman's sternum to her pussy, circling to open those lips before he cupped her and thrust his finger inside. The woman moaned for more, grinding against his hand, but the man brought it back to his mouth and licked his finger while she lifted her hips higher still. The woman's blatant imploring left Lori as aroused as a teenager, when just thinking about someone fingering her was enough to make her cum.

Brandon slid behind Lori as she watched, wrapping his knees around her hips. He lifted her hair and brushed the back of her neck with his lips, breezy and scintillating, careful not to disrupt Lori's view. She leaned in closer to the computer, her mouth practically touching the bodies on the screen. The man finally connected with his partner's clit, thumb rubbing fast while he fingered her inside greedily. Brandon moved up and down slowly while Lori arched her hips to meet his erection rubbing her ass through the seam of her sweat pants until Brandon suddenly shifted to her side. Lori buckled, but Brandon held her with a hand tucked under her belly and then pulled open the drawstring on Lori's sweatpants. He rolled them leisurely over her bottom and down her thighs before returning to caress her ass in slow circles with his fingers, each time moving closer to her opening, then drawing away to scratch lines on the delicate skin with his nails. Lori felt luxuriant. She elongated her back, still watching the couple as she purred into the screen. The man moved to enter his partner, and the woman grabbed his ass to guide each thrust as the pair grunted unabashedly. Lori badly wanted Brandon to move his fingers further down and inside of her. Another part willed him to wait. Let time stop, she thought, forever in that state of delicious, expectant craving.

Brandon seemed to understand. He continued to stroke down her backside and then her legs, sliding up her inner thighs with the back of his hand, each time getting closer but still not touching her pussy. Again and again. Closer and closer, only to draw his hand away at the last moment, instead to smooth her arched, clenched ass. Lori may have actually licked the screen as her purring turned into a groan.

"You want more?"

"God, yes, *pleeeease*."

"What do you want?"

"Touch me."

"Where, baby?"

"You know where," Lori blurted out.

Brandon drew his finger between her ass. "There?" Brandon's voice was as teasing as his fingers.

"Don't stop."

He mercifully continued further, capturing some of her wetness as he moved towards her clit, circling slowly, still not making a direct hit. "There?"

"You're killing me."

"You've got to tell me what you want."

"Touch my clit. Make me cum."

"Good baby." His finger closed in finally, fast and firm on

her clit, while his thumb fondled her anus. Lori arched her hips, curved her backside into his hand as far as she could go until she collapsed into a startling orgasm, knocking over the computer.

"No worries," Brandon said. "We don't need it anymore."

He shoved the computer aside and turned Lori quickly by the shoulders. Laying her back on the rug, he spread her legs until one bumped the table. Lori giggled, but Brandon leaned in and licked her pussy with a broad, firm tongue. It was a final flourish that made Lori's entire body shudder. She watched Brandon stand and strip off his pants. Lori squirmed the rest of the way out of her sweats before Brandon was over her. Arms flexed, hands pressed against the floor, Brandon locked his legs around Lori's and entered her. "Can you cum again?" Brandon asked, shifting his body forward so that his quickening penetrations engaged her clit to a frenzy.

Lori's eventual, rasping "yeeessss" met Brandon's final thrust. He held himself deep inside with his climax as if grabbing hold of her answer; then, he collapsed from his prolonged pushup. They stayed that way, Lori savoring the full weight of Brandon's body until he rolled away, half stuck under the glass tabletop.

"I don't want to crush you to death."

"I can think of worse ways to go," Lori chuckled, her released body suddenly as light as a feather. "Thank you."

It was Brandon's turn to laugh. "For what?" He asked. "I had just as much fun."

They made their way to her bedroom at some point, tiptoeing and shushing when they bumped into walls as if forgetting that no one else was there. They slept in late enough that Lori woke anxious about completing her last project. "We'll come back for a nap," she promised, "before I take you to the airport."

"That will have to do." Brandon reluctantly slipped out of bed.

After downing quick cups of coffee, they worked, side by side, to finish priming and painting the fireplace.

"Wow." Lori stepped back to take it all in. "I never imagined the fireplace could look so beautiful. It's transformed the room." Lori sat on the couch and patted the seat next to her. "Come sit down and admire your work."

"It looks good."

"It looks great! How did you learn to do all this stuff?"

"I worked as a carpenter for a while."

Lori grinned and asked with a hint of sarcasm, "Was that before or after you got your Ph.D.?"

"So it took me a lot longer than most people to figure out what I wanted to be when I grew up."

"We should all be so lucky." Lori laughed. "Do you ever miss being Professor McManus?'

Brandon grimaced. "I never made it past visiting assistant professor, but no. I loved being a student. I could have done that forever. Stuck at the front of a classroom, not so much." Brandon shrugged his shoulders. "Besides, academia is a tough market, and we had Fiona by then and so many bills to pay."

"You seem to really like being an FBI agent?"

"Yeah. It's a rush..., the danger and saving people. I think it takes me back to my roots. Where I grew up, all the dads were cops and firemen." Brandon paused for a moment. "Some days, though, are harder than others...," he shook his head, "to see the god-awful things people do to each other, and we can't always rescue the victims. I've been warned the burn-out rate is pretty high."

"You could always be a carpenter again." Lori pointed to the fireplace. "Look what you made."

"I didn't do it alone. We do good work together." Brandon winked at her. "We always have."

"I could never have done any of this without you. Thank you."

"You say that too much."

"I don't think it's possible to say it enough."

"In that case, I'll sketch out some plans to fix up the screened porch. We can work on that next time."

"Really?!" Lori jumped up, pulled Brandon from the couch, and spun him around despite the risk of acting like a toddler on Christmas morning.

Brandon held her out. "I'm not sure I can hire you again." He grinned. "Sloppy worker. You're covered in paint."

"It comes off!"

"Does it?" Brandon's question sounded like a dare. "How about I scrub you clean before we take that nap you promised."

"Sounds perfect," Lori answered as he led her back upstairs.

The bathroom Lori shared with Catherine was basic; the way bathrooms were built before people started believing that where they did their business should look like the Taj Mahal. Ben's bathroom was even smaller since Lori gave him the primary bedroom downstairs, but Ben was compensated by the privacy of a separate floor. They were honest, practical rooms, but Lori could not help thinking she and Brandon missed an opportunity.

A few years back, Lori and Peter undertook the de rigueur remodeling of their home, installing a custom kitchen and a bathroom with an extra-large, jetted soaking tub and shower enclosure with a fancy spigot that massaged your body from all angles. Catherine snuck many a bath in her parents' tub, but somehow Lori never found time to take advantage of the spa.

She could at least have enjoyed the extravagance when Brandon visited her while Peter was still living in the house he rented when they first separated.

It was another life... Lori let that realization wash away her resentments as she moved under the weak current of her rust-stained shower head. She switched places with Brandon so he could get wet, but when she shivered a little, Brandon moved her back under the water. He glanced at the jumble of shampoos and conditioners that, between Lori and Catherine's various experiments, filled every corner of the tub. "Do you really need so many hair products?"

"Don't ask! Pick one. I suspect they're all the same."

Brandon squeezed out a handful and began working it into Lori's scalp. It felt so much better than at the hair salon, where her neck always strained backward over the sink. Brandon kissed Lori while the water from the shower fell down their faces and into their mouths. It was a lovely sensation, like being kissed under a gentle waterfall, until the suds started to mix with the water. Lori tilted her head back to rinse as Brandon planted kisses on her neck and shoulders, lingering at each stop. Eventually, he grabbed the soap, lathered up his hands, and smoothed the foam around her breasts, working his thumbs on her sharply erect nipples. He lifted her arms, one at a time, and washed her underarms, then lathered up again and put his hand between her legs, moving from her pussy to her ass and back again. Lori felt her body sinking into his hand.

"Your turn," she grudgingly conceded. They did a little dance so that Brandon was under the stream, but he kept his hand tight against her pussy, even as she tried to squeeze the bar of soap under his arms. Lori giggled and gave up; instead lathered the soap like Brandon and rubbed it over the muscles of his shoulders. She relished the strong, hard feel of them, finally cupping his crotch and rubbing with whatever small amount of soap remained. Brandon turned off the spigots.

"Let's take this to the bedroom."

"That would be safer," Lori said, grabbing Brandon's proffered hand as she climbed out of the tub. He toweled her off, then gathered up Lori's hair and gave it a squeeze. Brandon dried himself quickly and led her back to her bedroom. He lay down first on the bed.

"I want to see all of you," he said in a low sort of grumble. "I want to watch you when you cum."

Brandon's words pricked Lori's already primed body. She was more than ready. Relaxed from the hot shower, wet and aching for Brandon, she kneeled astride him so her pussy could nestle his cock. Lori raked back her damp hair, elbows wide to make a show of her body. As she rocked against him, Lori watched the hunger rise in Brandon's eyes until they strained, mirroring his swollen cock stretched to bursting. She slipped him inside and rode Brandon slowly as the walls of the room reflected back their groans. Brandon did not touch her beyond the fixed hold of his eyes, narrowed like an animal about to capture or be captured. Lori used her own hands to cup and fondle her breasts as they bounced in tempo with the impact of Brandon's body. She moved faster, meeting Brandon thrust for thrust. Lori needed that. She needed more, a part of Brandon inside her after he boarded the plane and flew away.

Chapter Five

It seemed to take forever, but a board member from the foundation finally called. Lori did not get the job. They had lots of nice things to say but decided to hire someone with more "recent and relevant" experience. Lori answered the phone in the grocery store and fled to her car when tears sprung unexpectedly. As certain as Lori was that she would not be offered the position, Lori was confident that she would; that the foundation would go for maturity, real-life experience, and a fucking, free lawyer. Lori sagged at the thought of having to find work the hard way, searching websites and trying on the strange new descriptions of jobs. There would be hours spent scouring Linkedin, making lists of everyone she knew who might have a lead. Then asking strangers to meet for coffee, followed by thank-you notes and cover letters, each one unique and tailored, not avoiding the uncomfortable follow-up calls. Lori read the how-to books. They made her feel old and exhausted, as out of date as an expired can of stewed tomatoes, and that was before she really started looking.

She waited a week before asking Jeanette out for coffee. Brandon said all the right things about the bad news, even when

Lori confessed that part of her was glad to be rejected, worried that the job might interfere with scheduling their blissful weekends.

"You get the job, and I'll do whatever it takes to see you," Brandon reassured Lori.

Telling Jeanette would be different. Lori got to the Starbucks first and grabbed the last empty table. Jeanette was running late and came in with a rush of air-kisses and apologies. "I had to bring Jason the textbook he forgot this morning. That boy would forget his head if it wasn't attached. Chloe needed some new running shoes, although I swear I just bought her a pair. And since I was at the mall..." Jeanette plopped a pile of shopping bags on the extra chair, and one fell off as she sat down. She kicked it under the table. "The traffic these days." She finally stopped talking and took a breath. "So..." Jeanette's voice was coy. "Are we here to celebrate?"

"I didn't get the job."

"What!? I don't understand. You were totally overqualified."

"They wanted someone with a special education degree and, I'm guessing, more youthful vigor."

"Don't they know that life *is* experience?" Jeanette asked. "You've learned more from helping Catherine succeed than anyone who merely studied the topic."

"I guess they didn't buy it."

"Did they hire a millennial?" Jeanette asked skeptically.

"Yup."

"Wait till they get wind of his or her work ethic. They'll be sorry they didn't hire you."

Lori couldn't help but smile at Jeanette's attempts to console her. "I probably shouldn't have expected to get the first job I applied for."

"But it's the perfect job for you."

"It was."

"So now what?"

"A full-fledged job search, I guess."

"You're not going to work full time?" Jeanette asked Lori, but it sounded more like a statement. "That would be crazy with your responsibilities for the kids."

"Part-time jobs are hard to find."

"You'll have to say no if they won't agree to fewer hours."

"I'm not really in the driver's seat, Jeanette."

"Why not? After all, do you really need a job? You get alimony."

"I don't want to depend entirely on Peter." Lori's rushed words sounded more aggressive than she intended. "It makes me feel...," Lori slowed down, searching for the right word, "beholden," she added finally.

"Pshaw," Jeanette said with a wave of her hand. "That's what Peter gets for leaving."

"Yes, but if he doesn't like how I'm handling the kids, or anything else, he can miss a payment and make me squirm when I can't pay the bills on time. Men do it all the time."

"Peter is not going to risk pissing off some judge or looking stingy with his kids."

"Maybe, but I don't get alimony forever. In fact, it hardly seems like much at all since it has to last."

"You'll just have to save carefully."

"You sound like my lawyer." Lori patted Jeanette's hand. "Anyway, I need a job for…, well, for me. I miss feeling part of something worthwhile. I want to have an impact before it's too late."

"Isn't that what raising a family should be?"

"The kids are growing up, Jeanette. Fast. Sometimes it feels like they're already half out the door."

"You'll be surprised how often they come back, bags in tow

and looking for your help." Jeanette was wagging her finger. "Your kids are young, Lori. Catherine still has most of high school to get through, and you have to get Ben into college."

"I think Ben needs to get Ben into college."

"Not with boys. If you don't do it, it won't happen."

"I'm starting to think that's the problem, Jeanette. We do too much for these kids."

"That's the way things work these days. All we can do is accept it."

"Honestly, I don't know why our generation was so resentful of our parents' neglect. Those long afternoons, when my mom said, 'get outside, keep your sister safe, and don't come back until dinner time,' that was when we learned how to take care of ourselves. Our kids know nothing about freedom or responsibility."

"We're lucky we came out of childhood alive," Jeanette said, shaking her head as if terrified to think about it. "What without seat belts and bike helmets and lifeguards."

"We did fine though, didn't we? Now we're so busy protecting our kids, we've forgotten our other talents and dreams." For a moment, Lori fidgeted silently with the straw wrapper on the table. "There was a time, Jeanette, when I believed I was going to change the world." Lori looked up in search of understanding, but Jeanette was making a face as if to say you're being silly. "Maybe it's too late for that," Lori added, "but I want to do something more meaningful than orchestrating my kids' success."

"I'm sorry. I have to disagree. It's an incredibly important job, and our families depend on us. It's more than enough for me."

"That's okay, Jeanette. Really," Lori added, in a tone, she hoped expressed her sincerity. "I may not have that luxury anymore."

"You worry too much." Jeanette sat up sharply. "Anyway, I have another bone to pick."

"Excuse me?"

"Wendy Wilson tells me she met Brandon. I'm mean, really, Wendy and not me? She's not even a friend."

"It was by accident, Jeanette. We bumped into Wendy at the deli. Didn't she tell you? I would have brought Brandon around to meet you and Richard, but we got so busy with house projects, and he was only here a few days."

"I want to meet him next time he's in town. No excuses." Jeanette's voice turned coy again. "Wendy says he's quite the looker."

On the drive home, Lori realized that introducing Brandon to Jeanette had never occurred to her. Despite the times that Brandon came east, Lori didn't feel compelled to make the rounds and demonstrate to friends that she was doing fine and did not need their pity. Anyway, Wendy's gossip would take care of that. Lori found herself wondering, though. Was her reticence somehow knit together with her swift exclusion from, how did Brandon put it, the circles she ran in?

Lori understood that Peter's abrupt exit from their marriage would shift community allegiances. What she had not anticipated was how profoundly it would gut her social life. So much of what they did socially was connected to Peter's work; his colleagues were many of their friends, and events she and Peter attended were often for his law firm's benefit. She and Peter annually hosted one of the most popular summer associate dinners. Lori might have resented it, but she'd been a gracious participant. Her reward was entry to the hottest restaurants, tickets to sold-out plays and concerts, star-studded galas, and sporting events. Their refrigerator yearly boasted a lineup of coveted invitations to holiday parties thrown by and for the city's elite. That spigot dried up the moment Peter walked out, as if Lori had died, not been abandoned; as if she'd never been part of the firm despite that she was employed there not so many years ago, and all of Peter's time and attention Lori and the kids sacrificed for his clients. For a while, Lori was too shell-shocked to notice, and the partners' wives who had become her friends still called. Really, though, Lori's departure from the hub of that social wheel was fast and absolute.

Of course, they had friends from the neighborhood and the kids' school and sports activities. When her kids were younger, there were so many weekend events with the same group of folks they had no choice but to all become friends. Peter was usually a no-show, but that did not lessen Lori, Ben, and Catherine's admittance, without question, as a full-fledged family. That had changed just as definitively. Maybe it wasn't all the divorce, Lori thought. She moved homes. It was amazing the change a few miles could make. Lori strolled down different sidewalks, and activities were a lot less family-centric with both Catherine and Ben in high school. Still, there were less and less last-minute, bumped-into-at-the-grocery-store invitations to barbecues, brunches, or potlucks. As if their presence, the broken family, was too awkward or dangerous. Lori hoped she was imagining things. She'd been trying to get to know her new neighbors but often felt an outcast. As far as Lori could tell, she was the only unmarried woman on the block.

One Friday night, Lori found herself with a glass of chardonnay for company. Catherine was sleeping over at a friend's house, and Ben was out with friends after the usual, tedious exchange.

"Where are you going?" Lori asked.

"To Sam's house."

"Just you and Sam?"

"Probably some of the other guys will come over. Jack and Matt, maybe Eric, if he's not working."

"Will Sam's parents be home?"

"I don't know."

"You need to text Sam and find out."

Ben returned three minutes later. "His parents will be home."

"I hope you're telling the truth. I might call them."

"I'm not lying." Ben's tone was borderline rude.

"How are you getting there?" Lori asked.

"Can I take the car?"

"No. I might need it."

"Are you going somewhere?"

"I have friends too, you know." What Lori was really thinking was how untethered she would feel without her car in the driveway in case someone called (except all her friends would be with their husbands or family on a Friday night) or Catherine needing something.

"I'll ride my bike," Ben said.

"Be home by midnight, and wear your jacket with the reflector tape."

"Mom, no one has a curfew senior year."

"Obviously not true, since you do. And no drinking."

"So says the woman with a glass of wine."

"Ben!"

"I'm just saying. Everybody drinks, Mom. Dad lets me."

"You're at my house, and I say no. Not even a little."

"Whatever," Ben said, closing the basement door.

Lori felt dread at the sudden silence. She still was not used to evenings home alone. In theory, she wanted to revel in it; the quiet to read a book or her backlog of magazines; the freedom to watch a movie or television show that was inappropriate for Catherine; time to sort out the clothes she never wore that were cluttering her tiny closet. In reality, Lori fumbled with the possibilities; she scrolled through channels, uninspired, scanned book titles on her Kindle but couldn't settle, plucked a few old jackets into a pile for Goodwill, then felt despondent at the sight of the mess. That night, the hours waiting up for Ben felt more depressing than a few texts from Brandon could lighten. He was working late, so Lori didn't want to call him.

Lori suddenly remembered a small notice she had spied in the county newsletter about a gathering for divorced women at a local restaurant on the second Friday of the month. That night. It still shocked Lori that she didn't know another divorced woman locally, and when was the last time she went out for an evening drink? Lori paused from her excitement. These women would be strangers to her and might already know each other well. Lori reminded herself that she could leave if it was awkward and pretend she had a kid to pick up. She threw on her best jeans, some mascara, and lipstick and grabbed her phone before she lost her nerve.

The restaurant was crowded, but Lori spied a group of women who all looked between forty and fifty sitting around a table near the bar. It seemed the likely target, and Lori approached.

"Excuse me, but is this the group for, um…"

"Divorcées," one woman said with a fake, French accent, and everyone laughed.

"But of course," another said. "Are you eligible?" There was more chuckling.

"Actually, yes."

"Hello then. I'm Susan." The first woman who had spoken stood up, dropped the silly accent, and embraced Lori warmly. "Let's get you a chair." Susan grabbed an empty one from the next table and squeezed it beside her own.

"And a drink," another woman added. She had large, kohl-embellished eyes, curly, dark hair, and exotic earrings. "I'm Jill." She put out her hand. They quickly went around the table with further introductions while Jill motioned for the waitress.

Lori was about to ask for a glass of red wine but noticed all the women seemed to be sipping real drinks. "What are you all having?"

There was a chorus. "Vodka martini," "cosmo," "margarita," "manhattan."

"I'll have one of those, a manhattan."

"Good choice," Jill said. "We like women who are serious about drinking."

There was more laughter followed by an awkward pause while they waited for Lori's drink to arrive. Then another woman, Leslie, a blond wearing a preppy blouse and pearls, raised her glass. "To our new member, Lori."

"To Lori." The rest of the group chimed in, lifted their glasses, and drank.

Susan, Lori noted, was on the younger side, a little plump, with auburn hair in a ponytail, soft, pretty features, and no makeup. She looked at Lori intently and asked, "Sooo..., what's your sob story?"

"Um..., My ex..."

"Wait..., let me guess. There was a younger woman," Eliana said. She was the last of the foursome, sitting at Lori's other side, a striking brunette with expertly applied makeup and wearing a silk blouse.

"No, though I..."

"I know!" Jill jumped in. "He's a workaholic or a narcissist, or, wait..., a narcissistic workaholic."

"I'll drink to that," Leslie said, and everyone laughed.

"Actually, you're not far off, my ex..." Lori was cut off again.

"Don't bother with the deets, we can guess. Give us the

stats," Jill said. "Kids? How many? How long since the divorce?"

Lori gave her stats. She'd never thought of her family quite that way before. Jill and Eliana volunteered that their stats were similar.

"What made you decide to join us tonight?" Susan asked, turning to Lori. "Dad's weekend?"

"Actually, my kids are with me, but they're both out with friends, and I was rattling around the house feeling sorry for myself."

"I used to dread weekends when my kids were with their father," Susan said. "I've got three boys, ten, twelve, and fourteen, and the house feels so empty. Then I realized I dread when they come back; my peace and quiet shattered. But that only lasts a day before I'm too swamped by the chaos to notice."

"Three boys, that sounds hard," Lori said.

"Especially since they're all at different schools this year, elementary, middle, and high school. All three are athletes," Susan added proudly, "so there's a lot of driving to practices and games. I feel like I live in my minivan."

"Amen to that," Leslie added.

"I bet your girls have their own secret world going on," Susan said to Leslie. "I think girls are harder that way."

"Mine are pretty easy these days," Leslie responded. "Only because they're both holed up in their rooms on social media. It cannot be healthy. I never thought I'd say it, but I miss their needing me to entertain them."

"I'm so tired of the fight to get mine to turn over their devices," Susan added. "Of course, there are no rules at their dad's house, so I have to be the bad guy. Have you seen the articles on how smartphones are destroying our children? Literally, making them depressed, anxious, suicidal…"

"Can we change the subject?" Eliana asked, followed by a

68

dramatic pause. "I want to know how the dating is going, ladies."

There was a chorus of ughs. "What dating?" Susan asked. The other women laughed halfheartedly.

"Lori," Eliana said, turning in her seat to face Lori, "have you started dating?"

"I'm in a relationship."

"That was fast." Jill whipped her head towards Lori. "Tell us your secret." Jill was smiling, but Lori sensed a slight blanket of hostility wrap around the table. She stayed quiet.

"How did you meet?" Susan asked Lori.

"I've known him since we were in high school."

"The long-lost love, that explains it," Jill said. She circled the table with her hand. "This group's been stuck with hookups on Tinder or dates with old men who only want to take a lady to the opera."

"I prefer the term mature," Eliana said, "and they're not all bad. It can be nice to be treated well."

"If you want to be bored to death."

Eliana looked at Jill sharply and called over the waitress, announcing that they needed another round.

"You all use Tinder?" Lori asked, looking around the table.

"Actually, I think it's only me," Jill answered, one eyebrow raised, "when I get an itch for a non-masturbatory orgasm."

"How does that work?"

"I hope you're not asking me how to get yourself off."

"Of course not," Lori said, blushing. "I mean Tinder."

"It's easy, girl," Jill said the last word with a sassy flair. "We're living in the digital age."

"I could never do that," Leslie interjected.

"And that's why you're slowly dying from lack of sex."

"Jill, that's mean," Susan said. "We don't do that here."

"So you have sex," Lori interrupted, "with a stranger?"

"You should try. It can be quite liberating."

"Do they come to your home?" Lori asked with genuine curiosity.

"It depends. We usually meet at a bar for a drink so I can make sure the guy's not a serial killer. I've got a good spidey sense. I generally swipe younger guys, the kind that like to show an older woman they know how to please." Jill gave the group a broad smile.

"For goodness' sake," Susan said. "How can you tell that from a Tinder profile?"

"It's easy, sweetie. There's code language. You've heard the term MILF?"

"I don't get it," Susan interrupted, "sex is so intimate. How do you do it with a perfect stranger?"

"All your exes were strangers once," Jill answered.

"But we didn't jump into bed back then without knowing each other first," said Leslie. "At least I didn't. I think it would be too hard...," Leslie glanced around the table in search of allies, "to have sex with someone totally unknown after having sex with the same man for so many years."

"That's making a big assumption," Jill said, eyebrows raised again, "but that's the point. No baggage or another person to clean up after in the morning."

"That part I like," Leslie said, nodding.

"Look," Jill added, in the tone of someone who has seen it all, "we're all just bodies, mechanisms designed for pleasure. A stiff drink is all it takes to loosen up the important parts."

Lori couldn't help laughing.

"Actually, I like someone needing me in the morning," Susan said, looking down at her drink. Leslie reached out to touch Susan's hand.

"How come you're not with your boyfriend tonight?" Jill asked Lori.

"He lives in Seattle."

"What?!"

"We see each other one weekend a month. We take turns traveling."

"I see how that could work." Jill pursed her lips and nodded. "A guaranteed weekend of great sex each month. I assume the sex is great."

Lori felt herself blushing again. She was a little drunk and feared her cheeks were cherry red, so she stared into her manhattan. When Lori lifted her drink to take a sip, she could see all eyes were on her.

"Spill the beans, Lori," Jill said. "Hearing about great sex is almost as good as getting it."

"It's good," Lori said after a pause.

"I don't believe you're flying cross country for sex that's just good." Jill was shaking her head.

Lori took another sip of her drink. "It's really good, actually, and that still surprises me because I hadn't enjoyed sex for, like, a decade."

"I think that throws a wrench in Jill's theory," Leslie said. "Women are not like cars or washing machines. We have complicated feelings tied up with sex."

"Maybe...," Jill paused for effect, "or maybe some men are much better mechanics."

The whole table laughed. The attention thankfully diverted from Lori's sex life and took a turn to the mundane. The recent weather, the drudgery of schlepping kids, and did the town really need another Whole Foods? Lori looked at her phone for the first time all evening. "Wow, it's getting late. I better get home before I'm too drunk to drive, especially since I insisted my son not drink tonight."

"We'll let you off the hook once." Jill winked at Lori. "Next month, you have to share the juicy details."

Lori felt a little wobbly getting to her car. It was barely a mile to her house, and she only had two drinks, but they were stiff manhattans. She took it slow, pulled into the garage with inordinate care, and sat with a big glass of water at the dining room table. It was already twelve-thirty, and no sign of Ben. At twelve-fifty-five, Lori was about to call Ben when he stumbled in. Literally. It sounded like he was falling up the basement stairs.

"Hi, Mom," Ben mumbled as he crashed through the door and into the dining room. "Whatcha doing up?"

"You're late," she answered sharply.

"Barely."

"An hour is not barely. Are you drunk?"

"A little." Lori cringed to see Ben's goofy smile.

"What did I say about not drinking?"

"Mom, you're so out of touch."

"What does that mean?"

"All my friends drink. I've been drinking since last year."

"What?!" Lori needed a moment to absorb that information. "You said Sam's parents would be home."

"They were, Mom, upstairs, probably partying too."

Lori's head was swimming. Sam's parents, not that she knew them well, struck her as people who would care. "How did you get home? I can't imagine you rode your bike."

"Nah, I left it at Sam's. He drove me."

"Was Sam drinking?"

"Mom," Ben said her name like she was asking a stupid question.

"Are you crazy, Ben?" Lori hated the needling, anxious sound of her voice.

"It's, like, barely three miles."

"I can't talk to you right now."

"'K, Mom. Love you."

"Go to bed," Lori responded, her angry voice trailing Ben as he glided towards his bedroom. "I have chores for you in the morning."

Lori gulped back the rest of the water. She felt gutted, anything but tipsy; another portion of what Lori thought she could control yanked away, like a magician pulling the cloth out neatly from under an elaborately set table. How could Ben have been drinking all that time without her knowing? Did Peter know? Had Peter known and not discussed it with her? What was Lori supposed to do?

She slept badly. Ben's insouciance smoldered inside her like a volcano cantankerously readying to erupt. He's exactly like his father, Lori thought, but that hurt even more. By morning, disregarding her better angels whispering that anger was never a productive emotion, Lori drummed the table with her fingers, becoming angrier still while Ben slept like a baby. Catherine texted to be picked up around noon. When they returned to the house, Lori had enough. "Ben," she called loudly into his room.

"Mom, what the…"

"It's past noon. Time to get up."

"I'm tired."

"Now."

She closed his door roughly. She wasn't ready to talk, but she could make him work his butt off. Something she should've started doing a long time ago. Lori suddenly wished she'd never hired the yard guy or the cleaning woman. Lori was used to other people doing the messy jobs, but why didn't she think to give her kids those chores. Hell, she was bussing tables and scrubbing restaurant toilets at fifteen. Thankfully, the yard guy hadn't made a recent visit.

"You can start by raking leaves," Lori said when Ben joined

her and Catherine in the dining room wearing only sweatpants, his eyes squinted against the daylight.

"Everything in the backyard needs to be raked up and dragged to the curb."

"Put on your shirt Ben," Catherine said. "It's gross."

"I need some coffee," Ben replied.

"There's some in the pot. It's probably cold. You can heat it up in the microwave."

"Can you make a fresh pot?"

"I'm busy." Lori's voice was flat.

"Doing what?"

"Making you a list of chores."

Ben groaned and slumped into a chair, head sunk in his hands.

"What's wrong with you?" Catherine asked Ben without looking up from her phone.

"I'm hungover."

Catherine's eyes shot to her mother, clearly curious how Lori would respond.

"Ben drank too much last night. He wasn't supposed to be drinking, but he'll pay the piper today."

"What does the even mean?" Ben lifted his head enough to ask.

"Google it. And when you're finished with the leaves, the garage needs to be organized. It looks like a tornado touched down in there." Lori could see Catherine trying hard not to giggle.

"And you, young lady, can clean your room. It's disgusting. And straighten up your crap in our bathroom."

"But Mom, I didn't…"

"It's not a punishment, Catherine. It's not fair for me to do all the work around here."

"Isn't that why you hire the cleaning lady?"

"Don't take the attitude with me, Ben, and, no, I didn't hire her to clean up after you two. You need to start taking responsibility for your stuff."

"Whatever…," her kids said in tandem.

"I don't ever," Lori leaned heavily on the last word before continuing, "want to hear that word again. It makes you both sound snarky and stupid." She made a show of leaving the table in disgust as if departing some failed diplomatic negotiation. Lori went to her bedroom and closed the door. She could try to make them feel guilty enough to take some responsibility. Lori picked up a book; it was pointless. Catherine knocked several times to ask what she should do with this or that. "Figure it out, Catherine," Lori repeated, "and close the door behind you."

Lori grew more annoyed to hear the sound of Ben's occasional, desultory raking punctuated by long silences. She suspected he was probably texting his friends about what a bitch his mother was, then felt that stabbing pain again to be thinking such things about her son. Lori deployed her breathing exercises. She was trying out yoga and meditation classes, but she was supposed to practice new skills every day, not resort to them when she felt under attack. Somehow, Lori managed to stay behind closed doors for a few hours. When she emerged and looked for Ben, Lori found him in the garage, seemingly shuffling junk from one place to another.

"That's not cleaning, Ben."

"I don't know what you want me to do in here."

"Throw stuff away that you don't use anymore. Put things where they belong. You must have ten lacrosse sticks scattered around, and you haven't ridden that scooter in years."

"It's not all my mess, Mom."

"Can you please try to do something without making excuses," Lori said before walking out and closing the garage door behind her.

Dinner was inordinately quiet. Lori tossed out a few openings, but both kids were mopey, their hands in a constant, unsatisfied search for the phones Lori insisted they leave in their bedrooms. "Catherine," Lori said finally, "bring the dishes to the sink, then go to your room. I need to talk to Ben."

"I want to stay. It's my house too."

"Catherine, please, not tonight."

Catherine left begrudgingly after clearing the dishes at a snail's pace. It had taken her several trips to the kitchen, as Catherine made sure to get every last thing off the table. Lori steeled herself for the conversation with Ben. By the time they heard Catherine hit the top stair—it seemed to take forever—Ben started squirming.

"Can I get my phone?" He was half out of his chair. "My friends are probably texting me."

"They can wait, Ben. I'm concerned about your drinking."

Ben twitched back into his seat. "Don't make that a big deal, Mom. It's not a big deal."

"You lied to me, Ben. That's a big deal."

"I didn't lie. You said don't drink, and I didn't answer."

"So you ignored me."

"You're kind of old school, Mom."

"So you've said, several times now. Do you drink every weekend?"

"Usually."

"Do you drink a lot?"

Ben smiled. "I like to get a little lit, like the rest of my friends."

"What would happen if you didn't?"

Ben paused. "I don't know, Mom." His tone grew more sincere than snarky. "We've gotta blow off steam. All we hear is, 'you need to get good grades. You better kill the SATs. If you don't get into a good college, you're fucked.'"

76

"Language, please," Lori interrupted. "I don't say that," she continued. "I only ask you to do your best, not waste your talents or the advantages you've been given."

"Same thing."

"Look, I hear you, Ben, and I'm not saying it's easy..." Lori took a deep breath to acknowledge the truth in what he said. "Expectations are high for kids like you."

Ben nodded vigorously.

"The alternative isn't much fun," Lori added quickly. "I assume you don't want to flip burgers or work at the mall the rest of your life. To have the things you want, you've got to put your best foot forward. Everyday. I'd be a bad parent if I didn't help you stick with your commitments."

"Then why'd you get divorced? You broke a pretty big one there, the whole *till death do us part*."

"Is that was this is about?" Lori's voice was tight, feeling the sudden, sharp point of a knife to her heart as she thought to herself, is that what everything will always be about?

"Mom, my friends are waiting."

"You're not going out tonight."

"What?! I did all your chores. It's not fair."

"Not open for discussion, Ben."

He left the room in a huff, but Lori was relieved to be alone. She sat with Ben's comment and the pain it caused her. Lori was being judged by her own kid when it was his father who did the leaving. She knew that what she wanted, for Ben to choose sides, her side, was something she should never ask of her children. What hurt most was that none of it really mattered. The damage was done, and no matter how many times Lori tried to meditate, she would feel guilty regardless of fault.

Lori was also confident that Ben would sulk and waste the night away mindlessly scrolling Instagram. She didn't have the energy to make him do something more productive. Lori asked

Catherine if she wanted to watch a movie. They cuddled in Lori's bed with bowls of ice cream and watched *Brave* for what seemed like the hundredth time. Catherine stayed with her when the movie ended, snuggled like besties at a sleepover until Lori woke with a start at six in the morning. She decided to get up and make coffee. Lori quietly opened Ben's door as she passed. His bed was empty. She checked the bathroom and the kitchen, then rushed down the basement stairs. She checked the garage. Her bike was gone. Had he already gone out that morning? Not her sleep-till-noon son. That meant…

Lori called Ben's phone but it rolled over to voicemail. She texted him.

Where are you?

It took him over half an hour to respond while Lori's anger grew like a snowball rolling downhill.

I went with Sam to get breakfast.

You never get up this early. Where are you?

At the diner.

Lori didn't believe a word of it but Ben wouldn't flat out lie to her. She grabbed her keys and drove the few miles to the diner. She didn't see her bike. Maybe Ben went to Sam's house and they drove together. She parked the car and went inside. There were a few old men drinking coffee. She texted Ben again.

Come home now.

Then she drove back and sat at the kitchen table, her anger soon percolating, drip by drip, until it formed an ugly sludge. Ben didn't come home for another hour.

"Did you get my text?" Lori asked before Ben closed the door behind him.

"We were still eating breakfast."

"I went to the diner. You weren't there."

Ben paused. Lori could see him recalibrating. "How do you know which diner we went to?"

"There's only one in town, Ben. You went out last night, didn't you? You stayed out all night after I told you that you weren't to leave."

"Mom! I'm going to college next fall. You can't tell me when I'm there what I can do and where I can go."

"You're not in college yet. You're still under my roof."

"Yeah, well maybe I'll leave. I can go live with Dad."

"Is that a threat?" Lori tried to control herself.

Ben stared for a long moment before he turned and walked away. Lori just sat, her mouth twisted around a bitter taste of deja vu and that painful thought again... Ben was behaving like his father.

An uncomfortable détente followed. Lori and Ben passed each other in the house like combatants forced by proximity into a reluctant truce. Ben followed Lori's rules, but there was no real kindness. Catherine moped around like a leery peace-keeping force of one. It was a huge relief for Lori to find herself suspended thirty-five thousand feet in the air. Feelings that constrained her breathing like a slow-moving boa constrictor—anxiety about Ben; lingering sadness about losses Lori could not always identify; the myriad obstacles to her relationship with Brandon as threatening as sheer rock face—loosened their hold, bit by bit, as the plane lifted its nose, pushed through gravity and settled into cruising altitude.

Not that Lori hadn't struggled with leaving. She knew how hard it was for her kids to compete with Peter's work responsibilities, but they were with their father. That meant something, though what, exactly, was a bit of a mystery. As best Lori could tell, Ben was content at his dad's, left alone and few rules imposed. Peter seemed occasionally to pull himself from work to spend time with Catherine. They carved a pumpkin not long ago, nicely executed, Lori noted, as it was posted on Peter's Facebook page; optics mattered to Peter. Both kids let slip about game nights that even Ben deigned to join in. Lori confessed to Jeanette that she was jealous. Lori wished they had done more things like that as a family. Her kids were suddenly enjoying time with their father because Lori wasn't there. That hurt. Did it have to?

Lori toyed with that question with hours to go until she landed in Seattle. It was more than time to be pushing her kids out of the nest, even if that meant leaving them to navigate a relationship with their father. And, no, that didn't mean she shouldn't force Peter to address Ben's use of alcohol. The last shove Lori would give Ben into wide-open air was sure as hell to be scary—for both of them. Ben needed a healthier crutch. Lori waved away the flight attendant's offer of wine thinking about her own vulnerabilities. It was true that she never, ever, would have walked out on Peter, walked out on their family. Perhaps it was time to let go of that awkward badge of honor. It seemed to award Lori greater loyalty, she clung to that, but it also hinted at Lori's cowardliness. Strapped tight in her seat, soaring in midair, Lori felt the vibration of the plane's engines jostling something loose inside. Lori tried to identify the ticklish feeling. Was it regret for how long she neglected to spread her own wings, or the thrill that she was already flying?

Chapter Six

Lori was surprised to see Brandon waiting for her just beyond security. She dropped her bags before he scooped her into a tight embrace, momentarily blind and deaf to the throngs of travelers moving past.

"I could have met you outside," she said when Brandon finally unclasped her.

"I thought you might need a hug as soon as possible." His lips grazed her nose, then her lips, lingering briefly. Brandon's smell, touch, and taste were so familiar to Lori as if his matched chromosomes had always been snuggled tight in her DNA.

"It's been a hell of a few weeks," she agreed, shaking her head.

Brandon grabbed Lori's suitcase and took hold of her hand. "Want to make a pit stop?" He asked. "Do something fun for a change? It's not far."

"That sounds like just what the doctor ordered." Lori flashed him a grateful smile.

Almost immediately upon exiting the airport, Brandon pulled into another parking lot. There stood a lone, large store, not a bar, as Lori expected, and named to give a good idea of what merchandise was sold. The main floor boasted a large selection of sexy lingerie. Brandon walked Lori past the displays and to a back staircase where they descended a stairwell covered floor to ceiling with striking, erotic photographs and posters. The lower level looked almost like a kitchen supply store. Walls of packaged items hung from hooks with a few bright items on shelves and in glass cases.

"Look around," Brandon said, squeezing Lori's hand once and releasing her.

Lori stood for a moment, unsure how to browse for sex toys. She decided to head for the colorful cabinets like it was an ordinary shopping trip. After parsing out catchy names and descriptions, Lori recognized that she was looking at the latest innovations for women's pleasure—fancy vibrators with very fancy price tags. Lori moved on towards some racks of... props —that was Brandon's word—eye masks, handcuffs, and a variety of whips. Some looked quite gentle, though others would scare Lori if she found them in Brandon's hand. Lori shifted towards the next section, flustered as she realized she was looking at rubber penises in an uncountable array of shapes, sizes, and skin colors. Lori instinctively reached to touch one. She recoiled, surprised at how closely it mimicked actual flesh, and bumped into Brandon.

"I see you found the cocks."

Lori gave a laugh. "Um, yes. What exactly are they used for?"

"I bet you can guess." He smirked at Lori. "You might enjoy one when you want to bite something."

"No thanks." She looked at him sharply. "I haven't ever bit you there, have I?"

"No." Brandon was trying hard not to laugh. "You seem to enjoy something in your mouth, though."

Lori made a face.

"Did you find anything you like?" Brandon asked.

"No!"

"Keep looking. I want to buy you a present."

Lori's browsing became more urgent, but it took time to settle on a set of Ben Wa balls. She recalled something about them from the erotic books everyone was reading a few years back. At least they weren't expensive, and they looked innocuous. "Here." She handed the package to Brandon and hung back as he paid for them and a few other things he apparently thought they needed. A fluttery thrill gripped Lori's lower belly until she noticed Brandon flirting with the young woman at the checkout who was flirting back. Probably de rigueur when making purchases at a sex shop, Lori thought, but it invoked feelings that surprised her, something sharp and territorial.

Brandon asked Lori if she wanted to look at the lingerie on their way out. Lori considered it. She could try on a few things and pose for him to spark the tantalizing mood the store was surely meant to inspire, but Lori was tired. "Let's do that sometime when I'm less cranky with impending jet lag."

"All right, baby. Let's get you home."

Lori realized those simple words, not only *baby*, but *home*, were exactly what she needed to hear.

Lori exhaled with relief as they pulled up to Brandon's craftsman bungalow with its gracious porch. It seemed only a minute later, and she was comfortably nestled into Brandon's leather couch, a glass of whiskey resting on her chest, some snacks within reach on the table, her feet snug in Brandon's lap. He massaged her arches, pressing hard into the knots. It was excruciating and marvelous. Lori's lingering worries were being macerated and whimpering in defeat.

"That feels sooooo good." Her words dribbled out. "I've almost forgotten the drama back east."

"I want to hear all about it," Brandon cooed. "It might be easier to talk after you've had some time to relax."

Would she ever tire of his sexy, teasing voice? "Any ideas for how?" Lori asked.

"I've been thinking of a few." He rubbed harder.

"Ouch."

"Sometimes, you need a little pain to exorcize the demons."

"Really?"

"Pain before pleasure."

"Keep rubbing then."

"I don't want to put you to sleep."

"You better stop then." Lori laughed, pulling her feet back and grabbing the whiskey glass before it tipped over. "What else you got?"

"That sounds like a challenge."

Lori quirked her eyes to signal, if you want it to be...

"To the bedroom then." Brandon patted her butt to get a move on, grabbed the shopping bag, and followed. There were no dimmed lights or candles, Lori noticed, probably just as well if she wanted to stay awake. "Get naked, baby, and get comfortable."

"Good thing we didn't waste any time on lingerie."

"Enough talking," he said with a wink and gently plopped her on the bed.

"Yes, Sir," Lori responded and then frowned. "I really might fall asleep."

Brandon put his finger to Lori's lips and bent down to slip off her shoes.

"I forgot how nice it is to be undressed," she said, then managed, with only a few giggles, to remain limp and less than helpful as Brandon removed her clothes. Lori lay down on her

84

stomach, stretching and curling her toes into the thick comforter, snuggling her face sideways against the soft pillow. Just a little nap..., she was thinking before she heard Brandon rustling the contents of the shopping bag. Lori was suddenly alert, ears pricked like a guard dog. She heard his belt being unbuckled, the rub of jeans against skin, the little hop of Brandon's step as he pulled them off. After a moment, he slipped a velvety-soft mask over Lori's eyes. There was another long moment. Expectation gripped Lori's belly before she felt a trail of soft, flat bands of cloth brushed against her cheek and fluttering over one shoulder. She breathed a deep sigh and exhaled into the comfort while Brandon slowly brought the bewitching cloth down her back, over her ass, the backs of her legs, and then a return trip.

Lori's tired body awakened. Of its own accord, her ass lifted and squirmed against the undulant strips of fabric. Brandon paused for a beat. Lori's whole body thrilled, expectant, awaiting the next swirl of texture, hoping the cloth would fall between her legs. She could feel her pussy swell, his loving gestures like a homecoming, then Brandon swatted her ass. That was a new experience. Lori felt immediate anxiety but then thought about about all the trouble her fear had caused in her life. Lori took a deep breath instead, intent to see where things would go. She elongated her back and jutted her hips to ask for more. There was another swat. Pain before pleasure, she breathed into her new mantra.

"Roll over," Brandon said in a throaty whisper.

Lori turned, moving her arms, unsure what to do with them.

"Put your hands over your head."

Soft strands again flirted with her lips, brushing her throat on their way to tickle her underarms, then circling her breasts until there was a narrowing movement around her nipples. Lori's breath came quicker as the cloth moved down her

85

abdomen, a swirl around her navel, then polished the top of her bush. Everything below her belly button tensed and tingled. Again Brandon stopped. She heard a slight rustle before his hand was on her inner thigh, opening her legs. Lori embraced the command in that gesture. Anticipating where his fingers would aim next, Lori lifted her hips invitingly before she remembered. There was just enough time to contract her pelvis before a stinging swat. Lori grabbed a sharp intake of breath, then exhaled into what she assumed was the next strike, but Brandon surprised her again. He drew yet a different toy slowly through her pussy lips. The material was more assertive than cloth, firm but buttery, and deeply textured. She pictured strips of leather. Their movement forced Lori open, touched, and aroused so many places at once. She lifted her hips to welcome more of the complex pressure. Swat. Her clit stung, yet at the same time, a chord struck inside her at an exquisite, sharp pitch.

"Kiss me," Lori groaned.

Brandon responded by swirling his tongue around the edges of her pussy, languorously avoiding her clit, teasing her into articulating some kind of demand.

"Oh, god, pleeeeease."

Then the kiss she needed; the penetrating fire of pointed flesh on raw nerves. His tongue lapped and swirled between moments of focused attention; then, he sucked on her clit until a sudden orgasm ripped through Lori in clenching waves as she lifted her torso from the bed. She threw off the mask and reached for Brandon to make him stop. The feeling was too intense, but he stayed put, tongue replaced by his soft mouth gently kissing her. Lori stole a quick glance at the props dropped beside her on the bed, curious at what caused her body such a fierce response. They looked ordinary enough, the soft one more like a tool for dusting than a whip. Brandon nuzzled his nose between her legs and inhaled gravely.

86

"I've missed your smell," Brandon said, lifting his face to look at her. "I can conjure the feel of you, but not that smell. It's incredible."

"Let me feel you, Brandon. Inside me. It's what I miss most."

"Not more than cunnilingus?" He asked with a wicked grin.

"Yes." Her look was serious. Could Lori ever express how much she wanted him? Brandon began to crawl over her, never breaking eye contact. Like a hunter collecting his trapped prey but wanting it to know how much he would appreciate the meal.

"I believe you," he said before his mouth surrounded hers, his tongue and cock plunging inside her at the same moment. His thrusts came deeper and faster, and Lori feared she could not breathe, but his orgasm erupted, and she gulped in air when their lips parted. Brandon, too, was breathing hard. He collapsed upon her, chest against chest, their pooled sweat mingling until he rolled off. "There's nothing, I mean nothing, like reunion sex," he said as he tucked his arm under Lori's head.

"It almost makes up for the time apart," Lori grumbled as she burrowed in, trying to get as close to Brandon as humanly possible.

When Lori stuttered awake later, uncertain where she was, she felt a kernel of anxiety nestled below her rib cage. Lori eyeballed her surroundings, recognizing she was in Brandon's bedroom, lying snug against his warm, solid chest. It can't be missing this, she thought. Was she worried about Ben or, really, the coming confrontation with Peter? Lori knew she could not fix things with Ben without taking on her ex. She lay still, trying to puzzle out why their drama seemed more perilous than when they were an intact family. It was as if divorce inevitably shifted fault lines leaving its victims clinging to the edges without certainty of rescue. Lori saw how hard it was for her kids to navigate the displaced terrain. What about me? Lori thought. Was she crazy to be already trying to realign allegiances with a man entrenched in a difficult job, the badge, his only daughter? Lori could practically hear Emily's voice in her ear, too many complications!

There is time to work it all out, Lori told herself as she took a deep inhale and exhaled her ujjayi breath. Thank goodness for the yoga. Reassured by Brandon's steady breathing, she cupped his dawn cock. It was sleepy and relaxed; a contented kitten curled around itself. Lori shifted to hold his balls like comfort stones, softness and strength in her hand. With his stretching moan, Lori knew Brandon was awake. She didn't say a word but used her palm slowly, from tip to base, to entice his cock harder. Strength meeting power, she continued to add pressure with each pass. It wasn't long before Brandon felt ripe enough to burst. Lori shifted down between his legs and took him in her mouth. She soaked the entirety of his shaft with her saliva, then moved to envelop his balls, shifting her mouth to wet them as well. Lori looked up, finally, ensuring their eyes locked when she tongued him up the swollen vein of his cock. As Brandon's eyes rolled back, Lori bit, not hard, just grabbing a sliver of skin, but she could feel the shock register.

"Pain before pleasure, right?" Lori asked, lifting her head.

Brandon's glower widened into a smile. "Get over here." He pulled her towards him, and Lori planted herself over his chest. She squiggled like a child trying to settle into exactly the right spot before moving her hips to lengthen contact, adding her juices to the wet from her mouth until his cock was a slippery slide, and Lori sat up to direct him inside. She rode Brandon, back arched, arms stretched behind to brace herself against his thighs. That was how she felt him the deepest. Lori moved faster against each of his thrusts while Brandon fingered her clit until they both came, and Lori collapsed onto his torso. She nuzzled into the crook of his neck and gave him a soft nip.

"Someone's feeling her oats this morning," Brandon said.

Lori grabbed another small bite, that time holding the skin a little longer.

Lori didn't stir again until, it seemed, hours later. A soft rain was falling outside. Brandon was already awake and staring at the ceiling.

"Morning," he said and kissed the top of her head.

"How long have you been awake?" Lori asked.

"Not long."

"Whatcha thinking about?"

"Nothing."

"I don't believe you."

"No, really. I'm enjoying that the morning feels perfect."

"It does, doesn't it?" She joined him in staring at the ceiling. "I like the sound of the rain."

"It gets depressing when it hangs on for days," Brandon chuckled, "but it gives you a great excuse to stay in bed."

"I could get used to that."

"Hey, I forgot to ask." Brandon lifted his torso up from the bed. "Want to go out tonight with some friends of mine?"

"Sure. Sounds fun. I want to see more of your life here." Lori looked up shyly. "Do you think they'll like me?"

"How could they not?" Brandon kissed her and sat up further. "I've known John since I started working at the Bureau. John Bartlett and his wife, Abby. She works for the city, urban planning. Very no-nonsense, you'll like her. They have two girls."

"What time do we meet?"

"Probably not till after eight. They're night owls."

"What should we do until then?"

"My horny girl."

"No!" Lori grabbed his side, teasing. "I was simply asking."

"Actually, I was hoping to get to the gym," Brandon said. "Want to come?"

"I don't know. I haven't been to the gym in a while."

"It has a sauna and a hot tub."

"Well, in that case, sure."

"First," Brandon said, giving her a funny look, "we should check out your new toy."

Lori looked confused.

"You know, your balls."

"I already had fun with them this morning." Lori reached to fondle Brandon.

"Your Ben Wa balls."

"Oh, those. I'm not sure what we did with them."

"Right here," Brandon said, twisting to open the drawer of his nightstand.

"Ever the Boy Scout...," Lori chuckled, "always prepared."

"Yes, ma'am." Brandon flipped open the box, and two black glass balls spilled into his hand.

"They look harmless enough," Lori said, sitting up and tentatively fingering the items. They reminded her of kids' marbles, only bigger. She looked at him hesitantly. "Haven't we done enough fooling around for one morning?"

"We can never fool around enough considering how much time we're apart," Brandon answered.

Lori laughed. "That's true, except it feels a bit like whiplash when I'm here with you. Like I've been magically transported from real life to a fantasy called Pleasure Island."

"Is that a bad thing?"

90

"I guess I wonder if I deserve it, considering everything that's happening back at home."

"We all need a break sometimes."

"But is this real?"

"Of course it's real, Lori," Brandon said with conviction. "It's the reality we're making..., for now," Brandon added when he saw Lori's look of concern. "I know you, baby. I get that you want more...," he was searching for words, "integration of our lives. We'll get there, I promise. We might even be sorry when we do."

"No," Lori said emphatically.

"If you say so, but for now, can't we just enjoy ourselves?"

"There's no harm in that." Lori felt more relaxed as she said it.

"Then lie back, and let's have some fun."

Lori complied as Brandon squirmed down the bed, shoulders hunched, rolling the balls in his hand like a gambler intent on throwing the winning dice. "They should be warm," he explained, throwing a wink in Lori's direction, "when they go in." Brandon danced the fingers of one hand along her inner thigh, through her bush, and over to her other thigh and back again. "Relax," he cooed as he suddenly slipped the first one inside, his thumb against her clit as a counterbalance. It seemed to go in easily enough, and Brandon pushed it deeper. "You're soaking wet."

"Or course." Lori chucked. "I didn't say I didn't like all this fun."

Brandon laughed with her. "Ready for the next one?"

"I guess."

"Ta-da," he said when both were fully inside her. "How does it feel?"

"Nothing too exciting."

"You should walk around."

Lori rose from the bed. Standing, she could feel them, a sensation of fullness and bounce. She took a few steps. "I get it," she said as she exited the room, danced a little twirl, and came back to the bed. "It's like adding a little jingle to your step. I'm not sure I'd have an orgasm walking down the street, though."

"I can take care of that." Brandon took her hand and pulled her onto the edge of the bed.

"Is that safe?" Lori asked.

"Of course." Brandon knelt before her, spreading her knees wide. Lori noted a familiar tension, feeling herself both transgressed and desiring to be. It still excited Lori. She fell back onto her elbows and watched Brandon nibbling and nipping like a finicky cat. When he tucked in greedily, Lori was forced to catch her breath. Brandon's mouth seemed everywhere at once, licking, flicking, sucking, then faster. The Ben Wa balls shifted inside, further agitated by her clenching pussy. The balls downright rumbled as Lori groaned into her climax. All she could do was fall back onto the bed. Brandon licked up the wetness dripping down her thighs.

"I like them," she said finally, lifting her head and laughing.

"We can try some other things." He kissed his way up her body until he was stretched out next to her and took her in his arms.

"That's enough for now," Lori said emphatically, then excused herself to remove the toys. She was in the bathroom a few minutes when Brandon called out to ask if she needed help. "I'm fine, thanks," Lori said, trying to hide her panic. She couldn't remove the damn things. Lori had her finger curled around one of the balls but couldn't dislodge it. She got off the toilet and squatted as she did birthing her children, hoping that might help. Finally, she dislodged one with a huge sigh of relief. "I'm almost done," Lori called to Brandon, fingering herself to extract the second ball. She couldn't even find it. This is what happens when you get kinky, Lori thought, and she hurried back into the bedroom, sounding distressed. "I can't find one of the balls. Is it lost? Has it gone up into my body?"

"No, baby, it can't do that." Brandon pulled her onto the bed and rubbed her shoulders. "Want me to try?"

"Okay, please, but only after you rub some more." Lori rolled her neck in rhythm with his kneading.

"Take some deep breaths," Brandon said. "Do you want to lie down?"

"I got the first one out squatting."

"Let's try that."

Lori squatted in front of Brandon, her hand resting on his shoulder. He fiddled around inside her. She tensed.

"I know it's difficult," he said, "but try to stay relaxed. After all, I'm giving you a finger job."

Lori burst out laughing.

"I've got it!" Brandon extracted his finger like a little J hook; the offending object tucked inside it. He showed her. "See, nothing but a little ball."

Lori flopped on the bed with relief. "Sorry I panicked," she said sheepishly, "but thank you for staying calm."

"Nothing to be sorry about. I had tons of fun getting it out."

Lori slapped at him playfully. "I think I'm getting too old for new tricks."

Chapter Seven

Brandon had offered Lori some of Fiona's workout clothes, a few loose-fitting, athletic shorts, unlike the barely-cover-the-butt shorts Catherine kept trying to slip out of the house wearing. There was no way Lori would fit into Fiona's bathing suit, so she was not going hot tubbing, but Lori took a peek around the corner at the rest of the gym while Brandon signed them in. It was a bit intimidating. There were so many people weight lifting. More than a few of them women, younger than Lori to be sure, but at the racks, like the men, with fat, tire-like weights on the ends of bars that rested entirely on their shoulders. Ouch, Lori thought.

"Come," Brandon said. "I'll show you around." They walked past a clutch of women coaching each other. The one currently holding the bar was squatting at the knees, head tilted up, butt sticking way out, not exactly sexy.

"Lifting dead weights is great exercise for the core," Brandon remarked. When Lori gave Brandon a horrified glance, he added with a wink, "Those bumper weights are not as heavy as they look."

"It hurts my neck just watching them."

"There's a right and wrong way to do it. I'll show you if you want."

Lori was grateful to spy the cardio machines in the back corner. They looked similar enough to the device in her basement that she could figure out how to operate one. "I'll just head to the ellipticals," she answered as she hustled away from a chorus of grunts towards the aerobic equipment. They were lined up, all solid, contained aggression, with a row of people pumping hard like a front line of soldiers. Lori remembered why she exercised at home. She'd taken their elliptical machine despite that Peter liked to use it too and that she had to give the movers an extra tip to consider touching the heavy piece. Peter could pay for a gym; there was a fancy one right in his office building. Lori, on the other hand, was supposed to be careful with her money, and she didn't like leaving Catherine alone when the urge to work out hit her in the evening or on the weekend. Mostly, though, she enjoyed the privacy.

Lori got on a machine, pressed the setup buttons, and plugged in her headphones. She scanned the open floor as she warmed up. The place was filled near capacity. So many people, women as often as men boasting extravagant tattoos, and most of the guys with enormous, bushy beards. *Toto, I've a feeling we're not in Kansas anymore...* Lori smiled to think it before she got into her zone and stopped noticing. She worked out longer and harder than she expected, enjoying the graceful pace of high-end equipment. When she had enough, Lori went to find Brandon. He was seated on one of the weight machines, back straight, eyes focused ahead, forearms against pads, pulling bars towards his chest. "Hey there," Lori said from behind when he stopped to rest.

"Hey."

She glanced at the stack of weights he was lifting. "That's impressive."

He smiled. "It's not that hard; I'll show you."

Lori paused, considering. "All right. I'll give it a try."

Brandon sat her down, adjusted the seat height, showed her where to put her arms and how to set her legs. "You want to breathe in when you're dropping the weights, exhale when you're lifting."

Lori took a deep breath, pulled her arms toward her chest, and met a wall. Nothing. She made a face.

"Oops," Brandon said. He bent down and moved, almost to the top, the peg that was inserted into the weights.

"That's kind of embarrassing."

"Look around you," Brandon said. "Do you see anyone paying attention to anybody but themself?"

"Good point." Lori tried again. "Now it's too easy."

"Okay, Goldilocks. Remember, it gets harder after you do some repetitions."

"I'll be fine," Lori smirked. "Go do the rest of your workout."

She tried a few other machines. It was like sampling a restaurant buffet, a few pulls on this, a couple of pushes on that. The mechanics were relatively easy to figure out from the helpful drawings on the side of the machines. Lori kept her eyes closed as she lifted. The better to concentrate, though she did occasionally spy on her neighbors to see how much they were lifting, and on Brandon, enjoying his look of deep concentration.

"Looking good." Lori's eyes popped open at Brandon's voice as she was extending her legs in a modest battle with a reluctant metal plate. "You almost ready to go?"

"Absolutely." Lori scurried off the machine. Her posture between extensions felt a little too much like a pelvic exam. "I think I've done enough for my first day."

"You look sweaty."

"Yeah, I sweat. Hope that's okay." Brandon answered by nuzzling into her neck and licking the salty residue. "It's mostly from the elliptical," Lori said, squirming. "The weights didn't feel like a workout."

"Actually, you burn a lot more calories from lifting. It comes from the afterburn."

"So many things to learn." She grinned, then asked Brandon, "Why don't you listen to music when you lift? You're the only person in here without headphones."

"Another habit from my job, I guess."

Lori squinted her eyes, not understanding.

"I'm always paying attention to my surroundings," he said, "watching who comes in through the door."

Lori shook her head. "That must be exhausting."

"I guess, but I can't remember what it's like not to."

"Huh." Lori was still pondering Brandon's reply as they headed to the car, and Lori was surprised by the vibration of an incoming call. She usually managed to orchestrate her east-coast life to remain politely hushed the few days she was in Seattle. Lori saw Catherine's face on her screen, also unexpected. Catherine had taken to texting Lori, even when they were only steps away from each other.

"Hi, Sweetie, what's up?"

"Mom," Catherine said, sounding teary. "I want to come home."

"You are home. With your dad."

"I mean your house. I can't stay here."

"Why?"

"Dad's being so mean." Catherine's voice was an anguished rush.

"Slow down and tell me what's going on."

"He's being such a... *uggggh*. He won't let me have a friend over, and everything I do, he's like, 'Catherine, you're making a mess, Catherine, the TV's too loud…'"

"He probably has a work crisis. His job can be pretty stressful."

"He doesn't have to take it out on me."

"You're right. He doesn't."

"When I said 'what is your problem,' he sent me to my room like I was five years old."

"That was disrespectful, honey."

"*Pleeeeease*. Can I come home?"

"It's your dad's weekend."

Lori and Peter had finally agreed that Catherine and Ben would spend every other Friday, from after school until Tuesday morning, at Peter's house. Lori remained skeptical about whether it was in teenagers' best interest to be unsupervised after school, but she gave in when her lawyer told her that the judge might award Peter more time with the children. "What does that even mean?" Lori had groused. "'Time with the children'… Even when Peter's home, he's locked in his office." Lori's attorney seemed unmoved. She probably heard it all before, from so many divorcing clients, helicopter moms involuntarily weaned from the controls, and newly empowered dads asserting their rights. Lori returned her focus to Catherine, still sniffling into the phone, repeating that she wanted to come back to Lori's.

"It's really important to your dad that he spend time with you and Ben," Lori told Catherine, trying to say the right things.

"Can I come over for a little while? I'll tell Dad that I need to pick up something for school. He won't even notice I was gone."

"You can't, sweetie. I'm not there right now."

"But I need you, Mom. Please come get me."

"Catherine, I'm in Seattle this weekend."

"What?!"

"I'm sure I told you."

"I don't remember that."

"Well, I am, and my flight back isn't until tomorrow night." Lori was about to offer that Catherine could come home after school Monday. She stopped herself, aware that if Lori and Catherine agreed to a plan that differed from the written custody agreement, Peter's lawyer would be calling her lawyer, who would be calling Lori before she had time to pull the car out of the garage to get to the bus stop. Where do the kids' needs fit in? Lori felt, more than heard, these thoughts as a pain constricting her heart.

"But Mom...," Catherine's voice reached an octave higher. "It's so unfair."

"It feels that way because we're all still learning how to adjust."

"Yeah, but, like, I don't get to go away like you do."

Ouch. The pain strained one notch tighter.

"Why don't you go to a friend's house?" Lori suggested. "You can walk to Natalia's."

"She's got horseback riding today, and Ella's hanging out with Regan."

"Can't you join them?"

"Ella's being bossy and not letting Regan invite me too."

"Want me to call Chloe's mom and see if you can hang out there?"

"Yes! Please."

"All right, I'll call now. Promise me you'll take it easy and won't pick any more fights with your dad, okay?"

"Okay, Mom. Thank you."

Lori called Jeanette while Brandon drove them back to his house. Jeanette quickly offered to call Peter and ask if she could

100

borrow Catherine to help Chloe with a school project. "I don't mean to sound like a broken record," Lori told Jeanette, "but I don't know what I'd do without you."

"You can take me out for a drink when you get back. Preferably some night when Chloe really does have an assignment that she's trying to get me to do for her."

"Everything okay?" Brandon asked when Lori hung up. They'd arrived back at his place and were parked in front of the house.

"Peter's being difficult, and Catherine wanted me to come get her."

"Oh."

"They're only with their dad a handful of days each month. You'd think they could make it work."

"Why do that when you're so much better at taking care of things," Brandon said with a conspiratorial chuckle.

"I should be annoyed," Lori said, turning towards Brandon, "but I feel guilty."

"Why?"

"I'm not there when Catherine needs me."

"First of all," Brandon said, taking her hand, "you did just kind of fix things for Catherine, and second, does she really need you?"

"No, but does that really make a difference?"

Again, he chuckled. "No."

"I get that it's better if I let them figure it out, but..."

"What?"

"For so long, that's been my only currency of value, providing the indispensable glue that keeps everyone's shit together and a safe place to land. If I can't be those things, what good am I?"

"You're selling yourself short, Lori."

"I *do* need to protect them sometimes. It's terrible to say that," she added, quickly turning away, "but Peter can be such a bear when he's stressed out."

"It's not terrible to want to protect your kids."

"From their parent?"

"Sometimes that's the most important job," Brandon said, turning her cheek gently to face him. "I know from experience."

"I'm sure, but my kids are going to need things from Peter. I don't have the kind of money to buy them a car or pay for college. They'll have to learn how to push Peter's buttons…, the right way."

"I'm guessing that sounded crasser than you meant it."

"Yeah." Lori's shoulders sagged. "They need other things from him, a little of his attention...and admiration." They grew quiet. "My parents' approval mattered so much to me," Lori said after a while. "It's probably a big reason why I married Peter." Lori suddenly brought her hand to her mouth. "I can't believe I said that."

"Is it true?" Brandon asked.

"It might be," Lori said, shaking her head. "Of course, I also resented how much my parent's approval mattered." She smiled. "They never liked lawyers. So what did I do? I went to law school and paid, well borrowed," Lori gave a small laugh, "my entire way. I never asked for money from my parents. That meant I could make my own choices, right?"

"That kind of independence runs deep. You'll be financially independent again and able to help your kids."

"I don't know, not like Peter..."

Brandon shook his head to disagree.

"There's an irony here," Lori said, her eyes squinted in thought. "I genuinely wanted independence, but in the end, I guess I wanted security and my parent's approval even more. Peter and I were one of those smug couples in *The New York Times* wedding pages, equally stellar educational credentials, and fancy jobs. You can bet my parents showed that to their friends."

"Wait," Brandon interrupted. "You weren't really in the Times' wedding section?"

Lori made a shamed face but nodded yes. Brandon started laughing.

"I'm serious, Brandon. I hate to think of the power Peter's money gives him over our kids."

"Peter loves them."

"Of course, he does…in the abstract."

"I know all about that." Brandon dipped his head in thought. "Jocelyn has changed," he said eventually. "She's built trust and closeness again with Fiona, even if she still manages to disappoint when being a mom doesn't fit in with her schedule."

"Are you ever secretly glad when Jocelyn messes up?" Lori asked shyly.

"What do you mean?"

"Honestly," Lori said, looking earnestly at Brandon, "part of me wants Peter to fail. I mean, why should he get a second chance at being a good dad, especially after he had the audacity during our custody mediations to blame me for his terrible relationship with our kids?"

"I get that, I do, and believe me, I've felt the same. Ultimately, any joy in triumph is wiped out when you see your kid's pain."

Lori let that sink in. "You're very wise," she said after a while, "and a great father, I hope you know that."

Brandon laughed. "I'm barely adequate to the job." He reached for the door handle. "Let's go in, and I'll make you a fire. That's something I'll confess to being good at."

~

They met Brandon's friends later at a whiskey bar aptly named The Whiskey Bar. As they walked through the door, John stood up from where he and Abby were seated at one of the few tables sipping cocktails. Lori tried to gauge them quickly. They looked younger than she expected. John, in particular, had the fresh face of a teenager, with straight, dark hair, sharp features, and bright eyes. He was adorable. Abby was rounder in every way, though not overweight. Wavy, dirty-blond hair surrounded her face and fell past her shoulders to a deeply plunging v-neck sweater. Abby's deep-set eyes crinkled into a smile the second she spied Lori and Brandon at the door.

"Hope this place is okay," John said when they reached the table and made quick introductions. "It seemed like a central location with a name even Brandon could remember."

"I noticed the name," Lori said, smiling. "Does this city ever feel too ironic for its own good?"

Everyone laughed. "I like you already," John said. "Let's get you guys some drinks."

Brandon ordered manhattans for them both, in rocks glasses, extra cherries for the lady. "You remembered," she said to Brandon, then Lori turned to John. "Your comment surprised me. In my experience, there's nothing Brandon forgets."

"Not the important things," Brandon said, "but the rest goes in and right back out."

"I guess everything I say is in the latter category," John said, feigning hurt.

"Not true."

"Where did Abby and I go on our last vacation."

"Um...someplace sunny and warm?"

"Everyone in Seattle vacations someplace sunny." John looked back at Lori. "We happen to favor Mexico." That started a run on vacation mishaps until Brandon and John fell into a conversation about an investigation at work.

"Shop talk," Abby said to Lori in a conspiratorial voice, "always happens. So tell me about your kids." By the time they'd finished a second round, Lori felt like she'd known Abby forever. John suggested that they order some food.

"I better eat," Lori said, "if we're gonna keep drinking."

"Lori's still a lightweight." Brandon winked at the group.

"If we're ordering food then," John said, "we better order another round."

It wasn't long before Lori was feeling fairly intoxicated, despite the heavy appetizers. As was everyone else, she noticed, even if they weren't lightweights. Apparently, it was becoming her habit to get drunk with strangers.

"I went out a few weeks ago," Lori said after a rare pause in the conversation, "with a group of divorced women. They meet at a local bar once a month."

"Smart women," Abby said.

"Somehow, we got talking about sex…"

"Of course you did," Abby interjected again. "That's all I talk about with my friends."

"Really?" Lori asked.

"I'm exaggerating; we also talk about our kids once in a while."

"All you and your friends talk about are the kids," John added, winking.

"I never talk to my girlfriends about sex." Lori laughed. "I guess there wasn't anything to talk about."

"I bet that has changed," Abby winked at Brandon.

"When the divorcées heard I had a boyfriend," Lori continued through her blushing, "they were clamoring for intimate details. I managed to fend them off."

"I wouldn't have minded if you scandalized them with a few stories," Brandon said.

"That's what scares me."

"It shouldn't," Abby said. "Maybe those women needed some inspiration."

When the laughter died down, Lori said to Abby, "One of the women confessed that she meets younger men on Tinder. Would you ever…, I mean, this obviously doesn't apply to you since you're happily married to John, but..." Lori looked at Abby imploringly, "would you sleep with a perfect stranger, I mean, like fifteen minutes after you met him on some app?"

"No," Abby said.

"Of course not," Lori agreed with relief.

"I sometimes sleep with other men, though."

"What?" Lori nearly choked on her drink.

Abby looked over at John, seeming to ask if it was okay to go on.

"I don't understand," Lori interjected.

"John and I have a kind of open marriage."

"So... you're happily married, clearly," Lori was stuttering, "but you...sleep with other people?"

"Yes, but…"

John broke in. "We sleep with other people, together."

"Now I'm really confused."

"We're part of a group that enjoys mixing things up," Abby said.

"What does that mean, exactly?"

"We spend time with other couples who like to share their partners," John explained.

"Like other couples who...are your friends?" As Lori asked the question, she threw Brandon a wary look. He seemed to be in cop mode, just listening to the facts.

"We don't always know them well. There's sort of a grapevine where you can find other couples that are interested."

"Wow." Lori was shaking her head. "I never imagined…"

"That's what fun about it," John said.

"It's what got me interested," added Abby. "The chance to experience something pretty intense that I'd never imagined myself doing."

"Did you know about this?" Lori asked Brandon. When she heard her harsh tone, she turned to Abby and John. "I'm sorry, really, I'm not criticizing. It's your marriage."

"Please, don't worry." Abby put her hand on Lori's. "We know it's not for everyone."

"And please don't think we brought you here to make a pass," John said to Lori. "I haven't seen Brandon so happy in—well, I don't know how long," he added with emphasis. "We wanted to meet the person who was responsible." John reached for Lori's other hand. "Thank you," he said to Lori, then John turned to Brandon. "You have our approval. Lori is wonderful," he added before lifting his glass. "Another round?"

"No more, John," Brandon answered.

"You guys are great," Lori said, "but I think Brandon and I better get going if we're going to make it home in one piece."

Lori and Brandon were quiet in the car, exaggerating their concentration on the road, knowing neither one was really sober enough to be driving. They pretty much crashed upon arrival, barely making it to the bed. Not surprisingly, Lori woke with a headache. The price of her new habit, Lori chided herself, as she downed some ibuprofen before heading to the kitchen to make coffee. She needed both immediately. The sun was trying to peek through the cloud cover, so Lori took her coffee to the dining room, painfully squinting but enjoying the warmth of the pale light coming in through the patio doors. Lori grasped the mug in front of her with both hands and stared at the curlicue of rising steam. Had she imagined the conversation? There was a lot of alcohol involved. No. They really did talk about swapping partners.

"You look like you're trying to solve the mysteries of the

universe." Brandon suddenly appeared in the doorway with a cup in hand. "Thanks for making coffee," he added, sitting down next to Lori.

"Did you take me last night hoping for a swap?" Lori's tone registered between hurt and anger.

"Whoa. Back up."

"Did you?"

"No."

"Then why?"

"They're really good friends, Lori. They've saved my ass, like a thousand times, as a single parent. I wanted you to meet them."

"Okay," Lori paused to consider that she might have overreacted, "I get that, but did you know about their…?"

"Sex lives."

"What they do?"

"Not really. John and I spend a lot of time together. We've been through a ton of shit, and you share things. I knew they had some sort of open relationship. I guess I assumed it meant that John could fool around without Abby minding."

"That's a big assumption."

"Agreed. What they do is a lot more interesting."

Lori shot him a look.

"What?"

"I wasn't talking about the swapping partners, Brandon, but you assuming that Abby didn't get to stray."

"I see. Point taken, counselor."

Lori liked how he called her that. She let it sink in. "So you think it's interesting what they do?" Lori asked eventually. "That's a genuine question, not a judgment."

"Appreciated," Brandon said, meeting her eyes, "and yes. For one thing, it makes more sense."

"How?"

"I could never quite imagine John having affairs. They have such a good marriage, really solid. I guess the Catholic boy in me doesn't square that with infidelity."

"That's good to hear."

"What they do sounds different."

"Not infidelity squared?"

"Not if they're enjoying other couples together. To me, that sounds more like mutual exploration."

"I think it still sounds a lot like being unfaithful," Lori said.

"John and Abby don't strike me as a couple that would tolerate faithlessness. The thing is, they met when they were young. They've been together a long time."

"It does seem like monogamy is the death of good sex."

"That and raising kids," Brandon added.

"God, yes."

"Maybe they're looking for a way to keep the spark alive, by giving each other the freedom to explore, but keeping it, you know…in-house. It becomes something that connects more than separates them."

"That's quite a theory," Lori said, raising an eyebrow.

"Haven't you fantasized about sex with a stranger? A *ménage à trois*?"

Lori started to say no but then paused to ask herself why she was so quick to be the prude.

"There's certainly a long and ancient history of bacchanalias, orgies, and…"

"Ever the scholar," Lori interrupted. "Honestly, I've never imagined a three-way." She squinted her eyes into a question mark. "Is the third party always another woman?"

"Doesn't have to be."

"Two men, wow, that's a concept."

"There you go."

"I confess," Lori said after a pause, "I've stared at a cute guy, a total stranger, imagined him naked, and thought, what if?"

"Never acted on it?"

"Who has the time," Lori answered with a strained laugh.

"Do I detect disappointment?"

"Not really. I bought into a faithful marriage; to stray is wrong." Lori paused again, longer that time. "Maybe being honest about desire, even acting on erotic impulses, isn't necessarily bad." She gave Brandon a hesitant look. "Maybe it's the start of something...enlightening."

"Now, who's the philosopher?"

Lori gave a small laugh. "I'm probably too shy."

"You know…, I wouldn't mind sharing your new insights with others."

"What do you mean?"

"I might enjoy watching other people appreciate your sexuality, especially when you let the wild out."

Lori gave him a strained look. "Really?"

"Maybe, yeah."

"That's the hardest part to imagine," Lori said, "letting go with, basically, strangers. Don't you think it's because I trust you that I can embrace my uninhibited side?"

"You're giving me too much credit. I think you're realizing your own power."

"Kind of you to say, and, of course, it's fun to speculate. Doing something like that is another thing entirely." Lori gave him a sharp look.

"Message received," Brandon said crisply as Lori got up to grab the coffee pot from the kitchen. She topped off both their mugs, went to put the pot back, and returned with the carton of half and half.

"We could start with something safer," Brandon spoke with an upturned glance, waiting for Lori to sit back down.

"Excuse me?"

"We could role-play one of your fantasies."

Lori wondered if she would ever be able to resist Brandon's sexy smirk. "Let's walk around Green Lake," she answered, "and see if I can work off this hangover."

Chapter Eight

Lori loved Green Lake Park. The vibe of the city captured in a three-mile circumference with the iconic Seattle skyline etched into its extended view. On a sunny weekend before the rainy season, it felt like pedestrian rush hour. Cyclists and skateboarders, joggers and dogs, small children wobbling askew on scooters, all wanting to partake of a slice of fair weather. To Lori's eyes, every adult was sporting at least one colorful tattoo. It occurred to her how monochromatic the joggers on DC's Capital Crescent Trail would look in comparison.

Lori and Brandon traversed the circular path without speaking. Building to a steady pace, they held hands until they split to pass a group of slow walkers, interlocking fingers again to fall back into a rhythm. They were halfway around before Brandon broached the topic.

"Do you have a recurring fantasy?"

"You're my fantasy."

"That's nice of you to say, but I bet there's something more. When you were a kid, did you ever play doctor?"

Lori thought for a moment, "I did, actually, with my cousins, who we only saw once a year."

"You see?"

"They were girl cousins."

"Even more interesting." He gave her a raised eyebrow. "What about now? When you pleasure yourself, or even when you're with me, is there a scenario you use to get turned on?"

Lori gave him a how-could-you-think-that look.

"I won't be insulted. We all need our go-to fantasies in a pinch."

Lori laughed skeptically, but after a moment, she said, "Obviously, it's not the same thing, but when Ben was little, he cajoled me into playing make-believe all the time. Elaborate schemes involving bad guys and action heroes. He could stay in character for hours. Not me," Lori added, "even though I knew how important it was for Ben. I felt compelled to get back to the dirty dishes." She looked over at Brandon. "Why are we so quick to give up play?"

"You don't have to." Brandon gave her a conspiratorial grin. "You can tell me your fantasies, Lori. I promise to keep a straight face."

Lori knew her fantasies, but it felt uncomfortable to say them out loud.

"I can see you working," Brandon tapped her head. "Up here. Don't overthink this."

"I'm not. It's just... they don't seem appropriate."

"I won't judge."

"You say that, but they usually involve some kind of... violation, not a crime, but still something that if it really happened would probably be awful or, at least, highly improper."

"Maybe that's what fantasies are good for; to work out our darker natures."

"But they turn us on..." Lori's said, her mouth twisted with discomfort.

"What if sinful and pleasure are two sides of the same coin?"

"Please! Not another perplexing duality."

"What can I say, Professor." Brandon squeezed her hand smiling. "Tell me about them."

"Really?"

"Why not?"

"What if they're weird? Or involve men besides you, wouldn't that bother you?"

"Nope. You're naturally curious, Lori, with an expansive view of the world. I like that."

They walked some more in silence.

"Well…," Lori started, then paused for a few more strides. "They involve men. I've never fantasized about being with another woman."

Brandon turned quickly to look at her, but Lori stared straight ahead.

"They're in positions of authority…," Lori was glad they were walking, it made it easier to talk about, "and the woman is inexperienced, and not forced, but induced, into sexual contact."

"We can work with that."

"Sometimes, it's a bit more forceful than inducement." She looked up at Brandon but quickly turned away. "I'm not sure I want to work with those."

By that time, they had completed the circuit.

"Want to stop for a bite to eat?" Brandon asked

"Sure, and maybe a drink." Lori cringed. "I can't believe I'm saying that after last night."

"You drink, and I'll drive," Brandon offered.

They found a little cafe with outside tables facing the lake. Lori ordered a glass of white wine. "To fantasies." She lifted her wine glass.

"Cheers." Brandon clinked with his glass of water.

"I want to hear yours too," Lori added quickly.

"I promise to tell, but you still haven't let me in on what's happening with Ben."

"*Ugh...* It was top on my list of things to talk about, but it's been nice to forget for a while."

"Is it school?"

"I'm not sure. He's drinking, a lot I think, and lying to me."

"Is there something going on, with friends maybe?"

"He's under a lot of pressure. Everyone makes such a big deal about getting into a good college like their whole life depends on it."

"It sort of does."

Lori sighed. "He played the I'm-going-to-college-you've-got-to-let-me-grow up-sometime card."

"He's right, but so are you. You can have reasonable rules when Ben's under your roof. He should respect them."

"Ben drove home with a friend after they'd been drinking."

"That should be an absolute no."

"Even if we don't always follow that rule." Lori made a guilty face.

"Yes. Holding boundaries is really important. I see kids on the street; some look well-off, I suspect from caring families, but their parents stopped paying attention." He took Lori's hand. "It doesn't end well."

"Sometimes, I wish you had a different job," Lori said with an uncomfortable laugh.

"I'm not saying that's gonna happen to Ben. Maybe you can come up with an informal contract. List the rules that are non-negotiable and what happens if he breaks them. The most important thing is to stick to it."

"Easier said than done."

"True, but the rest, you let him know you're willing to talk about it. You'd be amazed at how well that combination works."

"I can do that."

"Keep it short, though, not too many words." Brandon grinned. "That's hard for you lawyers, but he's a teenager, and male, so consider the attention span."

"Point taken." She smiled back. "By the way, Ben has taken to remarking whenever I have a glass of wine."

"We did that to our parents."

"You're right! Emily and I were awful." Lori chuckled to remember it. "I think it was middle school. The health teacher told us that someone was an alcoholic if they had a drink every night. We promptly announced that verdict to our parents because they always shared a martini before dinner."

"That actually sounds kind of romantic."

"I know! Thank god we grow up and stop seeing the world in black and white."

"I'll drink to that." Brandon lifted his water glass.

"I'm guessing if I set boundaries," Lori continued, "I have to try, at least, to get Peter to hold the line. I am not looking forward to that conversation."

"Maybe he'll surprise you. Some rules are no-brainers."

"Maybe..." Lori sipped her wine shaking her head vaguely. "I could *never* have a conversation like this with Peter. Anything constructive would be sabotaged by the lurking question of whose fault, that, and Peter always has to be right."

"That must be hard."

"I could be subversive. Let Peter think he won, then do what I wanted."

"Did you like that?"

"No. I like to win honestly." Lori laughed. "Just kidding. No one has to win, especially when it comes to our kids, right?"

"Believe me; I've been sucked into the win/lose trap."

"I've *so* gotten into that with Ben," Lori rushed to add. "I'm so angry when I talk to him; I want him to feel my pain. I should wait until I'm calm."

"That's true, but you're only human. It sounds like Ben's been pushing your buttons."

"The worst part is his attitude. Ben seems to have absorbed from his father that women are lesser beings." Lori looked down and ran her finger around the rim of her wine glass. "Maybe I've taught him that too, unintentionally." She felt tears coming. "I get scared by what we've shown him."

Brandon leaned over and kissed her cheek. "I'm sorry, baby. You're a great mother, and you deserve respect, always."

When they got back to Brandon's house, he went off to check his email while Lori promptly claimed the couch. She felt her head drop as she flipped through the pages of a magazine. Crying always made her tired, not to mention wine at lunch. Lori considered napping for a minute, suddenly bolting awake when she felt the sag of another body next to hers.

"Hello, Miss…," Brandon said, looking down at some blank papers on a clipboard in his lap, "Miss Smith."

"Miss? You flatter me."

"Would you prefer Missus?"

"Miss is fine."

"Very good. I'm Doctor Dare."

Lori gave him a skeptical look. "I see."

"I understand you are here to participate in our research project on the subconscious mind."

Lori started to laugh, then stopped herself, seeing the sober look on Brandon's face. Were they really doing this? She asked herself, taking a few deep breaths to wake up and

118

switch gears. "Yes, that's right. I'm here for the research project."

"Thank you. It's difficult to find qualified subjects. You meet all the criteria."

"Good to hear."

"Are you ready to get started? I can explain the process as we go along."

"Okay. I guess. Sure."

"Why don't we head to the examining room."

Those few words gave Lori a jolt, well, more of a tingly thrill in the places that matter. Brandon led her to the bedroom. He'd made it look slightly clinical, having stripped the bed and placed a white sheet on top. "Please undress."

"Excuse me?"

"We'll be applying probes to your body. There's a robe for your comfort."

Lori noticed it on the bed.

"It should open in the front," Brandon said stiffly.

"I see."

"When you're ready, you can lie down."

Lori quickly undressed, put the robe on, and lay down. Brandon was turned away but seemed to be fiddling with things on his dresser.

"Let's get started," Brandon said as he walked back to the side of the bed. "First, I'll check your vital signs." He reached for her wrist to take her pulse. Lori tried hard not to giggle, wondering, had Brandon done this before? "Everything looks fine." He quickly slipped one panel of the robe off her shoulder, exposing Lori's breast. She shivered. Brandon ignored that and instead began to rim his finger around her nipple, bringing it immediately erect.

"Is that really necessary," Lori said. "It doesn't seem very…clinical."

"We need to check baseline reactivity."

"I see."

He slid off the robe to expose her other breast and repeated his fondling. Lori wished there was a genuine way that Brandon could measure her heightened bodily reactions.

"Excellent. You seem to be very reactive."

"Is that good?"

"Yes. Now please bend your knees and slide your bottom down to the edge of the bed."

"That seems unnecessary for a brain study."

"Please follow my directions. There are only a few more preliminaries."

Lori wiggled down slowly, keeping her legs tightly shut. He moved to the bottom of the bed and put his hands firmly on her knees.

"Please relax and open your legs."

"Really?"

"Yes," Brandon answered as he pressed them open, overpowering Lori's not entirely feigned resistance. "Please cooperate. It's important we get relevant data." With her legs spread wide, the robe fell away too, exposing her whole body. "I hope you don't mind if I don't use gloves; the findings are more accurate."

"That doesn't sound very proper." Even as Lori was speaking, he pushed a finger deep inside her. "Oh my."

Brandon lingered there, then rubbed her wetness around the tips of his fingertips when he pulled out. "Very reactive. Please stay as you are while I place some probes on your body."

"I thought this study measured brain activity," Lori said, closing her bent legs.

"Yes, Miss Smith. In fact, I'd like you to make your mind blank. No more questions, please. I'm going to cover your eyes." He slipped on an elastic blindfold. "We will be measuring your brain's reaction to various stimuli. I'll begin now."

Lori felt a sharp pressure, like a pin, move down the length of her outer arm. The movement was repeated, moving inward. When Brandon passed over the dimple in her inner arm, Lori shuddered, surprised at how powerfully the sensation registered deep inside her. He continued down the side of her body, tracing her curves, each time drawing the line closer to her belly until he passed over her breasts. The object caught at her taut nipple, and he changed direction, circling the hard bud until Brandon stopped suddenly. Before Lori could protest, she felt the shock of something clamped there.

"Ow!"

"I'm sorry. Does that hurt?" Brandon's voice stayed in character.

"No. Not really."

"Good." He clamped the other nipple.

After her surprise, Lori focused on the sensation. It was complex, like a sip of good wine, a layering of pressure, and a sensual sting. She breathed in sharply as Brandon's lips fluttered over her vigilant flesh. At the same time, he gently tugged on the device. Lori's breasts felt untethered, as if they existed apart from her body. Brandon continued to suck her nipples, alternating with a flick of his tongue or a tug on the clamp. She exhaled an *ohmygod*. Her breasts had never felt so sensitized.

"Shhhh," he whispered, "concentrate." He slowly released one clamp. Lori felt an exquisite shiver as circulation and feeling rushed back; then, he released the other. Lori experienced the lovely effect all over again. She squirmed a bit, hoping the clamps would return.

"Relax," Brandon said as he rubbed her belly in a circle. "We'll move on." Lori heard lust creep into his voice, then Brandon's movement in the room, a rustling of items. The air fluttered as he approached again and laid his hands firmly on her knees. "Please spread your legs." Those words, again, and her pussy was on fire imagining Brandon examining her. "Wider, please."

His hands commanded her open, then paused. Lori felt a draft flow over her pussy, aware both of unease and hunger at its blatant exposure. Brandon touched her again with the sharp object, that time drawing it down the insides of her legs, a different route each time, finally circling the soft flesh of her inner thighs. If her pussy had a voice, it would have screamed, "stroke me," but Brandon simply held her legs open with an almost clinical touch. Lori felt a pinch of cool metal clamping the delicate skin. There wasn't pain, but a heaviness, as if the object was weighted. He added several more, lining her labia, then Brandon started to manipulate them gently. Lori could describe it only as a deeply sensual massage, activating nerves in places she'd never felt before. It made her legs tremble. Lori was sure her pussy must be leaking from the effects of Brandon's enchanted rubbing down. He stopped abruptly.

"We're done. Thank you very much for your participation."

"No!" Lori gasped, surprised at her own voice!

"That's all the tests we require."

"Doctor," she sputtered, "you can't leave me like this."

"What do you mean, Miss Smith?"

"You haven't finished...that is...what you started. I'm begging you."

"I see." He paused a beat too long. It was killing her.

"Do you want this?" Brandon drew his finger tautly from her ass through her pussy like he was bowing a violin. There was a slip in tension as he passed through her wet hole.

"Yes!"

He slowly grazed her clitoris; a string tightened to its breaking point.

"Shit!"

He moved away.

"Noooo," Lori moaned in an extended syllable until Brandon returned, inserted his finger, moving in and out of her pussy, his thumb circumnavigating and moistening her labia. Brandon moved in rhythm with Lori's voice, a sonorous purr urging him to tighten the circle until, finally, he landed on her clit. She climaxed almost immediately, calling out to him, "Brandon."

"You must mean Dr. Dare."

Lori collapsed into laughter. Ripped off the blindfold and grabbed Brandon's arm to pull him down towards her. "You never cease to amaze me," she whispered into his neck.

"I told you fantasies can be fun," Brandon answered, punctuated by a gentle kiss.

Chapter Nine

Lori found herself back east again too quickly, where things with Ben were anything but fun. He left for school every morning, barely saying two words. When Ben returned after soccer practice, Lori would be in the kitchen or on her computer at the dining table and would ask about his day.

"Fine," Ben mumbled, discharging his backpack in the hallway before slinking into his room and closing the door. Dinner was more of the same forced conversation. Lori insisted that they eat together if there were no conflicting activities. Lately, she wondered why she bothered. Lori had such fond memories of family dinners with Emily and their parents. Maybe it was the patina of nostalgia, but Lori recalled long meals, her father always at the table, in fact, always at the center of things, directing lively conversations about current events.

Early in her marriage, Lori took pride in preparing an evening meal, even if it meant eating near midnight by the time she and and Peter got home from work and she whipped up something. It was some of their best times, laughing at the absurdities of client demands and partners' foibles. Then came children. Lori usually fed Ben early and waited to eat with Peter. After Catherine was born and Lori quit the law firm, it became painful, at least for Lori, to hear the deep divergence in their daily rituals and responsibilities. Lori found herself instead eating with the kids, but even that often felt stunted. They talked to each other, Lori made sure of that, but it never had the freewheeling quality she recalled from her own childhood. When Peter infrequently made it home on time, he was more interested in table manners—something Lori concededly cared little about—than joining in the conversation. In desperation one night, Lori pulled out *Table Topics* cards that someone gave them as a hostess gift. Players took turns picking a card and asked the question written on the back intended to spark conversation. It worked! All four of them stayed at the table for over an hour, talking, laughing, and surprising each other. Its success became a touchstone for Lori's growing disappointment.

She was tired of the recent fights about whether Ben and Catherine could bring their phones to the table. If Lori won, it felt like pulling teeth to get them to talk. Worse, with Ben giving Lori his sly take on the silent treatment — responding with just enough not to be called out as rude — Catherine seemed torn between sides. Catherine usually shared everything with Lori, but Lori could sense Catherine holding back, afraid to be the traitor. Lori found herself composing an angry list of house rules during the silence as if she could legislate quality time and respect.

∾

They had finished another stilted evening meal. Peter was coming over for a family meeting. The irony of the term was not lost on Lori, but she insisted. Ben was balking at chores. He often slipped past curfew and was drinking on the weekends. That was not how Lori wanted to send Ben off to college. When Peter arrived, he and Lori sat across from each other in Lori's living room, waiting for the children to join them. Peter surveyed the room, assessing Lori's decorations perhaps, or, more likely, her spending habits. She called the kids a second time and Catherine came bounding down the stairs, crossed the room to give her dad a hug, then sat down next to Lori on the couch. It took a third shout to get Ben to the room. He shuffled in and took the seat next to his father. There was a long silence. It felt to Lori like she and Peter were opponents, each with their second, squaring up for a duel.

"Lori," Peter said finally, "as you called the meeting, why don't you start."

"Okay. I want to talk about some family ru—," she stopped herself, "guidelines that we can agree to in both our homes." Lori was determined not to be the bad guy or make it seem like they were there to gang up on Ben.

"I've got something I want to talk about," Ben piped in.

"Okay, Ben. I'd like this to be a family discussion," Lori said.

"I need a car."

"That wasn't exactly what I was thinking. We could start with…"

"Actually," Peter interrupted, "I've been thinking about buying a car for Ben."

"Excuse me?" She shot Peter a look. "I'm confused about why we would give Ben a car when he hasn't kept up with basic responsibilities as a member of this family."

"That's not true, Mom. I'm going to school and keeping up my grades. You always say my job is to be a good student."

"That's true, Ben." Lori was trying not to take the bait. "So is taking on responsibilities," she added, trying to soften her tone. "You remind me frequently that you're going off to college. You'll need skills, like how to clean your room, do your laundry, budget your spending money."

Ben glanced at his father as to say what did I tell you.

"Having your own car is a big responsibility. Who's going to pay for car repairs, insurance, and gas?" Lori asked, her equanimity slipping. "You won't look for a part-time job."

"How am I supposed to get a job, keep up with classes, and get my college applications done?"

"If you got off your phone, there'd be plenty of time." Lori hated how she sounded, but not more than she resented being made the family nag.

"Perhaps we can get back to the guidelines," Peter said.

Lori took a breath. She looked from Ben to Catherine, noticing both brought their phones with them, and Ben was sneaking glances at his. "I think we need to come to an under-standing about phones. They are a privilege, and we need some reasonable restrictions." Lori made sure to look at both kids in turn. "For example, phones should not be brought to family meals. They need to be put away during a set time each day so you can do your homework uninterrupted. I would like the phones out of your bedrooms by eleven at night, nine o'clock for Catherine."

Lori noticed Ben give his dad another conspiratorial look. "Look, you guys." Lori grew exasperated. "These are entirely reasonable requests. You have no idea the damage smartphones are causing your school life and your mental health."

"Mom, I promise to put my phone on my desk at nine," Catherine offered.

"That's not good enough. I don't want texts waking you up in the middle of the night or you grabbing the phone first thing every morning."

"So what are you going to do, lock them up?" Ben asked.

"Sarcasm is not necessary," Peter said.

"Actually, I was going to ask you to bring your phones to the kitchen and leave them there."

"Mom, I'm not giving up my phone at night. That's the only time I get to connect with my friends."

"You see your friends all day, and you need to get a decent night's sleep. Every study shows..."

"Can we please skip the science lecture?"

"Ben," Lori cut him off abruptly, "you need to be more respectful."

"Your mother is right," Peter said. "Are there other things you want to discuss, Lori?"

"I think we should talk about a curfew for Ben, and Catherine too when she's older. My concern is having the kids drive or be driven home when drunk drivers are out on the road."

"No one has curfews, Mom."

"As you keep informing me, Ben, but..."

"What would be a reasonable curfew?" Peter asked no one in particular.

"What do you think, Ben?" Lori tried her best to give Ben a respectful look.

"Look, I'm going to college in a few months."

"It's more than a few months, Ben. You're still living in our homes, and it's our responsibility to keep you safe."

"Mom, you've got to stop treating me like a baby."

"All right, let's have a grown-up conversation." Lori sat up taller and looked directly at Ben. "I am concerned about your drinking."

Ben shot her a hateful look, and Lori could feel Catherine shifting to attention on the couch.

"Dad," Ben said, looking at Peter with confidence, "would

you please explain to Mom that you're fine with me having a few drinks on the weekend."

Before Peter could respond, Lori said, "Well, I'm not fine with it. There's a reason the drinking age is twenty-one."

"We have to be realistic," Peter said. "Ben is going to college and, while it may not be legal, there will be drinking. It doesn't make sense to pretend otherwise."

"I'm not oblivious to that fact, Peter. He's not there yet; he's barely eighteen."

"Yes, but I would like him to learn how to drink responsibly before he goes to college."

"What does that mean?" Lori asked.

"A drink or two on a Saturday night is not a big deal," Peter answered.

"Have you seen him come home on a Saturday night?"

"Mom!" Ben growled.

"Ben is very honest with me about his drinking," Peter said.

"I see," Lori said sharply. "Last Saturday, Ben didn't make it upstairs when he came home. He fell asleep, fully dressed, on the floor of the basement. He didn't get up until two in the afternoon Sunday and walked around like a zombie the rest of the day. Was that from one or two drinks, Ben?"

"This is bullshit."

"Wow." Lori felt anger coil around her concern and over-power it. "Is that all you have?"

"That's not helpful, Lori," Peter volunteered.

"Mom, you need to get an actual life and stop worrying about mine."

Lori knew better than to answer. The cruelty she felt rendered her speechless anyway. "Please excuse me." She got up with as much dignity as she could muster. As she walked up the stairs, she could hear Peter ask Catherine to give him a few minutes alone to talk to Ben.

In her room, Lori sat on the edge of her bed, trying to get her emotions under control. She was not going to leave the conversation like that. Ben needed to hear her, Peter too. She smoothed her hair and opened the door to her room but froze at the top of the stairs.

"I want to come live with you," she heard Ben say.

"That's not a good idea," Peter responded.

"Why not? I want to spend more time with you. You get me."

"I'm sorry, Ben, but your mother has more availability to take care of you and your sister."

"You think that's a good thing? She sits around waiting for us to come home so she can start in about schoolwork and her new obsession with chores and wanting to know exactly where I was and who I was with. It's like prison."

"Ben, she's your mother, and she's doing her best to care for you."

"You pay her for that, right? You give her money?"

Lori crumbled onto the stair.

"That's none of your business."

"Because you should keep it. She doesn't do anything for us."

"Ben, this is not an appropriate conversation. She's your mother and..."

"If I come live with you..."

"That won't work."

"But..."

"I have an engagement tonight."

"Do you have a date with your girlfriend?"

"Enough, Ben, I need to go. When you come next weekend, we'll work on getting you a car."

Lori staggered back to her room so Peter wouldn't see her. She could last a lifetime before looking at Ben again. He might as well have spat at her. She wanted to scream, or cry, or at least have Brandon there to fold her in his arms. The best she could do was call him; he'd still be at work.

Lori texted Brandon.

Can you talk?

Not right this moment. Everything okay?

Call me when you can.

As soon as I get out of this meeting.

Lori wasn't sure she could wait to vent the angry bile.

She called Emily, sobs coming before she could get out any words.

"Lori? Is that you? Are you okay?"

"I'm not sure." Lori took a stuttering breath. "I'm so angry... and hurt. I don't know who I'm more furious with."

"What happened?"

"We had a family meeting."

"Oh boy."

"It was awful, Em. Ben said hurtful things to me, and worse, about me, to his father."

"The apple doesn't fall far..."

"Don't say that. I don't want to think about Ben that way. Peter was cruel to him, too, totally dismissive when Ben asked to live with him. I feel hurt for Ben... I feel so hurt *by* him too."

"Sister, that's the juggling act called motherhood. You're expected to manage everyone's crises and bad moods, never letting them down. Then someone throws the occasional knife in your direction to see if you can handle it."

"This felt like a knife in the back. I hate when parents say,

'After everything I've done for you,' but Em, how could he? Why would Ben want to live with his dad?"

"I don't know, Lori. I'm so sorry."

Tears came again. Lori was trying to bring them under control when she noticed that Brandon was calling her.

"Em, Brandon's trying to reach me. I asked him to call so I should pick up. I'll call you back later."

"Don't worry about it. And Lori, take care of yourself. You're allowed."

Lori hadn't switched calls fast enough. She called back Brandon.

"I'm sorry, I was talking to Emily."

"What happened?"

"It's Ben." The tears started again.

"Is he okay?"

"He's fine; he just hates me and wants to go live with his dad."

"He told you that?"

"No. I heard him ask his dad." Lori snuffled up her tears. "You see, we had a family meeting, you know, to talk about some reasonable house rules."

"Was Peter there?"

"Yes, and Ben started to be snarky, so I left the room, and that's when I heard them. The two of them sat in *my* living room saying terrible things about me. Ben told his dad that I don't do anything and he shouldn't pay me to take care of them." Repeating it, Lori felt the blow all over again like she'd been punched.

"He said that?"

Lori was grateful that Brandon sounded as shocked as she felt. "Yes," she answered.

"Peter gave him a good lashing, I hope."

"He told Ben he should respect his mother and that I'm

doing the best that I can," Lori repeated the comment with all the contempt it contained coming out of Peter's mouth.

"What an ass."

"Then Peter's telling Ben that he'll get him a car."

"I thought Peter was smarter than that."

"I guess it was the consolation prize since he told Ben that he couldn't live with him."

"What message does that send to Ben? Does Peter know how much Ben is drinking these days?"

"He's being willfully blind," Lori answered.

"Binge drinking and a car, not a good combination."

"Peter doles out the goodies then leaves me with damage control, despite that he believes I'm a barely adequate parent."

"I'm so sorry, baby."

"God, I miss you. I wish you were here."

"I wish I could be."

"I can't believe we're not going to see each other until Christmas," Lori grumbled.

"It's hard for me to travel east two months in a row, and we agreed it doesn't make sense for you to come here in December if we're both going to be in New York for the Holidays."

"I know, I know. But that's like seven weeks. It feels like forever."

"We used to make it three and four months between visits."

"How did we manage?"

"Lots of sexting."

"Dammit," Lori nearly growled. "Why do we have to be sensible and dependable when everyone else gets to act like selfish assholes?"

"Because we're the parents in charge. Somebody's got to do it."

Lori exhaled an audible sigh. "I'm sorry," she said after a pause. "I'm acting as bratty as my son."

"You're fine, but what're you going to do about Ben?"

"Honestly..., I don't know." They both were quiet, listening to the other's breathing through the phone. "What happened to the little boy who looked at me like I hung the moon?" Lori asked finally.

"He'll come around. It's trial and error, but they figure out who's really there for them."

Ben and Lori were still giving each other a lot of space. When Ben wasn't driving around in his car — at least Peter went for something used and not fancy — he was complaining about college applications. Lori suspected he wasn't actually doing much. He refused her help with his essay, which Lori decided wasn't a bad thing. Ben should rise or fall on his own efforts. She hoped it wouldn't backfire with a string of rejections. To be fair, Lori wasn't much fun either. A constant anger simmered just below the surface and turned her into somebody she didn't like, a lurking spider poised to strike. The proverbial straw that broke the camel's back came when Lori told Ben he needed to earn his gas money, and Ben solved the dilemma by wheedling a credit card from his father.

"We need to talk," Lori told Ben on a Saturday morning when there was nothing on their calendar. She braced for his cringing, wondering, yet again, what happened to the little boy who ran to her headlong with open arms every time she walked into the room. Lori was ready, though. She had practiced her breathing, determined to get things right, even if she only planted some seeds.

"Mom, I've got to..."

"This is important."

He slumped into the dining room chair across from Lori.

"I miss you, Ben."

She could feel him crawl further inside. Don't get sentimental, Lori reminded herself; the kiss of death, Brandon had warned her.

"Don't worry," Lori added. "I get that you're going off to college. I'm ready for that." It was a bit of a white lie, but Lori allowed herself, to keep things on track. "I'm excited for you."

"Okay," Ben said, sitting up slightly.

"The thing is, I'm not comfortable with how we've been treating each other," Lori said, adding, as Ben sagged again, "I've probably seemed like a real bitch at times."

Ben's eyes shot open.

"I'd like to change that," Lori said.

"Okay," Ben answered, warily alert.

"Is there anything you'd like to see change, Ben?"

"Yeah, I'd like you to stop nagging me about everything."

Lori took a depth breath before responding. "I get that. What would you like me to stop nagging you about?"

"Chores, curfew, school work, my college essay."

"So pretty much everything," Lori said, smiling. She thought she saw the slightest grin from Ben. "Is there anything you'd like to change about your own behavior?" That seemed a better strategy than listing his flaws.

"Um, I don't know."

Lori stayed silent.

"I guess I haven't been very nice to you."

Lori resisted the urge to bite.

"You're trying to do your best," Ben added.

Shit, this is hard, Lori thought. She wanted to yell at Ben, don't be a condescending ass like your dad. Putting down the other parent, though—not a good strategy. Instead, she asked, "Do you see how that statement might be hurtful to me?"

"Why?" Ben looked genuinely confused.

"Because it sounds pitying and demeaning of my job as your mom and, well, disrespectful to me as a person."

Ben stiffened again, defensive.

"I'm still your parent, Ben. You are becoming an adult too, but I'll always be your mother. I deserve your respect. I didn't always ask that of your father." Lori paused, worrying if that revealed too much. "That is a mistake I'm not willing to make anymore," she added, noting that Ben looked at her differently, in a way Lori couldn't identify. "I'm willing to let go of a lot, Ben, school work, applications, curfew even, if we can reach an understanding on two things.

"Okay..."

"No more lying."

"I haven't..."

"No more shading the truth then. And this gets to the drinking. I..."

"I know."

"I'm not sure you do, Ben. I think you lie about your drinking because you see that you are crossing some dangerous lines. And I can't help you with that if you're not truthful with me."

"I *do* know, Mom. Listen to me, please."

"Okay."

"It was really humiliating when you told Dad about that night I got so drunk, but you were right. It was really bad. I got scared thinking about it." Ben looked down and spoke into his lap. "I kinda didn't remember where I was when I woke up or exactly what I did the night before. I don't ever want to feel that again."

"Look at me, Ben," Lori said gently. "I don't love hearing that, but I like hearing that, if you know what I mean."

Ben broke into a genuine smile. It made him look relaxed and suddenly young again, like the toddler she played with in the park every day no matter the weather; the boy to whom she read his first Harry Potter book snuggled on the bed, thrilled. It was the innocent face Lori still saw glimpses of, even as a teenager, when Ben was asleep. Dare she push her luck?

"I gave up a lot to be a full-time mom."

"I didn't ask you to do that," Ben interrupted.

Danger zone. Lori changed tack. "Of course, you didn't, and I wouldn't change it for the world."

"Maybe you should have..."

"I'm not asking for your advice."

"I'm just saying..."

Lori cut him off again. "I consider parenting my job, Ben. Being there for you and Catherine cheerfully, consistently, no matter what else, it's as important as any job I could have. That's true even though, or maybe because, I don't get paid for it."

Ben seemed to wince.

"It's probably something you can't understand until you have kids of your own and see how much your kids need that. And even though it's vital," Lori added, "it is not a given that parents show up." Lori paused. If only she could remind her son of all the times Peter was absent, physically or emotionally, and how sad and disappointed Ben was. "I can only hope that I've shown you how important that is when your time comes."

Ben seemed to be nibbling on that.

"For now, and this is the other place we need to reach an understanding," Lori continued, "you have to treat me with the respect I deserve."

"You said that already."

"Would you say that to your boss?"

Ben looked taken aback. "Probably not."

"Why?"

"Because I might get fired for being rude."

Lori laughed. "Exactly, and because the boss, with *her* experience, might know a few more things than you."

"I get it."

"I won't ask you to do something unless it's important." Lori looked at him hard but said with a smile, "And then I expect one answer, 'yes, Mom.'"

Ben responded with a crisp, military salute.

"No need to go overboard," she answered, and they both laughed in what seemed like the first time in months. It felt good, though Lori knew not to expect miracles.

Lori left Ben to decide if he was too busy with college applications to make their usual trip to New York for Thanksgiving. When he said, "let's stay home," Lori accepted Jeanette's invitation to share the holiday meal with her extended clan. Jeanette added three folding tables to accommodate the raucous crowd. At one point during dinner, Ben was laughing so hard that he almost fell off his chair. He was seated at the other end of the table, but Lori was pleased to spy from her end —where Jeanette, not so discreetly, seated Lori next to Richard's recently divorced brother—Ben covering his wine glass. That was no easy feat as Jeanette's older brother, Barry, made sure everyone's cup was filled at all times. Lori felt surprised that despite Barry's efforts, Lori was not tipsy. It allowed her the luxury to observe someone else's crazy family dynamics without any of the angst. She noticed how Jeanette's younger brother used silly stunts to slip the shadow of Barry's oversized personality, and when Lori joined Jeanette at the sink to help with the dishes, she said under her breath, "I totally get it now about your mother undermining you."

Jeanette laughed. "So you heard the comment about how

the turkey would not have been so dry if I ordered it from her butcher?"

"Yes, and how her children would never have dared to wear jeans to a holiday dinner."

"You've got to choose your battles, right?"

"I'm definitely working on that these days," Lori agreed. "I'm not sure that I'll ever get around to forgiving Peter, but Ben and I are in a much better place."

Jeanette stopped rinsing plates, dried her hands, and swept Lori into a tight hug. "I'm so glad to hear that."

"Me too," Lori hugged her back. "I better go check that Catherine's not bothering your nephew."

Lori had noticed Catherine following Jeanette's adorable nephew into the living room, where he offered to play guitar for anyone not interested in watching football before pies were served. As she sat listening with Catherine, it struck Lori that being surrounded by someone else's family could never assuage the deep longing for her own. She wondered if they'd made a mistake not going to New York. It felt right to give Ben some autonomy. Her parents wouldn't be around forever, though, and she missed Emily and Thomas and their wonderful entertaining. There was something else too. Lori missed Brandon, maybe even more on a day designated to bring families together. It didn't help that Jeanette's less than artful seating assignment reminded Lori of her outward status — divorced and single. It wasn't true, but at the moment, she did feel alone. Lori exhaled a deep sigh and bent down to kiss Catherine's hair.

Later, after she had gone to bed, Lori was awakened by a ringtone. Groggy, anxious that something might be wrong with her parents, Lori fumbled for the phone.

"Did I wake you?" Brandon asked.

"No worries. Is everything okay?"

"I needed to hear your voice."

"It's good to hear yours. I miss you."

"Miss you too. How was Thanksgiving?"

"Fine. Fun. Jeanette's family's as crazy as everyone else's. They were really welcoming. Somehow, though, it left me wanting you."

"It was really hard not being with you and your kids."

"I'm glad your mom came out."

"Just the three of us, like old times." Brandon made a dismissive sound. "We never saw our dad for Thanksgiving."

"Did Fiona cook?"

"My mom announced she would be sous chef, but yes, Fiona planned the whole meal. She's a much better cook than her grandmother. She did great."

"Wow, that's impressive for a sixteen-year-old."

"We kept it simple."

"Thanksgiving's never simple. So many traditions to satisfy."

"True," Brandon chuckled. "Hey, since you're awake, can we FaceTime?"

"*Ugggh*, I didn't take off my makeup, and my mascara's probably smudged. I'll look like a raccoon."

"You'll still look beautiful."

"Flattery will get you everywhere."

"Do you have your iPad? I want to see all of you."

Lori paused. She could hear in Brandon's voice exactly where he wanted the conversation to go. It still came as a surprise to Lori that her first instinct was too demure, as she had done for so many years with Peter. Lori guessed it was a way to process her resentment that Peter seemed to prefer reading legal briefs to being intimate. It wasn't just me, Lori reminded herself. Their occasional lovemaking felt like going through the motions, about as fun as emptying the dishwasher. Everything was different with Brandon. He liked sex, a lot. Imagine that! Brandon seemed to understand lovemaking as a generous act, a kind of restoration. It could patch up insecurities and wipe away regret.

"You still there?"

"I'm here. I need to wake myself up for that."

"For what?" Brandon asked with a sexy purr.

"Damn, your voice... Give me five minutes, and I'll Face-Time you."

"I'll be waiting."

Lori flung herself out of bed. She tiptoed to the bathroom and turned the water on low to wash up, careful not to wake Catherine. Her face was flushed, she noticed in the mirror, but a glimpse at her pajamas made Lori cringe. It could be fun to wear something sexy. Lori tiptoed back to her room, pausing at the top of the stairs to make sure Ben wasn't up. She quickly rummaged through her panty drawer, conscious not to keep Brandon waiting. Lori found a lingerie slip that she'd worn exactly once. It was a gift from Peter. Was that creepy? She decided what the hell. It was elegant, made of genuine silk with a plunging v-neck. Lori put it on and returned to her bed, kneeling before the propped-open iPad. After steadying the device, she opened the FaceTime app. Appraising her cleavage, she pulled the slip down a bit before pressing Brandon's face on the contact list.

"Did you stop to make yourself a snack?" Brandon looked playfully back at her from the screen.

"I wasn't that long! I needed to get ready."

"Me too," he said, tipping down his phone. The screen filled with Brandon's flushed and swollen cock gripped in his hand.

"Oh my. I see." It felt close enough to touch, and Lori

142

couldn't help but lean in and graze the screen with her cheek. She closed her eyes to imagine the feel of his soft skin, the hard pressure of his erection against her face. "If only I could wiggle my nose and be in your bedroom," Lori said. "I'd make you cum before my kids noticed I was gone."

Brandon laughed. "What a concept, but live video will have to do." His voice slowed and deepened. "Tell me how you would do it."

Lori sat back against her heels as Brandon's face came into view. She looked into his eyes. They were bright and mischievous, melting her bashfulness.

"Well, um, I guess I would kiss you..."

"Can you be more specific?" He was grinning. "It's just us, baby, don't be shy."

Lori looked straight into the screen, took a deep breath, and shook her head to clear away the prissy cobwebs. "I would run my tongue up and down your cock to make you wet."

"Show me," Brandon said.

His gravelly voice made Lori's mouth water, and she flattened her tongue, drew it slowly around her lips, and smoothed it over her teeth. "Then I would nip you a little to let you know who was in charge."

Brandon looked hungry as he glanced down at her body. "As pretty as your little dress is, I want to see more of you."

"You noticed?" Lori grinned back, slipped a finger under one strap, and toyed with it before letting the strap fall off one shoulder. The silk followed, causing her nipple to harden as the slippery material slid over her breast. The resulting difference was arousing, one breast exposed to the slight rustle of a breeze through her window, the other covered in satin.

"You are so fucking sexy," Brandon said in a slow growl.

Lori sucked on her fingertip, then caught her lower lip as she smoothed the fingers of her other hand around her breast, then her nipple, entrancing it to hardness. "I would lick your balls," she cooed, opened her mouth, smoothing her tongue again around her lips, her mouth filling with saliva, "like this." Lori puckered her lips into a circle, sucking the edge of her fisted hand. "I would suck you hard."

Brandon's eyes were tensed, nearly closed, and she could sense, without seeing, his hand moving faster, feel, without touch, his cock tensing for eruption.

"Cum into my mouth," Lori said as she moved her face right up to the screen, mouth open wide. Brandon moved the phone down to capture the moment of his climax, semen splattering on the device.

"God, I can taste you," Lori said, catching a glimpse of her own eyes in the corner screen constricted with longing. Brandon's were closed like he'd gone somewhere for a moment.

"I knew I had something to be thankful for..." he said finally, eyes opened and crinkling with a smile, "the sexiest woman in the world is mine."

Lori laughed. "Not sure about that, but I am yours."

"Tell me what you're feeling."

Lori thought for a moment. How to describe the thrilling tightness, her desire wound to the breaking point simply by watching Brandon's rising pleasure and release?

"Remember when you were a kid, and a friend would spin you in a swing until the rope was all bunched up and then let go?"

"I do."

"I feel like that, right before the swing unravels."

"Wow. Grab your toy so we can set you loose."

"That's okay. It's enough to think about it."

"You're kidding, right?"

"I can take care of myself later," Lori said.

"And deprive me of the pleasure?"

"I'm really tired, Brandon, and before you think it, I'm not being shy."

"Are you sure?"

"Believe me, a few months ago, I never could have done what we just did."

Brandon laughed.

"Seriously, I'm trying to say how thankful I am for what you've given me." Lori paused, squinting. "Do you remember that time we fooled around in front of the mirror?"

"I think…"

"Of course you do." Lori chuckled. "I don't think I understood at the time, but you set it up so carefully, the chair just right, me on your lap, so I could watch. I barely recognized myself, but you helped me see what my body knew instinctively. I can still see how my pupils got so dark and wild-looking, how my legs fell open."

"I'm hard again."

Lori laughed. "Should we do something about that?"

"You should get some sleep."

"Okay, but I'm going to dream...," Lori smiled sleepily, "that I'm a captured maiden, and you, a mysterious stranger who, for a price, will set me free."

"I love that you're embracing your fantasies."

"I love you, Brandon. Sleep tight."

Chapter Ten

Lori decided to give the Friday night divorcées another shot. Ben was out with his friends, and Lori told Catherine she could fend for herself. Lori laughed as she said it. As if being home in a tidy, suburban home with a steaming hot pizza delivered to the door required any fending. Lori was hoping the ladies might have some advice on negotiating house rules with the ex. She and Peter had made little progress on guidelines about the kids' phones. Lori suspected it was because Peter was never separated from his own. At least he didn't want to be a hypocrite; she would credit him that. At the same time, Lori was composing an email she had yet to pull the plug on. To let Peter know she overheard his conversation with Ben, and if Peter continued to disparage her parenting abilities, she would ask the judge to require co-parenting classes, maybe family therapy. She recognized it as a long shot. Writing it, though, reminded Lori of her power to enlist backup.

She entered the restaurant to find the same clutch of women sitting at exactly the table they inhabited two months before. Lori took a moment to glance around. The other tables were filled with couples or families. The owners should appreciate the slightly exotic flare the divorcées gave the place. Jill noticed Lori and stood up to wave her over.

"Look who came back," Jill said, swinging an extra chair to the table. "We thought we'd scared you off."

"Of course not. Things have been really busy with the kids."

"Just with the kids?" Jill gave her a questioning smirk.

"You know teenagers," Lori answered without missing a beat. "How is everybody? It's good to see you all again."

"It's good to see you too," Susan said with a sweet smile.

"How are your boys?" Lori asked.

"You remembered! They're fine. Indoor sports have started, so at least I'm not freezing my tushie off during games."

That led to a discussion on how to keep warm during the outdoor-sports season. It took a while for the waitress to come take Lori's order.

"I'll have a red wine."

"What! No manhattan?"

"Last time, I was afraid I'd be stopped for a DUI."

"That's because you left too soon," Eliana said.

"Yes," Jill added. "You left us hanging."

"Can I ask you all about something?" Lori hoped the shift from her sex life was not too obvious.

"Sure," Leslie answered, "as long as it's not about exes. We try to keep this an ex-free zone."

"Not very successfully," Eliana added.

"It's not about exes exactly, but co-parenting. How do you all manage it and stay sane?"

The women responded with their bodies. Susan slumped, Jill groaned, Eliana shook her head, and Leslie nodded, but their faces all looked pained.

"We might need another drink before we can face that

subject," Jill said. "Eliana, how are things on the geriatric ward?"

"Ha, ha. I actually went on a very nice date last weekend. He's sixty-three, still quite handsome, and runs two marathons a year."

"But can he get it up?"

"You don't have to be crude, Jill," Leslie interjected. She turned to Eliana. "Tell us more."

"Thank you," Eliana said, throwing Leslie a smile. "He's had a busy career. Kids are grown and out of the house. He's starting to wind down at work and wants to travel the world. I think he's looking for a companion."

"Travel! The surest way to end a relationship. So much stress," Jill said.

"Or it can be a perfect way to see if you're compatible," Leslie added, then turned a schoolmarmish look at Jill. "How many Tinder dates, Jill, since we last saw you?"

"It's been slow, what with the holidays," Jill answered, seeming unbothered by Leslie's tone. "I'm probably the only woman on Tinder who single-handedly cooked for and hosted thirty people on Thanksgiving."

"At least you can make fun of yourself," Leslie said.

Jill patted Leslie's hand. "Let me know when you want to give Tinder a try. You're still young and pretty. You'd have a hookup in a second."

"I read an article." Susan piped in. "It said most people on Tinder never even meet their matches."

"What's the point?" Eliana asked.

"Turns out most people use it for a confidence boost," Susan answered. "Apparently, it feels good enough to get... What's it called, Jill?"

"Swiped."

"Right. Swiped."

"Good pun, Susan," Jill said.

Susan looked confused.

"That's the direction you swipe," Jill said, "if you're interested."

Susan cocked her head as if still baffled.

"Never mind." Jill looked around the table. "Anyway, why not get the boost from actual sex? Nothing beats that."

"Jill, you have a one-track mind," Susan said.

"I might have to agree with Jill on this one," Lori interjected.

"Finally, we're going to hear from the one person besides me actually getting some."

"What do you mean, Lori?" Leslie asked.

"It's changed me."

"A new relationship?" Leslie was looking at Lori intently.

"Yes, that, but also the sex."

"See," Jill said with a note of satisfaction.

"Lori's not having sex with a stranger," Susan added.

"That's true," Lori said, "but it's more than that. My ex and I had a pretty good partnership, at least for a while, but we never had sex that was daring. It does something to you."

"Exactly!" Jill added.

"Really? Susan asked. "Isn't sex, well, just sex. Maybe some men are more determined to find your G-spot," she shot Jill a look, "but isn't the day-to-day support what makes you feel loved."

"She's right," Leslie added. "Bottom line, women want a partner. Your Tinder dates are gone before the light of dawn, aren't they, Jill?"

"Absolutely, but I'm ready to conquer the world when I wake up."

"I don't buy it," Leslie said. "In the morning, all the same crap is clamoring for your attention."

"Maybe you've hit on it." Lori looked back at Leslie. "When you let sex be…," she paused to find the right word, "a bit reckless, you finally stop feeling so responsible for everything."

"So you and Jill find it necessary to retreat to the level of teenage boys," Susan said glumly. "I really don't need more of that in my life."

"No," Lori said, "I'm not advocating irresponsibility—reckless was the wrong word. It's more like… vulnerability."

"That's the last thing a divorced woman wants to feel." Eliana finally joined the conversation. "Everything about our situation is precarious. Divorce guts women financially. End of story. Sex, our ability to give or withhold it, is one of the few options we have to make sure we're not eating cat food in old age."

"So sex in exchange for security," Leslie said. "Is that any better than Jill's Tinder dates?"

"That's actually the vibe I get," Susan said, looking a bit sad, "when I'm with my girlfriends. They're not commiserating that I've lost the love of my life. They're kind of smug because they've held onto their security blanket, even if — and it's a fact — they only get occasional and boring sex."

"Here's the million-dollar question." Eliana looked directly at Lori. "Is your fella rich?"

"No," Lori answered.

"Well then, did your divorce leave you well off?" Eliana asked.

"For a while, I'm okay. Not forever."

"I've made my point."

"And what point is that?" Jill asked. "That the only reason Lori's new sex life is fulfilling is because she doesn't have to worry about money?"

"In my experience, it's rare to get both," Eliana said.

"I think I got us headed in the wrong direction," Lori chimed back in. "Maybe it's not the sex, exactly." She paused before asking the group, "You know how your identity gets wiped out by your role as wife and mother?" Lori saw lots of nods. "With a certain kind of intimacy, you can catch hold of yourself again."

"I don't think any part of *me* still exists," Susan said. Everyone stared into their drinks until Leslie volunteered, "Well, now that we all feel bad..."

"I'm sorry," Lori said. "Things at home have been rough. My son threatened to go live with his dad."

"Kick him out," Eliana said, "isn't that where your enlightenment takes you?"

"Eliana," Susan said angrily. "We're here to support each other."

"Susan's right," Jill said. "How are you dealing with that, Lori?"

"The crisis has passed. We've actually had some good talks lately. Anyway, his father said no."

"Ouch."

"It's hard to feel hurt by your kid when he's been hurt, right?"

"I'm guessing it's easy for your ex not to feel bad about the things he's not around to see," Jill said.

"How do they get off so easy?" Leslie asked.

"I hate to sound like a one-note Johnny," Eliana added, "but men still run the world."

"Maybe that's all I meant, Eliana," Lori said. "Women need to do whatever works to put ourselves back into the equation."

"Here, here," Jill said, lifting her glass. All but Eliana joined in. She told the group she needed to get going.

"Stay, Eliana. I should go," Lori said. "I promised my daughter I wouldn't be gone long." As Lori gathered her things, she leaned over to ask Jill quietly, "What's your number? Maybe we can have coffee sometime?"

Jill grinned and slipped Lori her business card.

Lori was standing at the back of the minivan, waiting for Catherine and Ben to bring out their suitcases. She was looking forward to the holidays, and not only because Brandon would also be in New York. For the first time since Peter walked out, Christmas felt like more than something to get through. Her kids put up the velcro advent calendar, taking turns to stick one decoration on the felt tree each day even though they had long outgrown the ritual. The three of them picked out a rather large tree which Ben helpfully corralled through the front door and set up in its stand. Lori sent out a Christmas card, for the first time since she shoved the stack of cards, with a professional portrait of their family of four, into the front hall closet in the weeks after Peter walked out. Her new card featured an unguarded snapshot of Lori, Ben, and Catherine that Jeanette took at Thanksgiving. It was one version of their new family that felt as honest as Lori's trimmed-down mailing list.

Other things had changed too. Lori left her kids to pack their own suitcases, schlep them to the car, shop for, wrap and load the presents they intended to give. That way, if they forgot something important, Lori was not left holding the bag. Catherine even surprised Lori by insisting on getting presents for Brandon and Fiona. All that was left was the long drive — plenty of time for Lori to fret over her and Brandon's attempt to blend extended families, and they'd barely tried to blend their own.

Ben appeared at the garage door, suitcase in tow.

"Load it in the back. Where's your sister?"

"Putting on makeup."

"For heaven's sake, we're sitting in the car for the next five hours." Lori yelled up the basement stairs, "Catherine, get in the car."

"I'm coming, Mom." Catherine appeared at the top of the stairs. "I'm right here."

"Where's your stuff?"

"Oh shit. Be right back."

"Language..." Lori shot back. "Ben and I are waiting on you."

Barely five minutes into the drive, Ben reached for the auxiliary cord.

"Please use your headphones," Lori said.

"But Mom..."

"You can plug in when it's your turn to drive."

It was such a small thing, but for years, Ben, then Catherine, got in the car, flipped off Lori's station, and plugged their phone into the car stereo. She accepted it; her only retaliation was to make them change songs when the lyrics were too crude. Instead, Lori plugged in her own device. She selected her driving playlist, which Lori made for the occasion to reflect a time before children when she loved a long stretch of highway and singing at the top of her lungs. By the time they exited the Capital Beltway to head north on I95, Lori was humming along quietly but still, out loud. Ben looked over at her like she'd grown a second head.

They stopped to get gas at a rest stop in New Jersey. It was swarming with people, and Lori felt oddly connected to that group of strangers, each heading to a unique set of complications but to a place they all called home. Lori and her kids waited in a ridiculously long Starbucks line while they took turns going to the bathroom. When they finally got back to the car, Ben said he would take the wheel.

"Thanks," Lori said. "It's a lot easier when you do some of the driving." She meant it, but braced for the onslaught of his new favorite music, high-pitched screaming that she didn't dare complain about for fear of sounding like her own parents. Ben surprised her, though, choosing a mellow song Lori liked. They sang along, Catherine piping in from the back seat. Three songs later, a smile still on Lori's face, Ben switched back to the screeching. Lori fumbled in her bag for her earbuds. Catherine plopped on her Beats. They were back to being three people alone together in a car.

When they crossed the state border into New York, Ben tapped Lori's knee. She took off her headphones, noticing the car was silent. Catherine was asleep.

"What's up?" She asked. "You want me to drive?"

"No. I'm good," Ben answered. "The thing is... I wanted to say... Look, I'm sorry for the times I've been such an ass to you."

"You haven't been an ass."

"Yes, I have," Ben said emphatically, then paused. "I've been talking to Gabe."

Ah, Gabe... Lori silently thanked Jeanette for recommending the hip but savvy adolescent therapist who recently set up a practice.

"I was really angry at you and dad for getting divorced."

"I'm so sorry, Ben."

"I'm still mad. I hate the divorce and feeling like a pawn..."

"Wait," Lori interjected, "I get your anger, but that's not fair. We try very hard to..."

"That's not true, Mom. You can't talk about Dad without telegraphing how much you hate him and that we should hate him too, and it's the same when he talks about you."

"Hate is an awfully strong word," Lori said before what Ben reported actually registered. "Your father hates me?"

"Of course he does," Ben answered. "You made him feel like we didn't want him around."

"Ben, I never wanted him to feel that way." Lori worked to control herself. "Your father," she began again slowly, "made choices between work and family, and he inevitably chose work. I picked up the slack. There was a lot of slack," Lori couldn't help adding.

"He tried...sometimes, and you shoved him away. Besides, he works hard for our family."

Lori took a breath and held her tongue. She felt confident that what Peter did, he did mostly because it was good for Peter, but Lori understood Peter's love language. His need to be stroked and appreciated for barely showing up and for how well he provided for them. Lori was too resentful to give him that. "I could have done a better job at letting your dad know how grateful I was for how well he supported us."

"Yeah, well, water under the bridge."

Lori shot Ben a look, surprised at his mature choice of words.

"I thought it was your fault that Dad left," Ben said.

"I begged him to stay. For you and Catherine."

"But not for you?" Ben paused; it cut like a knife. "Anyway, I get it," Ben continued. "Nothing's that simple. It's not fair for me to take my anger out on you."

"That's what mothers are for."

"Don't do that." Ben's tone was urgent.

"Do what?"

"Be a martyr."

Lori glanced over again and caught Ben's eye. "A martyr, huh. Who taught you that?" Lori had her guess.

"It doesn't matter," Ben answered sharply. "We all have to be responsible for our own feelings."

"Wow, Ben. That's incredibly wise."

156

"Are you being sarcastic?"

"No! Not at all. I'm impressed, and you're absolutely correct."

"I just wanted to apologize," Ben told her again, glancing over quickly, with no smile, as his hand reached to turn the music back on.

Lori let her head fall against the headrest. *Wow.* She glanced out the window letting her thoughts duke it out like in a school-yard brawl, lots of shoving and some blood, but no clear winner. Ben apologized. That was a first. It felt like real progress. But all that talk about hatred. What had they shown their children? Lori felt a stabbing pain. Could that kind of damage ever be repaired? Twenty years Lori gave to her marriage. It suddenly felt like twenty years wasted. But without Peter, there wouldn't be Ben and Catherine. There's the rub, Lori thought, and that she still cared what her kids thought about whose fault. Ben was telling her she didn't have to. *Wow.* It was the only word she could settle on, like that book Catherine loved as a kid, *Lily's Purple Plastic Purse.* Ben's martyr comment still stung. Everyone loved to accuse mothers of being martyrs, but wasn't that part of the job description? Was there ever a mother who did *not* sacrifice too much and never enough at the same time? Lori feared that might be a puzzle she would never solve.

They arrived at Emily and Thomas's house with Christmas Eve in full swing. Lori and Emily's parents, Joe and Mary, were already there, as well as the Brunos, her parents' oldest friends, Thomas's parents too, and his sister and her husband and a boatload of children — Emily's three from her first marriage, and Thomas's two, his sister's three teenagers. Christmas music gently filled the house. An elegant buffet was set. Flutes stood filled with prosecco. Lori's kids said quick hellos, filled their plates, and headed to the basement to join the other teenagers. Lori grabbed a drink and sat in the middle of the couch between the Brunos. Michael Bruno, still a flirt at near eighty years old, told Lori that she looked as young and lovely as on her wedding day.

"You're lucky you married such a charming man," Lori said, turning to his wife, Margaret.

"You should see him in the morning when I haven't made his coffee," Margaret responded with a wink.

"Well, it's great to see you both. I would have thought you'd be with your family tonight."

"How I wish, but Lucy moved to Chicago. She stayed home to spend Christmas with her husband's family. They alternate years."

"Sounds like a divorce," Lori said, adding "just joking," when Margaret looked confused.

"Thankfully, no divorces yet," Margaret paused, "but I can't quite get used to Christmas without family. Your sister was kind to include us."

"Everyone is family in Emily's book. Last year she invited her ex-sister-in-law's entire clan. They all got along famously. My kids thought it was weird, but I'm hoping they've come to see the good in it." Lori laughed.

"I'm sure you do."

"What about your son?" Lori asked Margaret.

"Bill's law firm sent him to Beijing for two years."

"That sounds like an adventure. Will you visit?"

"We're thinking about it. But it's a long trip at our age."

"I think you should go. You two hardly seem your age."

"We've had some health issues, but we're still here." Margaret knocked on the wooden edge of the coffee table.

158

"You're way too young to be thinking like that," Lori said.

"So you say, but you get to a certain stage in life, and the horizon starts coming at you fast." Margaret put her hand on Lori's knee. "I haven't seen you since your divorce," she said. "How are you holding up?"

"I'm good, Margaret. Thanks for asking." Lori thought for a moment. "Sometimes it still feels like a total shock, and other times..., I can't even remember being married to Peter."

Margaret laughed. "I've known you since you were a toddler. When your mother told me about Peter leaving, I knew you would land on your feet."

"I appreciate that. I always assume Emily is the strong one."

"She is, but you were always sure of what you wanted."

It was Lori's turn to laugh.

"Is that funny?" Margaret asked.

"On several levels, yes. The last thing I wanted was for my kids to be from a *broken family*," Lori said with air quotes, "but here they are..."

"I'm sorry, I didn't mean to be insensitive."

"Not at all. My marriage was in trouble, but it's not the kids' fault, and they seem to be paying the price."

"They come from hardy stock. They'll be okay."

"Your whole generation is hardy stock." Lori gave a small laugh. "Let's hope my generation hasn't ruined that."

"We certainly didn't get divorced. And we got married knowing a heck of a lot less than women these days when they say 'I do.'"

"Brides have gotten awfully cocky," Lori agreed with a chuckle. "It's a hoot to watch those wedding reality shows. I'm always thinking, oh my ladies; you are so missing the point."

"I confess, the confidence seemed justified with your marriage. I remember how your parents thought it was a perfect match of intellect and ambition."

"Really?"

"After the fiasco with Emily and her first husband, they were glad that you and Peter seemed so suitable, financially and otherwise."

"Like a good disaster movie, all calm until the storm hits."

"Is that how it happened?"

"Not really. I thought we were going through a rough patch. Normal, you know, in a long marriage. I couldn't imagine Peter would blow up everything."

"That did seem out of character."

"I still don't know whether to credit him for his honesty or hate him for being selfish."

"Hmmm. I guess it was easier for us. We never imagined we had the choice to leave."

Lori shrugged. "I certainly wasn't consulted, which, I suppose, may be what I deserved."

"Of course it wasn't."

"If marriage is about choices now, I'm pretty sure you have to ask for what you want and be clear about the things you're not willing to sacrifice."

"At least you're dating again," Margaret said, turning towards Lori in a conspiratorial fashion. "Your mom tells me he's someone from around here."

"Yes. Joanne McManus's son, but he lives in Seattle."

"That sounds very modern. How does it work?"

"We take turns traveling to see each other. I really love Seattle."

"How exciting for you."

"It is..., except when it still feels lonely."

"Well, you're getting a second chance." Margaret lifted her glass. "Here's to new relationships."

"Thanks," Lori said, lifting her own. "Looks like my glass needs refreshing. Can I get you anything, Margaret?"

"No, dear, I'm perfectly content."

Lori stepped up to the buffet, filled her flute with prosecco and sipped, glancing through the golden bubbles. The room practically glowed from the illumination of the fire and small circles of loved ones in warm conversation. Lori felt a pang of resentment that Brandon was not with her. He'd arrived in New York with Fiona that morning, but they agreed to spend the first day each with their respective families, more for Lori's sake. Her parents were still getting used to the idea that Lori was dating and already seemed serious about another man. Of course, Brandon was not a stranger to them, but that might have been part of the problem. Her mother saw Lori get hurt early on by Lori and Brandon's tortuous shifting between friendship and romance and friendship again. Lori also suspected that Brandon, the FBI agent, did not meet her mother's criteria of, how had Margaret put it, suitability, financial and otherwise. If Lori thought about it, that was one of the things she loved most about Brandon. He seemed to care more about the work than the outcome, more about fighting for the underdog than what would be gained, financial or otherwise. Lori hated to admit it—taking another sip of expensive prosecco—but when she married Peter, she made the same calculation as her mother.

Suddenly, the room felt unbearable to Lori without Brandon there. His mother's house was less than half a mile from Emily's, but the space between held a lifetime of *if only* and *what-ifs*. When Lori came home in past years, the town's landmarks felt like touchstones for something just out of reach. Was it really a surprise that Brandon found her again there? As if every decision, good and bad, led back to that place.

Lori was startled by her phone buzzing in her pocket. She slipped off to the bathroom to find a text from Brandon.

I don't know what we were thinking.
I need to see you. Can you slip away?

You read my mind! The party's winding down.
I'll text you when the coast is clear.

Like old times, sneaking around so
our parents won't catch us.

Brandon added a winking emoji.

Ha! This time we're hiding from our own teenagers.

Who could have imagined?

It still scares me to think… What if we hadn't
met up two Christmases ago?

It wasn't an accident that I came east for
the holidays for the first time in years.

But when I got into my car that day,
I wasn't sure I would drive to your mother's house,
or if you would even be there.

But you did, and I was…

162

And you took a chance and kissed me...

And you kissed me back, even if you
left me hanging for another nine months.

I'm sorry.

Don't be, baby. Just get out of there!

Lori and Emily cleaned up from the party and said their
goodnights. Lori made sure Ben and Catherine knew where
they were sleeping. She told them they could stay up with their
cousins but that she was going to bed. Lori texted Brandon to
give her ten minutes, and she would start walking to his house.
It would be nice to stretch her legs after the long drive, and Lori
would not have to explain if someone heard her car. She went to
the guest bathroom and brushed her teeth. Lori mussed the bed
for good measure, turned off the light, then tiptoed downstairs
and slipped out, grateful for people who didn't lock their doors
so she could get back in. When Lori turned from the door, she
was startled to see Brandon hovering under the street light. She
ran to him, ignoring that it felt like acting in a corny rom-com.
They didn't tumble into a passionate kiss, though, or even hold
hands, just stood there, staring.

"I was looking forward to the walk," Lori said finally.

"Let's walk back to Joanne's house." Brandon put his arm
around her shoulder as Lori circled his waist with her own.
They took an indirect route as if by agreement, walking in the
direction that took them past the house where Lori grew up,
then past the trailhead that led to the rock outcropping in the
woods where Lori and Brandon first made love. They spoke

only to point out places where they met up in years past, but each footfall felt like a step backward in time. The house was dark inside when they finally arrived.

"I guess everyone's gone to sleep," Brandon said. They stood arm in arm, watching the fog of their breath disperse gently into the night air.

"It's getting cold," Lori said. "Maybe it will snow for Christmas."

"Maybe."

"Can we go inside?" Lori asked after a while.

"I thought you'd never ask." Brandon kissed her hair. "I left the basement door unlocked." He released her, slipped her cold hand inside his warm one, and led them to the backyard and down the basement stairs. The lights were off, and they left them that way, as sneaky as mice, a recurring motif of their lovemaking, though for reasons that kept changing. He struck a match and lit the wick of one small candle giving the utilitarian room an inviting glow. Apparently, Brandon planned ahead. Lori noticed that he'd also laid a thin, narrow mat and several old blankets on the floor.

Brandon pulled her in, enveloped her with his strong arms, and held her for a long moment. It was hard for Lori to believe that two years had passed since Brandon similarly tucked her into his chest. She had released a flood of tears and fears about Peter's sudden desertion that were wiped away and replaced by a profound sense of security. Lori lifted her head and smiled as she met Brandon's waiting lips. It was a long, smoldering kiss, hands moving inside their coats and over each other's bodies. They seemed to be retracing the years with their hands, as their feet had done on the walk to Joanne's house.

Lori pulled away finally to shrug off her jacket, letting it fall on the floor. She began unbuttoning her blouse as Brandon slipped off his coat. It turned into a mute game of *Simon Says*.

Brandon followed Lori's lead and pulled off his sweater, then Lori slipped off one shoe, then Brandon his, the same with the other foot. Lori unzipped her skirt and pushed it down past her hips before Brandon unbuckled and pulled off his pants. He simply watched as Lori unhooked her bra and let it fall to the floor. They mirrored each other to take off their last article of clothing, then stood stock still, eyes locked. Inside, Lori's every nerve was jagged.

She finally took the first step. Brandon moved forward, and they both stopped barely inches apart. He raised a hand to smooth Lori's cheek, and she snuggled against it before he traced a line down her nose and across her lips, then lifted her chin, and they fell into another long kiss to warn away the cold, winter night. Eventually, Brandon turned Lori to lean back against his chest as he continued a slow tour of her body. He gripped her neck and kissed her temple, nuzzled her ear while his other hand slid down her décolletage, palm against her breast, thumb circling her nipple like a snake charmer raising the cobra from its basket. When his hand moved down to graze Lori's belly, she could feel the hardness of Brandon's erection against the small of her back. Lori reached for the nape of his neck and wound her fingers into thick coils of hair. Her grip tightened with anticipation as Brandon's fingers continued their stroll down memory lane, leaving a trail of sparks in their wake. It was a dangerous current mixed with her wetness, and Lori released a blistering sound when Brandon finally cupped her pussy and fingered her. She rocked her hips back and forth against Brandon's rock-hard cock, while his greedy fingers fondled her clit until she unraveled and nearly collapsed. Brandon caught her and lay her back on the blankets.

"I never want to be apart this long." Lori's voice was desperate, circling his neck and pulling him towards her.

"Never," he rasped in tandem with the first thrust of his

cock. She loved how Brandon held himself there for a moment as if to acknowledge the completed circuit and let her feel the fullness of him. Then came the energy of connection, the bounding friction that negated time and distance. They both choked back groans that released into laughter with Brandon's climax, hushing themselves and laughing again, seemingly at how crazy it was to be sneaking around at their age, until Brandon pulled Lori into his arms, so they both fit on the mat.

"It sounds silly," Lori said after they cuddled for a bit, "but I better get back to my sister's before they notice I'm gone."

"We're adults," Brandon answered. "Stay awhile." He tucked some of the blankets around her feet. "You should at least warm up your toes before we head back into the cold."

"Okay, until my toes are warm. By the way," Lori added, lifting her head to kiss Brandon, "I really like our grown-up sex."

"Better than our teenage sex?"

"Just different."

"At our age, different is probably better if we can keep it up."

"I'll remember that." Lori snuggled deeper, but she nudged him right before they fell asleep.

"If I don't go now," she warned, "I'll never leave."

"Fine by me," Brandon said, but Lori slipped past his playful attempt to hold her fast as she lifted off the mat.

They dressed quietly. Brandon blew out the candle and guided Lori to the basement door, where they slipped back into the night air. They took the direct route to Emily's. It led past Sharon's old house. There were remnants of a snowman on the front lawn. The last Lori heard from Sharon, her parents had sold it and moved to Arizona. A new generation of kids were growing up there. It struck Lori more as a feeling than a thought; what a short, transient thing life is. That the places of her girlhood milestones could be occupied so quickly, by other families, by other children who would never give a thought to the lives of those that preceded them.

"Do you ever think about her?" Lori asked as they stood gazing at the house.

"Not really. I'm not even sure I remember what Sharon looked like."

Lori laughed. "I don't believe you. There was a time you two couldn't keep your hands off each other."

"She knew how to kiss; I remember that."

"I'm sure she knew more than that." Lori threw a teasing glance at Brandon. "She was way more adept at how to act around boys."

"I liked that you never acted." Brandon turned Lori towards him. "Even back then," he added, "when everyone seemed to be playing a part."

They walked on, holding hands. "I remember what you were wearing," Brandon said after a while, "that day you led me into the woods."

"No you don't."

"Cutoff jean shorts and a white t-shirt."

"I think I wore those pretty much every day that summer."

"Your hair is almost as long as it was back then." He stopped again, turned Lori, and tilted her chin as he toyed with a short tendril falling on her cheek. Brandon filled his hand with a fistful of Lori's hair and brought their lips together. The tips of their noses were cold when they met, but their mouths were warm and moist, tongues entwined as if wending their way back to the beginning of an old story.

"I really need to get back," Lori said, finally breaking from his lips. On the sidewalk outside Emily's house, they stopped, and Lori stamped her feet a few times for warmth. "Tomorrow," she told Brandon, "the kids and I will come over for brunch like we planned, and we'll pretend we're seeing each other for the first time this visit." She held Brandon's cheeks and planted a firm kiss, like sealing a deal.

"Or not." He grinned as she pulled away.

"Always looking for trouble," Lori said, turning back as she ran up the front stairs, "that's what my mother would say." She slipped back into the house to find everything as she'd left it, the sounds of kids' voices floating up from the basement.

Chapter Eleven

Christmas Day was exhausting, navigating a house with three adults, five when Lori's parents showed up to open presents, and seven young adults, not to mention the never-ending exchange of gifts. Lori wondered if she'd gotten a little too used to the new solitude of life with two teenagers off in their own worlds. Lori and her kids escaped briefly to the relative quiet of the McManus's home. Ben and Catherine hadn't seen Fiona since their spring break trip to Seattle. Even though they had gotten along well, the three teenagers returned to their first, tentative wariness, seeming to understand that whatever was happening between their parents had grown in importance and would likely pull them into its wake. They would at least try for the dignity of resistance. Catherine was the first to fall. She told Fiona that she loved the cool star design on her nails and, when Fiona confessed to have done it herself, immediately insisted that they try it on Catherine. Ben and Fiona managed to connect again over a video game; then, over Ben's immersion in the IRL game of getting into college. Fiona seemed genuinely curious about the schools Ben was applying to. Ben seemed to enjoy the position of wise advisor by sheer dint of being ahead in the process. Lori recognized the obvious; Fiona's interest, since she was only a sophomore, meant Fiona would be way ahead of Ben when her time came.

"Do you think Fiona's too much of a tomboy?" Joanne asked Lori as they cleaned up together from brunch. "I've never seen a girl enjoy computer games as much as she does."

"It's their world now, Joanne. Better that than the makeup videos Catherine favors. She watches strangers talk about the stupidest things." Lori made a face. "Video games probably make them more computer literate. Good for their job prospects someday, right?"

"*Ach.* What do I know," Joanne answered. "I'm a dinosaur with these smartphones and gadgets."

"You and me both."

"Sometimes I wish Fiona had a sibling growing up. She's so solitary and serious."

"Fiona is a lovely young woman, Joanne. Grounded and confident. You should be proud."

"I am, dear. I just worry that she and Brandon are a little too, I don't know..., self-sufficient, maybe?"

Lori glanced over at the others. Fiona was patiently letting Catherine show her something on her phone. Ben and Brandon were huddled at the table. Lori tried not to eavesdrop, but she heard Ben politely ask Brandon why he became an FBI agent. Wonders never cease, Lori thought, smiling into the plate in her hands.

Brandon and Fiona came to Emily and Thomas's house for dinner the day after Christmas. It was the *big event* before Brandon and Fiona flew back to Seattle. Joanne begged off because she was getting ready for a visit from her sister. Still,

170

almost all relevant parties were in one room together. Lori's stomach wobbled with nerves.

When dinner was announced, the younger crowd clustered at the far end of the table, calling Fiona over when she seemed to be eyeing a seat next to her dad. On Lori's last run helping Emily deliver platters of food from the kitchen, Lori noticed their father, Joe, had slipped into the seat to the left of Brandon. Catherine sat on Brandon's right, the seat that demarcated the generations. Lori's father insisted on saying grace, shooting a withering look at the young persons who dared to start serving themselves. Lori looked at Emily as if to say Dad's in rare form. Joe's prayer was mercifully quick, and for a long time following, the only sounds were scraping utensils, the gentle babble of small talk, and enthusiastic comments about the incredible food prepared by Emily and Thomas.

"How long have you been an agent?" Joe asked after folks started serving themselves seconds.

"About fourteen years," Brandon answered. "I got into it late."

"I see. What did you do before joining the Bureau?"

"Mostly studying and teaching." When Joe looked confused, Brandon added, "I have a Ph.D. in philosophy and taught college kids for a while."

"That's quite a career jog. You don't see that too often."

Lori shot Brandon a look as if to say I'm sorry.

"I hear that a lot, Joe. Actually, more than a few agents have graduate degrees of one kind or another."

"Interesting. How's the retirement package?"

Lori cringed. She felt like a girl whose father was assessing her boyfriend's prospects rather than a divorced, financially-independent mother of teenagers.

"It's very good." As if to avoid more grilling, Brandon turned the tables. "How are you enjoying retirement, Joe?"

Smart move, Lori thought, smiling as she lifted another forkful of creamy risotto. Her father was describing his retirees' luncheons and twice-weekly tennis games when there was a commotion from the kids' end of the table. It was probably Sam, Emily's youngest, playing one of his pranks. Catherine was laughing uproariously.

"Young lady," Lori's mother said quickly, "please behave appropriately at the dinner table."

"Sorry, Nana." Catherine looked embarrassed and tried to control herself.

"And please remove your elbows from the table," Mary added.

Lori noticed Brandon lean over and whisper something to Catherine. It caused her to wiggle upright in her chair but also to grin widely. Lori's mother seemed to notice as well. Lifting her wine glass, Mary turned to Brandon.

"I understand from Lori that you have primary custody of Fiona. That's an unusual arrangement."

"It works for us," Brandon said, giving her mother his most charming smile.

"Has it always been that way?"

"Fiona's mother made some decisions soon after our divorce that shaped our arrangement."

Lori wished she could change the subject. She knew how hard Brandon struggled to raise Fiona when Jocelyn took off, sometimes for a year at a time.

"Every family's got to figure out what works for them," Emily piped in helpfully. "Thomas and I learned that the hard way. Do you remember those first few years, Thomas?"

Before Thomas could answer, Lori's mother asked Brandon, "You married Jocelyn Lane, is that right?"

"That would be Fiona's mother, yes."

"Lori took us to some of Jocelyn's dance performances if I

recall. On parents' weekends. Jocelyn was very good. Did she become a professional dancer?"

"She did," Brandon answered. "She traveled the world. Now she works with a Seattle dance company doing choreography and giving private lessons."

"I can still picture the dress she wore to Lori and Peter's wedding. It was striking."

"Mother!" Lori almost spit the food from her mouth.

"What?" Lori's mother gave Lori an annoyed look. "Who knows why we remember the things we remember."

"Can I get anyone more wine?" Thomas stood up quickly, bottle in hand. He threw Lori a supportive smile.

Emily directed her attention to Brandon. "I had a great conversation with Fiona. She's a lovely young woman. You've done a great job."

"Thank you, Emily. Fiona gets all the credit. Dinner was delicious, by the way."

"Wait till you see what's for dessert."

"I can't wait. Let me help with the dishes." Brandon stood when Emily got up to collect empty plates.

"I'll take you up on that," Emily said, loudly adding as she passed Mary, "I'll be sure to tell Joanne next time I see her what a good son she's raised."

Mary and Joe left promptly after dessert while the kids absconded to the basement. Emily, Lori, and Brandon moved to the living room carrying their wine glass. Emily pulled two chairs close to the fire and then sat in the love seat, where Thomas joined her, having followed them in with the remaining opened bottles of wine.

"I'm glad the inquisition is over," Brandon said, laughing.

"I'm so sorry about that."

"I felt worse for Catherine," he said.

"My mother can be hard on her. Catherine's never learned to do ladylike very well."

"You have to understand," Emily said, turning to Brandon, "Joe and Mary were trained badly by my divorce."

"What do you mean?"

"I was a mess. Three young kids, no college degree, and an ex without a steady job. They had to step in and practically raise my kids for a while. It's difficult for them to keep appropriate boundaries."

"One reason I stayed on the West Coast, I suppose. Joanne could easily have fallen into that trap."

"They were counting on never having to worry about Lori," Emily continued. "She was the perfect daughter. They thought she had the perfect marriage."

"That's not true." Lori's statement was a question.

"Yes and no. They never really liked Peter."

Lori looked shocked.

"I mean, they tried," Emily added quickly. "They thought he looked down on us from the deck of the proverbial Mayflower. Later, they didn't like how he was never around for you. But they knew he was a good provider. They could live with that, especially when they were busy paying my bills."

"That must have been hard, Emily."

"Oh, only modestly humiliating, Brandon. But you do what you gotta do to feed your kids, right?"

"That I can understand."

"It's why they like Thomas so much. He took me off their hands."

"Yup, that's all I'm good for," Thomas said, pouring them all some more wine.

174

"You know that's not why I love you." Emily blew Thomas a kiss.

"Why *do* you love me?" Thomas asked with a broad grin. "It's not my athletic physique." He threw a glance at Brandon.

"Hey man, I've got to stay in shape for work. They test us."

"I'm sure that's the only reason. You must hate the looks you get at the gym."

Emily squeezed the extra flesh at Thomas's waistline. "I wouldn't know you without these." She seemed about to make another joke but stopped. "Do you really know why I fell in love with you?"

"Why?" Thomas asked with dead seriousness.

Lori was trying to keep up with the sudden change of tone.

"You always accepted the chaos," Emily answered. "You never ran. In fact, the crazier I made things, the more you stuck around."

"It's true. I wouldn't let you scare me away." Thomas turned and gave Emily a tender kiss. Emily was animated again. "Now, you two..." She looked over at Lori and Brandon. "You seem determined to accomplish the impossible."

Lori and Brandon exchanged a questioning look.

"What do you mean?" Brandon asked

"You have three teenagers between you, and you're trying to build a relationship three thousand miles apart."

"When you put it that way...," Lori said, her face caught between a grin and a frown.

"On the other hand," added Emily after sharing a wistful glance with Thomas, "you get all that alone time together. The luxury of quiet, grown-up weekends. Can you imagine that, Thomas?"

"I miss us being all together," Lori said, ignoring Thomas's laughter. "I want the ordinary moments."

"Do you really want to spend more dinners with Mom and Dad?"

They all laughed then until Lori said, "Seriously, I like this. We've never hung out, the four of us. It's nice."

"I agree. I forgot how much I like you, Brandon." Emily winked at him. "Come by anytime."

"But we won't," Lori said pouting, "not for a long while, or get all our kids together."

"It's true, Sis, but maybe your relationship is meant for a different stage of life. Enjoy the freedom." Emily sighed. "Having all your children under one roof is only fun until they start fighting."

"I wouldn't have minded Mom and Dad being a little nicer to Brandon."

"They were fine," Brandon offered. "It's all new for them."

"I'd like them to know how...," Lori started to say.

"Rubbish!" Emily said. "You're too old to care what other people think."

"I'm not that old!" Lori slapped her sister lightheartedly.

"You know what I mean," Emily said. "You survived the worst. You got divorced in spite of that proper, uptight bubble you live in, and you're still standing. Enjoy yourself. Better yet, go a little wild."

"That seems to be a message I'm getting from a lot of people," Lori said.

Brandon squeezed Lori's hand. For some reason, Lori felt herself blush.

Chapter Twelve

It was Brandon's turn to come to Maryland in January, but since he came east for Christmas, they agreed again to skip a month. Lori would travel to Seattle in February. In the meantime, a funny thing happened. The foundation called and said the job was Lori's if she still wanted it. Apparently, their first choice hadn't worked out. The director was vague. Lori was bowled over, but suspected she might have a bargaining advantage. She said she would love to accept with one condition, she could have a four-day weekend each month for family obligations. What she really meant was time for Brandon. As much as she wanted the job, she could not survive if it made their relationship impossible. Thankfully, the director agreed. When the call ended, Lori's hand was trembling. She texted Brandon

I got the job!!!

Brandon called her back instead. What job?" He asked.

"At the foundation."

"I thought they hired someone else?"

"They did. I guess being fresh off a graduate degree isn't all it's cracked up to be."

"Congratulations, Lori."

"Thanks."

"How does it feel?"

"Um..., great. Terrifying. They want me to start next week. I think my life is about to turn upside down."

"Remember, it's just a job."

"Easy for you to say. I haven't had to dress for work, or answer to a supervisor, in fifteen years."

"Like riding a bike."

Lori laughed. "I suppose. I did those things once."

"You'll be the smartest person in the room. Don't forget that."

"Did I mention that you're hired as president of the Lori Brewster Fan Club."

"It would be an honor."

"I did ask for one concession."

"And she's ballsy too."

"A four-day weekend each month."

"Big ask."

"The director said yes. On the spot."

"Wow."

"I want us to still have our weekends. When I go to Seattle I need time to travel, and..."

"It's okay, baby. We'll make it work."

"I'll have to get Peter to take an extra night, and..."

"Four whole days." Brandon made a kind of whooping sound. "We won't know what to do with ourselves."

"I bet we can figure out something," Lori said.

"I like the sound of that."

"I hate having another four weeks without seeing you."

"I don't think our time in New York even counts."

"Agreed! Only one time alone, and it was freezing in your basement..."

"I'll take your body however I can get it," Brandon said, his voice lowered.

"My body definitely wants some more of that," Lori whispered back even though no one was home on her end.

"You come for a long weekend and I'll make it worth your while," Brandon said suggestively.

"You don't know what you just did to me."

"If I wasn't at work," Brandon's voice was even lower, almost a growl, "I'd make you cum."

Lori laughed aloud. A release of sorts.

Lori's first weeks at the foundation were exhilarating, if overwhelming. She made a good start, getting up at six in the morning on Monday so she wouldn't have to compete with Catherine for the bathroom. The Sunday before, she went to the grocery store, overloaded the pantry, and ironed three shirts so she would be ahead of the game. No matter, there was a backlog of projects awaiting her arrival, and Lori needed to get up to speed on things big and small, the major issues they were working on and where to find office supplies for her slightly shabby desk. By the third night, Lori fell asleep at eight-thirty after half a glass of wine and making mac and cheese for dinner. The kids were as thrilled as they had been with pancakes the night before. On the weekend, Lori somehow got all the laundry done and through a week's worth of mail. She even picked up a few things at Staples to brighten her desk, but she did not manage to get more groceries. The kids already had a field day with her overstocked provisions.

By the second week, a legal issue needed resolving, and

Lori scrambled to recreate what she knew about contract law, at the same time filling out a stack of forms from the office administrator. Lori was asked to make a presentation to the board, and she tried to hide her delight when the director said great job. Lori was late, though, picking up Catherine two days in a row. Lori and Catherine agreed that Catherine could walk home from the bus. Lori raced home the following afternoon, anxious that Catherine might be waylaid, or worse... Catherine was, of course, safely returned, peering into the refrigerator while sniffing at the milk. She made a sour face.

"Mom, there's nothing to eat."

"I haven't been able to get to the store. We can order Thai food for dinner."

"Great, but I'm hungry."

"This weekend, the three of us can go to the grocery store and get what you and Ben need for the week."

"*Ugh...* I hate grocery shopping."

"You know what? I do too. Always have, and now I have a lot less time for it. You and Ben will have to step up."

"That means me. You know Ben won't help."

"He's the one with the car, so he'll have to."

"He'll say he's busy."

"Don't let him get away with that."

"Yeah, right," Catherine said, biting into an apple. "It's mushy."

"It won't kill you."

"Thanks a lot, Mom." Catherine made her best super-annoyed face. "I'm not sure I like you having a job."

"Well, I like it," Lori answered crisply. "Quite a lot."

∾

The weeks flew quickly with all Lori's new responsibilities. Still, she was desperate to see Brandon by the time of their first long weekend. There was so much to tell him, but when she got off the plane in Seattle late on a Friday afternoon, there was only a text to greet her.

Work's gone crazy. Can't get to the airport.
Take a taxi to Abby and John's house.
I'll reimburse you. Abby should be home.
I'll get you as soon as I can.

Lori thought about going for a walk around downtown Seattle. It felt uncomfortable showing up at Abby's after meeting her only that once and they had all been so drunk. But it was dark, Lori was learning how short winter days were in Seattle, and she was tired. Lori ordered an Uber and arrived at the address Brandon texted. Abby and John's home was in a quiet neighborhood. Lori thought it might be somewhere near Green Lake. It looked like it was once a bungalow with a second floor added. There were lovely exterior details, including a cantilevered overhang with stained-wood wainscoting above the front door. Abby opened it before Lori could knock.

"Come on in." Abby gave Lori a tight hug.

"Thanks for having me. Your house is beautiful."

"I'm glad you found it. You must be exhausted."

"I'm always so tired these days," Lori answered, quickly adding, "I hope I'm not intruding. You must be about to feed your girls."

"No worries at all. I ordered some pizza."

"That's more interesting than what my kids got this week."

"I'm sure. Starting a new job! I want to hear all about it." Abby pulled Lori into the kitchen. "We can have a glass of wine while we wait for the 'boys.'" Abby smirked as she poured them healthy glasses from an already opened bottle. She yelled at her kids to listen for the pizza delivery and that they could eat in front of the TV. "That'll make their day." Abby gestured for Lori to sit at the counter stool. "To your new job," she offered, lifting her glass.

"To new everything, it seems." Lori took a long sip.

"So..., how's it going?"

"You've always worked, right?" Lori asked instead.

"No. I quit for about four years when our youngest, Amy, was three and Ida was starting first grade. I felt like I was missing too much."

"I didn't know. Did you like being home?"

"I loved it." Abby sat down at the stool next to Lori. "We took Amy out of an okay daycare center and put her in a lovely nursery school. Mornings were so much less chaotic with one less person needing to be somewhere dressed and on time. God, those first few months...," Abby pursed her lips as if still in the wonder of it. "I would come home in the pj's I wore to drop off the kids. I'd sip my coffee, listen to the radio, and take my time straightening up the house. Amy and I would have lunch while she told me about her morning at school, then she would nap before we strolled to pick up Ida. I'm sorry..." Abby interrupted her reminiscing. "You must be famished." Abby fetched some cheese and crackers and sat down again. "Ida liked school so much that we usually stayed a bit while she joined her friends on the playground. When Amy started kindergarten, I got super involved volunteering at their school and took up yoga, like, seriously. I don't think we ate takeout for two years. Nothing but organic, unprocessed homemade meals."

"Sounds like you were very happy as a stay-at-home mom."

"I felt like I was meant for the job."

"Why did you go back to work?"

"Money, mostly. We were doing okay on John's salary. I

was careful with our budget. Then we started looking at what it was going to cost to send two kids to college, and, well, here I am, working almost full time and with a body that is no longer so carefully fed... or supple." She laughed.

"You look great. Do you keep up with the yoga?"

"I try, but it's not the same."

"How did your kids handle your going back to work?" Lori asked.

"They hated it."

"Mine are about to mutiny," Lori agreed emphatically. "Well, Catherine, at least. Ben's got one foot out the door."

"I remember those days, but, ultimately, it's been good for us. Teamwork. Everyone has to pitch in." Abby raised an eyebrow. "Believe me; I'm not saying there aren't bad days. About every two weeks, no one has a pair of clean underwear, and either John or I think the other one is in charge of dinner. Thank the lord for takeout."

"So much for organic, unprocessed food."

"I know, right? There's been some big fuckups." Abby shook her head, wincing. "Ida's science project last fall was good enough that she was invited to the regional science fair. We showed up with her project Saturday morning only to be told that setup was required on Friday night, no exceptions. It was in the paperwork that neither John nor I had time to read."

"That sounds awful."

"Just mention science fair, and I'll start crying."

"I was the only parent who missed the eighth graders reading their graduation essays. Catherine was devastated." Lori told Abby. "It was the same week that I crashed my car. I think I was having a tiny nervous breakdown."

"Don't you love those? Wine helps keep them at bay." Abby topped off their glasses. "At least her dad was there."

"Of course he wasn't."

"Oh. I thought you said you were the only parent who missed it."

"You're right." Lori laughed. "I did. I guess I didn't consider it something Peter missed since he'd never have been there in the first place."

"Sounds like you've been a single mom for a long time."

"It's true. But not a working, single mom. That's a new trick."

"Even with two of us, it's hard to pull off. The worst is the after-school tango. John's line of work makes us painfully aware of what can happen to unsupervised kids. We make sure one of us gets home in the afternoon, but it's a mad scramble each day. Sometimes neither of us can get here until after four o'clock." Abby sighed, seeming to exhale remembered stresses. "Actually, it's good that the girls never know exactly when we'll show up. It keeps them honest."

"Clever."

"You've got to keep one step ahead."

"I feel like I'm always three steps behind."

"It's only been a few weeks," Abby lightly touched Lori's hand. "It gets easier."

"Maybe, but we have years of bad habits to break." Lori pulled back to take hold of her wine glass. "There's not much teamwork around my house. I still do pretty much everything."

"Did you like being at home?" Abby asked.

"I always thought I loved the job." Lori gave Abby a knowing smile. "You know, some kind of higher calling." Lori shifted in her chair. "If you'd asked me a few years ago, though, I might have said no. I was tired of being the household's cook, maid, and laundress. Then again," Lori shrugged, "in the past few weeks, I've definitely come to appreciate, maybe for the first time now that it's gone, the freedom it gave me to do things I enjoyed, especially as the kids were getting older."

"Will you stick with the job?"

"God, yes."

Abby laughed. "I wasn't expecting that answer."

"Being paid to be intelligent, and have something meaningful to contribute, feels even better."

"Good for you."

"And Catherine will survive some mushy apples and sour milk."

"Here, here," Abby said, lifting her glass again.

Lori and Abby had finished off the bottle of wine and sent the kids to bed before the "boys" showed up. When Lori and Abby teased them with that sobriquet, Brandon and John were ready with apologies. "A tough case, a big break..." The "girls," Lori was a little tipsy and smiled to think of her younger self, waved them off.

"We've been having a fine time on our own," Abby said.

"I can see that." John gave her an exaggerated kiss. "I like coming home after you've been drinking."

Brandon walked over to where Lori was sitting on a bar stool. He mouthed "sorry" before cupping her head and kissing her tenderly.

"Enough of that," John said. "First order of business is food. We haven't eaten anything since lunch."

Brandon pulled away slowly, leaving Lori a little flustered, even more tipsy and decidedly horny.

"What should we eat?" Brandon asked.

"I can think of something...," John answered.

Abby interrupted. "I'll see if the kids left us some pizza. I ordered two large ones."

"So you did," John said with a crooked grin as he pulled a

bottle of whiskey from the shelf above the refrigerator. "My private stash," he said to Brandon, pulling out some large tumblers. He added ice and a generous pour. John pushed one across the kitchen island towards Brandon. "We have some catching up to do."

"And I better slow down," Lori said, putting her hand over her glass as Abby tried to pour more wine from a newly opened bottle. Lori had noticed John's energy and innuendos and her gut tightened. She and Brandon were not going to be one of the couples that Abby and John had sex with, were they? Lori and Brandon hadn't even discussed the possibility. That would be a prerequisite, wouldn't it? Lori was asking herself, thinking that Brandon and John worked together, for goodness' sake. Still, Lori couldn't help following John with her gaze as he pranced around the kitchen. She forgot how cute he was and caught herself wondering if she would have kissed him if she had met him at a bar.

John seemed to have changed gears. They were all wolfing down pizza, refilling glasses, Lori's included, and laughing at John's stories. Lori felt like they were all the oldest of friends. At some point, Brandon excused himself to go to the bathroom. Abby went to check on their girls to make sure they had really gone to sleep. The energy in the room changed again. Suddenly, John was very close behind her. He put his hands on her shoulders and said softly, "It's really good for Brandon when you're around. He's like a different person."

Lori turned to look at John, squirming from under his grasp. John took her cue and dropped his arms, sitting instead in the bar chair next to her.

"I love being here with Brandon," Lori said. "It's like a weight is lifted the minute I get on the plane."

"It's nice to see your face light up when Brandon comes in the room. It can make a man jealous."

Lori looked down at her glass, hoping her cheeks were not too flushed from the wine.

John brought a finger to her chin and lifted her face towards him. "You're very beautiful, Lori."

"Umm..., thank you."

"I would love to kiss you."

Lori turned away sharply and picked up her wine glass. "I'm not sure how Brandon would feel about that."

"How would you feel?"

"I'm not sure," she said, giving him a small laugh. Lori realized she was drunk enough to acknowledge a what-the-hell freedom she had not felt since she was a teenager.

"Why don't we give it a try and see." John seemed inches from her face when he finished speaking.

Lori turned to say no thanks, and their lips met. John's lips were soft and warm, deliciously sweet. She turned away again. "You taste like whiskey."

John picked up his glass and took another swig. "Let me give you another sip," he said, drawing her head towards his. John kissed her with an open mouth. When Lori's lips softened, he answered with his tongue, filling her mouth with a cold, bracing burn. His ardor caused a rising heat in Lori's pelvis, but she put a hand on his chest to nudge him away as Abby's voice reached the room.

"They're sleeping like..." Abby stopped in the doorway, her mouth in a questioning circle as Brandon returned to the room.

"Did I miss something?" Brandon asked, staring hard at Lori with a look that asked are you okay?

"I was giving Lori a taste of the whiskey," John answered.

Lori suddenly felt the absurdity of what had happened. "With his tongue," she added, shaking her head. She looked directly at Brandon. "I'm sorry. I was taken by surprise."

Brandon walked over quickly and placed himself between Lori and John.

"Hey, man," John said. "I just gave her a kiss. I asked first. I swear."

Brandon looked at Lori, not angry but surprised. "Did you say yes?"

Lori shrugged, sensing the goofy look on her face. "I didn't say no."

John sat back on the stool. "That's true. She didn't say no."

"Huh," Brandon said. Lori could see his shoulders relaxing. "Okay then... I guess."

Abby joined them, standing across the island from the other three. Lori recognized Abby's tipsy smile as her own.

"Why don't we all go sit down in the family room," Abby said. "We can make a fire."

"That might put me to sleep." Lori felt the sudden exhaustion of travel and jet lag catching up with her.

"That's fine," Abby said. "I'll get you a blanket."

John led the way through a small, formal living room and into the family room. Brandon and Lori followed. Brandon was holding her hand tightly. The room was dark but for the small glow of a reading lamp. "That one is incredibly comfortable." John pointed to a long, deep-cushioned couch. Then he turned his attention to the fire and had a small flame started before Abby returned with a blanket. She tucked it around Lori, who was sitting next to Brandon, then Abby sat down on Brandon's other side. John plopped down next to Abby once several logs caught fire. They were sitting in a row like an audience watching the fire. It felt strange after all their talk and laughter. Abby broke the silence.

"This is interesting."

Lori laughed. "That's an understatement."

"I guess I'm a little mad at you, John," Abby continued quietly.

"Why?" John sounded surprised. "We kiss other people."

"That's not why."

"Then what?"

"I wanted to be the first to kiss Lori."

Lori was fully awake again. She sat forward to look past Brandon directly at Abby. "What did you say?"

"It's true. I have a little crush on you."

Lori fell back against the couch. Her head was swimming.

"Don't worry if it's not reciprocated," Abby added quickly.

"It's not that... I mean..." Lori was fumbling for words. "I like you a lot, Abby. I really do, and I appreciate what good friends you are to Brandon."

"You don't need to explain. This scene is not for everybody."

More soundless minutes passed. Lori focused on the reassuring feel of Brandon's hand, holding her own against her belly, his thumb rhythmically stroking the back of it.

"It's not that I'm not curious," Lori finally broke the silence. Brandon turned to her with a questioning look, and Lori threw him a shy smile. "I've never kissed a girl," Lori said, more to Brandon than Abby, but Abby chuckled.

"We're hardly girls."

"You know what I mean. I've never even thought about it."

"Really?" Abby sounded surprised.

"Really."

"You give off such a sensual vibe."

"I do?" It was Lori's turn to sound surprised.

"Very much." Abby got up and moved to sit on the edge of the small amount of couch that remained between Lori and the armrest. "Would you like to see what it feels like?"

Lori turned to Brandon with a look that was both panic and a question. Brandon answered with a nearly imperceptible nod.

"You might like it." Abby's voice was almost a purr, and she had loosened several more buttons on her shirt. "Only a woman can know how another woman feels," she added as she put her hand on Lori's leg and leaned in closer. Their lips touched. Abby's were smooth and soft, but Lori did not feel hunger. She couldn't deny, though, that there was something nice in Abby's gentle brushes and nibbles, and Lori finally welcomed Abby's tongue. Abby tasted of strawberries, a taste that reminded Lori of childhood and summer. Lori returned Abby's kiss with slow movements, feeling more like she was exploring a connection than igniting desire, and she broke the kiss, curious at the difference. Abby reached for Lori's hand and brought it to her breast.

"Would you like to touch me?" Lori nodded, and Abby guided Lori's hand inside her blouse. Lori brushed over Abby's bra and felt a shock when her thumb caught the edge of Abby's hard nipple and something else. "Let me take this off," Abby said, quickly pulling her shirt, still half-buttoned, over her head. She reached back and unhooked her bra, and let it fall. Lori stared. Abby's breasts were so much fuller than her own, with large areola and thick nipples, each with a small metal barbell pierced through it.

"Ouch," Lori said reflexively.

"Actually, it makes the sensation more intense," Abby cupped Lori's head and drew it to her breast, "when I'm kissed there."

Lori felt Brandon's hand reassuringly on the small of her back as she put her mouth on Abby's nipple. Lori had a moment to wonder what Brandon was seeing, what he was feeling before she was overtaken by exploring Abby's body. Lori traced her tongue around Abby's nipple, testing the cold metal before she began to suck gently, curious. She held her hand around the fullness of Abby's flesh, even as Lori recalled Brandon's mouth on her own nipple, then a flash of the primal joy remembering her own babes' suckling. It startled Lori, and she pulled away. "That was intense," Lori said, bringing her hands to her face as if to hide for a moment.

"That," John said, pausing for emphasis, "was incredibly hot."

"I'm glad you enjoyed it," Abby smirked sarcastically, "but it wasn't for you."

"Well then, continue as if we aren't... even... here." John slunk back against the cushions saying the last words slowly as if he could make himself invisible and watch unseen.

"That's not what I'm saying." Abby sounded annoyed.

"What do we do now?" Lori caught the eye of everyone in the room.

"Only what makes you comfortable," John said.

"You're sure your kids won't stumble in?" Lori asked.

"They sleep like the dead. No worries there."

"I've had a lot to drink," Lori said. "I confess I'm feeling a little reckless, and..." that goofy smile again took hold of her face, "a lot horny."

"I could help with that." John rose and extended a hand to Lori.

She glanced over at Brandon, trying to gauge his commitment to the unfolding events. Again, he dipped his chin once in agreement. Lori took John's hand, and he led her to a club chair in the corner of the room. "I need to catch up," he said as he began to unbutton Lori's blouse. John slipped off the sleeves and asked, "May I," before unhooking her bra, then he stared, seeming to drink in the sight of her half-naked. "You have a beautiful body, Lori," he said finally, brushing the back of his hand across her breast and catching her nipple between his fingers. "May I kiss you?"

"What will they do?" Lori asked, her squeaky voice betraying her sudden panic. She glanced over and noticed that Brandon was sitting against the couch with Abby tucked between his knees. Abby was drawing Brandon's hand to her breast.

John turned to Abby. "She's a worrier," he said as if Lori wasn't there.

"She's making sure everybody's taken care of. I like that." Abby smiled.

"It's just..." Lori stammered.

"I bet they can find a way to occupy themselves, right, Bran?"

Lori caught Brandon's eye. He didn't look uncomfortable.

"Abby does have a lovely body," Lori said to no one in particular.

"Thank you, Lori."

"So everyone's good," John concluded, stroking Lori's cheek to bring her eyes back to his. He leaned in, holding her chin, and kissed her skillfully. Lori's first sensations were of difference. With Brandon, each kiss felt like history, reclaiming a missing part of herself. John's kiss held the thrill of something new, a pure, physical awareness of those lips, that tongue surrounding her mouth, and then John cupped her breasts. Lori's mind registered a mental *oh my*, her body a continued sense of novelty followed by titillation. She was surprised to hear her own sounds of pleasure breaking through her silence. John broke away and nudged Lori to sit in the chair. He knelt in front of her.

"I'd like to remove these."

Lori nodded. John unzipped her jeans and pulled as she lifted her hips and wiggled out of them. He left her panties in place but spread her legs so he could move closer in between them.

"I love a woman's belly." John crooned at a deeper pitch, but his voice was still velvety smooth. He traced his finger from her belly button, catching it on her panties and pulling them down slightly. He kissed her there, nudging her panties down a little more with his nose. "I love the smell of a woman," John said, lifting his head to look at her with hungry eyes. Lori reached out to touch his hair, and John closed his eyes for a moment resting his head against her hand. Lori could see over John to spy Brandon, pants still on but on all fours over a supine Abby. Lori left her body for a moment, as if she was a mere spectator, before John lifted his head, blocking her view, and returned his attention to the triangle of cloth. Lori's pussy was thrumming and wet beneath the fabric, beneath the intensity of John's gaze. Lori wondered if he could feel her vibrating.

"I love a woman that wears lace," John continued, strolling his finger leisurely around the edge of her panties. He returned to their top edge, stopped, then drew his finger down the center line of her panties, adding pressure through the crotch. Lori breathed in sharply. He slipped his finger into one side, brushing back and forth between cloth and pussy hair.

"Oh god..." Lori groaned.

"There's something I love most of all." John's voice shifted to a deep baritone. Lori's panties were gliding off. He ran his finger again through her pussy, unclothed that time, and drew it back again from her ass through her wetness to her clit, a direct hit.

"You're so wet," he said, lowering his mouth to follow his finger with his tongue, and Lori's legs fell open, unable to resist the wave of pleasure that came over her. She closed her eyes so she wouldn't see what the other two were doing. Lori came almost immediately, quiet as a mouse, and tried to sit up. John restrained her with his hands on her belly. "I'll consider myself a cad if you cum only once."

Lori was too overwhelmed to argue. She let her head fall back as John began another long, slow teasing with his tongue. He finally lifted his head; his chest expanded as he stared at her mischievously for a long moment, then cupped her pussy and entered her with his finger. Lori gasped at the intrusion before capitulating to John's expert engagement with a particular sweet spot inside her while his thumb played a perfect rhythm on her clit. Lori ejaculated with her second climax and couldn't help moaning with the strength of her orgasm. She was shocked to open her eyes and see John drinking some of her squirt. She sat up quickly.

"You don't have to do that."

"It's wonderful. I've been dying to experience a squirt since Brandon told me about your special skill."

"He told you?" Lori's tone betrayed her shock.

"It's a guy thing. We like to compare notes."

"Did he tell anyone else?"

"Of course not. You should be proud. Abby is jealous."

"You discussed it with Abby?" Lori's voice was an octave higher as she stood up. Brandon and Abby turned their attention toward her.

"I think I've upset Lori," John said to the group.

Brandon came over to her quickly. "Are you okay?"

"Yes. No." Lori covered her eyes. "I don't know." She tucked her head into Brandon's chest.

"Can we go home?" Lori asked quietly, but apparently, John heard.

"Lori," John said softly, "there's nothing to be embarrassed about."

Lori shook her head.

"Anyway, you guys can't drive anywhere right now. I've got

194

a breathalyzer if you want to check," John added, "but I'm pretty sure neither of you will pass."

"Sleep here tonight," Abby said. "Use the guest room. Brandon, you know where to find it." She was sitting up languidly against the couch and reached her hand out towards John. Meanwhile, Lori fumbled to pick up her clothes, mumbling apologies, feeling utterly awkward, but John and Abby hardly seemed to notice. Lori threw on her shirt, noticing a goofy look on John's face as he sat watching. As Lori and Brandon walked past, Abby said loudly, "Get over here, Johnny. I need to be fucked."

Lori stumbled down the hallway putting her finger to her lips, remembering there were children around.

"They sleep upstairs," Brandon whispered. "I think on the other side of the house."

He steered them towards a small, tidy bedroom with twin beds. Lori flopped down on the closest one.

"What happened?" Brandon asked with urgency, sitting on the edge.

"What do you think happened. He went down on me."

"Is that why you're upset?" Brandon looked puzzled.

"Not really."

"Baby, I'm sorry if I misread the situation. I thought you wanted to try this."

"I did."

"Did John do something to hurt you? I'll go right now..." Brandon said, rising.

"No, don't." Lori held his arm. "Can we go to bed? I'm so tired."

"Sure." Brandon slipped off his jeans and pulled the covers from under Lori before climbing in and covering them.

"You sure you want to share this tiny bed?" Lori asked.

"Of course." Brandon spooned Lori as she reached to

195

switch off the light. She was asleep before her head hit the pillow.

She didn't sleep long, though. It was still dark when she opened her eyes. Lori's body felt cramped from the same position, so she turned to her other side. Brandon was facing her, eyes wide open. He kissed her nose.

"You're awake," she said with concern. "Have you slept at all?"

"Not really. I was worried about you."

"I'm feeling better. Really," she added when Brandon gave her a look. "I think I was overwhelmed."

"I'm glad you're okay." He kissed her softly on the lips. "I've been wanting to tell you how beautiful you looked last night."

"And I don't look so great now?"

"You know what I mean. You were very sexy when you were kissing Abby." He smiled. "I could tell you were thinking too much."

"Can't help myself." Lori laughed shyly. "I take it we've determined that you do, in fact, like watching?"

"I do," Brandon answered.

"What about watching John and me?"

"I didn't see much, but I could hear you, and it made me horny as hell. I'm still horny."

Lori reached down and encountered his erection. "I see..." She thought for a moment. "I guess you were the only one left... how should I say... unsatisfied."

"Apparently."

"Want to do something about it?"

"Absolutely. I haven't had blue balls this bad since I was twenty."

"I haven't heard that expression since I was twenty."

"You used to give me blue balls all the time back in college, saunering into the cafeteria and sitting down to pick a fight about something I said in class."

"If I recall, you were spending your nights with Jocelyn."

"But I had a hard-on for you."

"Why did we torture ourselves like that?"

"Because it made the sneaky sex that much better?" Brandon sounded half-convinced.

"That must be the reason." Lori gave a small laugh but then grew serious. "We've wasted so much time."

"I know."

"My mother's friend said something about getting to an age when the horizon starts closing in fast. Do you ever feel that way?"

"All the time."

"So why are we wasting our time having sex with other people?"

"Was it wasted? I think of it more as a new experience for us."

"But I've missed being with *you* all these weeks."

"You have me now."

"I want you," Lori said, moving on top of Brandon.

"I've been told," Brandon said as he grazed her neck with his lips and bit lightly, "part of the fun of swapping is that the reunion sex is amazing."

"You and John talk way too much about your sex lives. Please just fuck me."

"Yes, ma'am," Brandon grunted as his lips found her mouth, and he kissed her greedily, pushing up her shirt and filling one hand with her breast. He reached around to grab her ass with his other, reclaiming her body piece by piece until he rolled them and held her hands over her head. "I want you," he groaned, "more than I've ever wanted you before."

Brandon plunged inside her as Lori gasped and tightened her legs around his back.

"I'm yours," she responded, "yours," saying it over and over with each drive of his cock.

Brandon came loudly, his entire body shuddering before he fell to Lori's side, almost falling off the bed. They laughed with what to Lori sounded like relief, then fell fast asleep again, grasping each other towards the center of the small bed.

It was definitely morning when Lori's eyes opened next. A dull grey light pressed through the window slats, and the clamor of voices drifted in from the kitchen. The comforting sound of children eager for their breakfast. Lori nudged Brandon. "The natives sound restless. I think we should get up."

"I don't want to leave this bed," he said, hugging her tighter.

"I never want to leave you." Lori grazed her finger over Brandon's chest. "Plus, I'm a little anxious about meeting their kids."

"They're great."

"Don't you think they'll wonder why we're here?"

"I'm sure Abby and John explained that we drank too much to drive."

"You really think they don't know what we were up to?"

"They're too young to even imagine."

"I'll try to believe that," Lori said, rising up on her elbow. "I am curious, though. What exactly were you and Abby up to?"

"Don't worry. Not much more than mutual fondling. I was somewhat distracted by the sounds coming from the corner."

"I tried to be quiet."

"Why?"

"I didn't want you to think I was enjoying it too much."

Brandon sat up laughing. "That's the whole point!"

"Really?"

"Yes, baby. Your pleasure turns me on." Brandon traced

Lori's lips and leaned over to kiss her lips, her cheek, then her ear. "You seemed to like what he was doing," he whispered.

"John... " Lori brushed her hair against Brandon's face, "has definitely worked on some expert moves."

"So he tells me."

Lori sat up abruptly. "You two are worse than a pair of gossipy teenagers."

"I'm trying to keep that horizon from moving in."

"Maybe next time, I'll do the watching and see how it feels." Lori paused and touched her lips. "Last night... I kissed another woman. I fondled her breasts," she added, her voice trailing off.

Brandon gave her a broad smile. "I was wondering when you'd remember."

Chapter Thirteen

It was past noon by the time they got back to Brandon's house, fueled by several cups of coffee and too many of John's home-made buttermilk and blackberry pancakes. The weather felt spring-like in comparison to the below-freezing temperatures back east, and Lori suggested they sit on the patio. Brandon flung open the French doors and turned a lounge chair to face the sun. He beckoned Lori, and she snuggled between his legs and lifted her face towards the rays of light struggling to break through the clouds.

"I could stay like this forever," Lori said.

"Be my guest."

"You might get bored of me."

"Being with you is never boring."

Lori chuckled.

"What's so funny?" Brandon asked.

"That word..., boring. A month ago, I would have been embarrassed to describe my typical day. Talk about boring."

"I take it that it feels good to be working again?"

"Yeah. It really does. Don't get me wrong; it's turned life

upside down. I don't know how you survived all these years working and raising Fiona."

"I'm not sure I have."

"You don't give yourself enough credit." Lori slowly stroked the length of Brandon's arm. She felt the luxurious pull of a midday nap. "After last night," Lori mumbled, already half asleep, "no one can ever call us boring."

The sun had lost its fight against the clouds, and Lori woke chilled. She retrieved a blanket from inside but tucked it over Brandon when she decided to surprise him by making a fire. She forced down two glasses of water to stave off a headache and gathered some wood from the porch. Lori's time shepherding Catherine and her Girl Scout troop through their badges paid off. There was a nice flame going, enough wood to last a while, and Brandon had yet to come in. Lori grabbed last month's book club assignment, her tumbler of water, made a pile of pillows for her head, and grabbed an extra one to prop up the book—it was a thick tome; her book club decided to return to a classic—and snuggled into Brandon's couch. Despite taking a hiatus because of her new job, Lori promised to keep up with the book club's selections. At the rate she was going, two paragraphs in bed before falling asleep, Lori was unlikely to finish any of them. It was good enough to try, she thought, opening to her dog-eared page.

"What ya reading?"

Lori dropped the book. "You startled me."

"Sorry."

"How long have you been standing there?" Lori asked.

"A few minutes. I was enjoying watching you. Brought back memories of those long nights in the college library."

"Those couches were a lot less comfortable." She laughed and patted the cushion inviting Brandon to join her. He sat down on the other end and lifted her feet into his lap. "Do you remember that one spot we commandeered after dinner each night?"

"I remember," Brandon answered, massaging the toes and pad of one foot.

"That feels great."

He glanced at the book cover. "*Anna Karenina*. I'm guessing that wasn't your choice."

"I've lost voting privileges since I'll be missing meetings for a while. But, really," Lori pretend-struggled to lift the book, "who has the time." She shook her head slowly. "There was so much more time back then. We had no idea how lucky we were."

"Youth is lost on the young."

"That's what old people say."

"Then forget I said it. Nice fire, by the way."

"Another one of my hidden skills." Lori sounded a bit angry.

"Is that what happened last night?" Brandon threw Lori a serious look while he rubbed her other foot more softly.

"I can't be mad at you when you're making my feet feel like they're in heaven," Lori answered, "but yeah. I can't believe you told John about..."

"Squirting?"

"Yes."

"I'm guessing he would have found out anyway. Some things are too good to hide."

"Not funny." Lori made a face, but they grew quiet, mesmerized by the flames, Brandon stroking Lori's calf like a meditation.

"I've been thinking," Lori said finally.

"Why does that not surprise me."

"Again, not funny," she said, though with a smile. "As I was saying, I was thinking about John, and..."

"About John, really?" Brandon looked at Lori with raised eyebrows.

"It seems like sex is kind of a competitive sport for him."

"How do you mean?"

"Like he's working on his technique, racking up notches on his belt."

"So judgmental." Brandon squeezed Lori's foot. "What if it's just fun?"

"Shouldn't sex be more than that?"

"Does it have to be, I mean, all the time?"

"I guess I thought so."

"If no one's getting hurt, and everyone's happy..."

"Do you think Abby enjoyed last night?"

"Ouch."

"I didn't mean it that way."

"I may not have as many tricks as John, but she seemed to be enjoying herself. And I'm sure John took good care of her after we left." Brandon smirked.

"While we fell asleep."

"They didn't have jet lag. Anyway, John tells me they have great sex after they play with new people."

"Play?"

"That's what he calls it when they do the group thing. He says their sex is more intimate afterwards because they're coming back to the person they know and love."

"I can see that. Last night, with you, it felt different."

"How so?"

"It felt like something more than sex."

Brandon looked skeptical.

"It's hard to put in words, but it was like I was experiencing the emotional arc of our entire relationship."

"Everything?"

"Kind of. I was fully aware of what we have now but also felt the longing for what I couldn't have back then."

"Sounds deep."

"Again, with the sarcasm. Do you remember the times when we couldn't be together, not physically?"

"Painfully, yes."

"I swear it took all my strength not to pull you into the book stacks to make out, even when Jocelyn was sitting right there…, but you weren't mine."

"I know."

"I'm not sure you understand how badly I wanted you," she made an uncertain face, "or what it means to have you now."

Brandon reached to stroke her cheek. "I think I do."

"I've always loved you, Brandon." Lori gave a small laugh. "Even when I swore to myself that I didn't."

He laughed too but grew serious. "I've always known I loved you."

Lori paused as if absorbing the magnitude of Brandon's statement. She turned to him and asked, with dead seriousness, "Can I show you how much?"

Brandon leaned away. "Sure." His voice, for once, sounded uncertain.

"It won't hurt." Lori laughed as she stood up and slowly pulled off his shirt. She kneeled on the floor between his legs, playfully nudging Brandon's knees apart. She stared intently to observe his upper body, exploring his shoulders and chest with her palm as if molding, or memorizing, the contours of his torso. Lori's hand drifted lower, feathering the soft hair below his belly with the back of her hand. She slipped a finger under his waistband when she saw his erection pressing against the zipper of his jeans. Only then did she unfastened the button and pull the zipper down slowly, finally tugging his jeans past his hips. Lori let Brandon wiggle out of them. "Let me do the rest," she said, locking eyes to show him, however clumsily, what she was trying to say.

Lori stared at his erect cock for a few moments, enjoying the shiny, taut skin, the anticipatory bouncing of his shaft telegraphing need and desire. Then Lori fisted Brandon and raised her eyes to watch the effect of her stroking the full length of his member. Brandon's eyes smoldered, and she held his gaze even as she crouched lower, circled her lips, and traced her tongue firmly up and back down his cock pressed into her hand. Lori finally broke contact to nudge his legs farther apart with her shoulders, slipping her hands under his ass cheeks, tucking her head between his legs. She licked his inner thigh and used her tongue to fondle his balls before working her way towards his ass. It was new territory, but Brandon's arched hips and deep moans sent a clear signal. Lori circled his asshole with her tongue and slipped it inside a little. She was surprised by the taste, sharp, metallic, not unsavory. She spread his cheeks farther to explore deeper with her tongue, enjoying the role reversal.

"That feels so good," Brandon's said. His voice was tight, and Lori could tell that Brandon was stroking himself vigorously. When she felt him on the verge, Lori quickly lifted her head and took him in her mouth as Brandon's hand fell away. Lori increased her tempo; her entire body joined in the motion, all building towards his climax.

"I'm going to cum," Brandon groaned.

Lori firmed her mouth to make clear she wasn't leaving him to that moment alone. Brandon's body tensed, then loosened extravagantly, their eyes locked again as he watched Lori swallow.

"Now, do you know?" Lori asked mischievously.

"I might need more proof of your affection."

They laughed, and Brandon pulled her into his arms. He stroked her hair. Over and over, lulling her into a trance.

"I sound like a broken record, but I could stay like this forever," Lori said finally.

"Hold that thought." Brandon shifted Lori so he could get up.

"Hey! Where 'you going?"

"Be right back."

Lori started to settle into the warm spot on the couch that Brandon left behind, feeling like a flower opening to the sun, but he returned quickly.

"Oh no, not the magic wand!" Lori exclaimed. "You even remembered an extension cord."

Brandon belly-laughed as he plugged it into the far wall.

"You know," Lori said, "we can just lie here and bask in, if I say so myself, one incredible blow job."

"It was fantastic, but your pleasure is mine. I need this as much as you do."

"I suppose I can't refuse." Lori chuckled before asking, "Do you want to grab a towel? I never know if I'm going to squirt."

"We'll christen the leather." Brandon was pulling off her shirt.

As Lori stripped off her pants, Brandon lay back on the couch and propped himself against the armrest. He reached for Lori and pulled her down to lie with her back against him, so Brandon could watch the action over Lori's shoulder.

"Go for it," he said, handing Lori the device.

She fumbled to find the on/off switch. Lori still wasn't quite comfortable being watched as she played with herself; who wanted to be caught in their self-indulgence? But how then to explain Brandon's excitement?

"I want you to make a lot of noise. Let me hear everything."

Lori stalled for a moment, letting the thought settle that self-pleasure could truly be a source of mutual arousal. Then she waved the wand theatrically as if to prepare her small audience for a magic trick. Lori spread her pussy lips ostentatiously then she touched the spot. A gasp escaped her lips, and her body snapped to attention. That first hit; it must be what an addict feels.

"That's great, baby. Keep going."

It would have been easy to let the wand do the work and cum quickly, but Lori was starting to enjoy Brandon's appreciation.

"You look so sexy right now," he crooned.

Lori slowed down the speed setting and continued with more curiosity. The pleasure was almost unstoppable when the toy was directly on her clit, but she pulled it back and discovered a more subtle gratification when she grazed it around her pussy lips. When Lori brought the wand head to vibrate the edge of her hole, she felt a throbbing delight, as if her body wanted to pull the damn thing inside. Finally unable to resist, Lori cupped the device with her hand held tight against her clit. She immediately spilled over, a gush of fluid accompanying a detonation of bliss. Her legs were trembling when Brandon put his hand over hers, holding the wand head firmly on the spot.

"Don't stop," he said.

Lori experienced both a thrill and the fear that she would never be able to pull away from the edge, the continuing undulation of spiking pleasure and release. Lori clenched her ass against Brandon's hard cock and heard a gurgling; electronic vibrations mixing with the abundant fluid of her squirt that splashed back on Lori's belly.

"Amazing," Brandon swooned before Lori threw aside the vibrating toy. It fell, still drumming, on the hardwood floor. She was sitting in a puddle.

"That was more than a christening." Lori jumped up. "Let me get a towel."

"I'll go. You enjoy the aftermath."

Brandon turned off the device and returned quickly with a towel and a glass of water.

"Thank you."

"No. Thank you," Brandon said. "That was incredible."

"I couldn't have done it alone." Lori reached down to stroke the butter-soft skin sheathing his cock. She glanced back. "Sorry about the mess."

"No worries," Brandon said as he spread the towel on the couch and nudged Lori to lie back down. He grabbed another pillow and lay across from Lori. Their legs automatically entwined like plant roots securing themselves into the soil. Lori picked up her novel. Brandon took his book from the coffee table. They remained settled until Lori got up to fetch a snack. Brandon, at some point, threw a log on the sputtering flames and returned with his favorite bottle of whisky and some glasses of ice. After only a few sips, Lori's eyes were closing, and she vaguely felt the thud of her book falling on her chest.

"I'm not sure what happened to yesterday." They must have shifted positions at some point. Lori woke to them scrunched together, spooned. "Did we actually spend the entire day and night on the couch?" she asked.

"I thought it was perfect," Brandon answered, kissing her hair.

"You're right!" Lori snuggled tighter against him. "No need to feel guilty about a lazy day when you deserve it. Another perk of going back to work, I guess. By the way," Lori added, "your couch is my new best friend."

"It was my friend first," Brandon said, "but I'm willing to share."

Lori threw him a funny look over her shoulder. "I'm not gonna bite."

"I don't know what you mean," Brandon said, but his grin confirmed Lori's suspicions that he was referring to their night with John and Abby. Lori decided to make some coffee before taking that on. She brought back two mugs and sat back on the couch.

"I have to confess..." Lori paused to take a few sips of coffee, "I'm not sure how I feel about sharing you with Abby." It was her turn to grin. "So much for not taking the bait."

"It was purely physical," Brandon responded, "like a game, you know that, right?"

"Game nights for me usually involve *Pictionary*."

"From what you've told me about your friends, I'm guessing that's way more competitive than what we played."

"Some marriages *have* almost ended over a bad clue."

They laughed, but Lori grew serious again.

"What if the next time Abby wants more from you?"

"Next time?"

"I'm just saying..."

"You know, baby, that's the second time you mentioned a next time." Brandon raised his eyebrows. "I'm paying attention."

"Okay, so there was definitely something intriguing about what happened, but in the light of day..."

"Back in guilt-mode?"

"It's not that. I guess I'm doubting that sex is ever just physical?"

"Why not? Gratification and pleasure in the moment. Nothing more."

"You're a guy." Lori pulled her hand away. "Men are programmed for that."

Brandon feigned insult.

"I'm serious, Brandon. You know what they say. Women have sex with the man they want to hang around to raise the babies."

"Who's they?"

"You know what I mean. I can't imagine any woman having sex with you and not falling for the whole package."

"That's very flattering, Lori, but you're probably biased. Anyway, aren't we past the age when sex is ruled by procreation."

"I don't know. Are we?"

He looked at her strangely. "You want to have more children?"

"I didn't think so, but..."

Brandon's look changed from surprise to something Lori couldn't read.

"I sometimes fantasize about you being my kids' father. Is that weird?" Lori asked.

"No."

"Did you..." Lori bent protectively over her mug, "ever imagine us having a child together?"

"I did." Brandon paused. "I do."

"Wow," Lori said, pulling back. "This is so not a conversation I expected us to have. It's not like our life isn't complicated enough."

"We can always put a pin in it." Brandon reached out again for her hand.

"Not fair to use my favorite expressions against me." Lori wanted to keep the mood light, but she faltered. "Isn't our bulletin board a bit too *fucking* full of the things we've already put a pin in?" Lori winced. "I'm sorry. That sounded angrier than I meant. I get so frustrated sometimes."

"Believe me. I do too."

They fell back to sipping coffee.

"You know...," Brandon said finally, "that expression has an interesting history. It refers to putting a pin back into a grenade so that you can use it later."

"I had no idea..." Lori grinned. "But I love that you do." She paused, shaking her head slowly. "Having a baby... That would certainly throw a big, fat grenade into our lives."

Lori suggested a walk when it appeared that the hesitant sun might actually win out against the grey clouds. "I guess I *do* feel a little guilty about spending a whole day on the couch."

Brandon laughed but dragged his feet. Eventually, he drove them to a park not far from his house, where they set out on a wooded trail. Lori was falling hard for Brandon's forests. Not that they were so unlike the woods back east. A gathering of trees, ferns unfurling in the underbrush, a path of crunchy leaves. In the Pacific Northwest, though, canopies were always full and bright with evergreen foliage. Fuzzy, soft moss dripped from tree limbs. The air was enviably clean, lush, and moist, and footfalls were hushed by a blanket of fallen pine needles. Lori especially liked that their wanderings almost always led to a watery place, sea, sound, or lake, with, if clouds permitted, the sight of mountains beyond. Lori was never sure if it was the Olympic Mountains or the Cascades. It didn't really matter; the view was always breathtaking.

The path narrowed, and Brandon slipped behind Lori without speaking. Their steps fell in a matched cadence, the woods so quiet Lori could hear if their rhythm faltered. When they stumbled upon the inevitable shoreline, they kept walking, side by side again, holding hands, until they spied a fat log and sat down to stare at the view.

"That was a strange conversation this morning," Lori said finally, still looking at the mountains.

"Strange how?"

Lori tossed him a surprised look. "For starters, weird to speak so matter of factly about you having sex with another woman," she turned back to the view, "and crazy to be talking about having a baby."

Brandon didn't say anything, just teased a small stick through the sand.

"I guess you could say both those topics are about being open to possibilities." Lori looked over to Brandon, who was nodding slightly. "Or...," Lori continued, noting Brandon's sidelong glance, "they might mean that what we have is not enough." Lori's face scrunched as if it hurt to have to ask. "Is it enough?"

"I've told you, yes."

They stared out some more.

"I shouldn't have made that a question," Lori said after a while. "It's a bad habit. What I meant to say is..." She turned to look at Brandon. "I need more."

"More what?"

"More time, I guess. We've lost so much already."

"We can't turn back the clock."

"It's kind of a miracle we found our way back, no?"

Brandon answered with a smile.

"I hate to be the one that's always complaining." Lori turned away again, sad to meet his smile with her frustration. "And yet, despite that fact, it still feels like our life is not our own."

"It can't be, really, not once we had those pesky kids."

"But one weekend a month? I don't mean to be so negative, but how can that be enough? How are we going to build our relationship?"

"That's several questions, but no. It's never enough. It's what we have, though. For now."

They sat for a while more, staring at the water and the bit of mountaintop beyond that managed to peek through gathering clouds.

"What if we could make it two weekends a month?" Lori asked. "At least until we can figure out how to be together, you know, really together."

"I'd like that very much. It might be hard right now with Fiona."

"We could do some weekends with the kids," Lori added quickly. "I really enjoy time with Fiona, and my kids love being with you."

"It's not so much the kids but the money."

"What do you mean?"

"Fiona's been applying to private schools."

"You didn't tell me." Lori's shoulders lifted in surprise.

"It's Fiona's project, totally with my blessing, though."

"I didn't even know that was a possibility."

"Fiona's only got two more years of high school," Brandon continued. "Even two years at a good school would give her something important. I think I can swing the tuition, but it'll be tight."

"I see."

"I'm impressed with her initiative, and it would be so much better for her academically."

"That would certainly tie you to Seattle."

"No more so than now." Brandon's posture straightened defensively.

"Really?" Lori asked. "You've always said you would

consider moving, that you could transfer to an east coast bureau office. I'd been thinking, now that I have a house and found a job, some real independence from Peter, it was time to talk seriously about that."

"What about Fiona?"

"Our public schools are some of the best in the country."

"So she'd move too?"

"Of course. I'd never ask you to leave her."

Brandon shifted uncomfortably. Lori felt suddenly awkward like she was talking to a stranger. She got up and walked towards the water. Brandon followed and took hold of her arm.

"Please don't walk away from me."

"I'm not," she said sharply.

"Yes, you are. You're angry."

They both stared past the water to the mountains. The peaks suddenly felt imposing, encircling them like a trap.

"I'm sorry," Lori said. "Anger is not the appropriate response."

"I didn't say that."

"It's just… This morning we were talking about having a child. How is that going to work if we're living on opposite coasts?"

"Lori, we just started that conversation. Let's not get ahead of ourselves."

"It seems like we just ended it." Lori's whole body sagged. "At our age, it's not like we have years to decide."

"It's true, but there's a lot of moving parts. I guess I thought you might move here. You seem to like it so much."

"I do. I love it. But I found a job in Maryland. I have the ex from hell," she added, her voice rushed, "and a kid that started high school and would probably die if I told her she was moving."

"I don't know what Fiona would think about moving. She's gotten so excited about the schools she's applying to."

Lori sat down in a heap, head in her hand. "Fuck. What are we doing?"

"Managing as best as we can."

Lori made a pained sound. "Really?"

"I've always been clear that if our relationship is not working for you, I will..."

"Don't you do that?"

"What?"

"Run away at the first sign of danger."

"I am not running away; I'm asking you..."

"Or act like it's my dissatisfaction that's the problem, or..."

"Lori, stop."

She looked at him, her eyes filling with tears. Brandon reached out and cradled her hand in both of his, "I never turn away from physical danger," he said, then frowned, "but I *do* sometimes run from emotional risk. I can blame the job. Really, though, it's a bad habit." He gently nudged Lori's chin so that she faced him. "But Lori, please don't rush to conclusions. It scares me."

"Scares *you*? My life just flashed before my eyes. All my dreams for us went up in smoke."

"That's what I'm talking about."

"Okay." Lori took a deep breath. "I get it."

"We take things one step at a time," he said, squeezing her hand.

"Or you could get me pregnant. That would certainly force the issue!" She laughed harshly.

"Let's talk about that."

"I was joking." Lori looked at Brandon crazily.

"What if it happened?"

"Are you serious?" Lori asked, almost angry.

"I'm just asking, what if?"

"We can't get married," Lori answered gruffly. "I'd lose my alimony."

"I can support us, maybe not as well as you're accustomed to..."

"I'm not going to be dependent again," she snapped. Then dropped her head, conciliatory. "That's not what I meant."

"What did you mean?"

Lori took a breath. She learned something from not appreciating Peter's efforts as a provider. "I love that you want to support us. It makes me feel incredibly cherished and safe, but I still have a bit of PTSD from the way Peter left. I was so unprepared financially."

"I get that."

"Also, I *earned* my damn alimony! It's compensation for all that I sacrificed so Peter could be successful. I'm not letting him off the hook." Lori gave a small laugh. "It's not gonna make us rich. You'll probably still need to support me, but we'd have a rainy-day fund."

"That might be nice for a change," Brandon said, smiling back. "So..., we don't get married."

Lori's face was a mix of shock and awe. "Wouldn't our mothers love that? We'd be the new town scandal. Way beyond a decent age to be new parents, and the child out of wedlock to boot."

"Let them worry about that."

"I could get down with finally cutting the umbilical cord," Lori chuckled and nodded slowly, but she stopped abruptly. "Would our kids hate us?"

"That is something we have to think hard about."

Lori exhaled a sigh. "Where would we live? I don't think we can start a new family living on opposite coasts."

"Agreed. We'd find a way, though, if having a baby is something we both want. We'd ruffle some feathers..."

"More like yank them out by the shafts, but..."

"But?"

"I can't believe how this conversation has turned around."

"Is that a bad thing?"

"No. It's amazing." Lori grabbed his hands. "From anger to fear, then possibilities. How did you do it?"

"It wasn't just me." Brandon wrapped his arm around Lori's shoulder and pulled her close.

Lori breathed deeply, allowing her body to expand with what was possible. "I guess I'm not ready to decide the big things yet," she said finally.

"That's okay. I'm not either."

"What about where we started today. An extra weekend. Each month. I'll buy the plane tickets."

She felt Brandon tighten ever so slightly.

"I've got a job now," Lori said. "It's my pin money."

"You really like that word, but airfare is more than pin money."

"Look, if we can't solve the big stuff, can't I help with the little things? It's just money."

He shook his head. "We'll do another weekend," he paused, "and I'll pay my way."

"Okay," Lori nodded as if sealing the deal, "and just so you can think about it, I'm going to send you some information about the schools in my neighborhood."

Lori and Brandon jogged back to the car when the rain started. It was not a fat-raindrop deluge like what erupted during humid afternoons in the mid-Atlantic. Pacific Northwest rain fell as soft and fine as a mist. They barely got wet, though it was still fun to strip off their clothes at the front door, kissing and laughing until Brandon threw Lori a sweatshirt from his coat stand. She slipped it on, breathing in his smell, surprised that the fit wasn't overly baggy, just enough to be extra comfortable. Lori remembered it was Sunday afternoon and, just as suddenly again, that she didn't have to pack up, check in, or think about leaving. By that point in her previous visits, Lori would have been sulking, as if watching her lover left standing on the platform, knowing how gutted she'd feel when her train rounded the bend. It was a melodramatic vision but made all the better that her new schedule meant an extra night in Brandon's arms. She bounded back into the living room with her tumbler of water and flopped on the couch.

"You're in a good mood," Brandon said.

"I'm so happy to have another night with you," Lori responded, stretching her arms high and settling back into the cushions.

"Me too." Brandon reached out his foot and rubbed it against Lori's.

"And *not* just for sex," she added with a grin.

He laughed. "If you say so."

"Really, I love sleeping next to you. Everything about it, sleeping naked, waking in your arms no matter which way we turned during the night, how you stroke my hair when you wake up and kiss my nose."

"And you say I remember a lot."

Lori wiggled her toes against Brandon. "I love that you're so affectionate."

"Glad to know it's appreciated."

"Were you that way with Jocelyn?"

"She didn't really do affection."

Lori sat up, chuckling.

"What's so funny?" Brandon asked.

"Sorry, it's not you. I was thinking how we both got things so wrong."

Brandon looked confused.

"Peter also struggled with affection," Lori explained. "It worried me, but I married him anyway." She sat back. "I used to think if he held my hand or thought to kiss me goodbye in the morning, things might have turned out different."

"Maybe," Brandon said noncommittally.

"Probably not." Lori frowned. "As much as I wanted affection, I resented Peter so much that I withheld."

"Affection is an important emotional glue, and...,"

"When you hold me all night," Lori interjected, "like you're afraid to let me go...,"

"Afraid might not be the right word."

"You know what I mean." Lori squeezed his hand. "At least, I hope you do."

"To give affection demonstrates commitment," Brandon said, pausing, "and if you don't receive affection, you will never feel truly cherished."

"Getting philosophical?"

"Can't help myself."

There was another long pause. Lori propped her feet back up on the table, enjoying the feel of her hair, frizzled from the rain, as she lolled her head against the soft leather.

"I like how at home you look right now," Brandon said, returning his foot to wrap around Lori's.

"I hope you're not regretting that you introduced me to your couch?"

"Never." Brandon let his own head fall back.

"Do your friends think we're crazy?" Lori asked after a few moments.

"Why would they?"

"Because we live on different coasts. We've fallen headlong into a relationship." Lori gave him a strained smile. "Because we're entertaining the thought of having a baby."

"Do you think we're crazy?"

"No." Lori paused. "Maybe." She smiled. "Sometimes it feels a little nuts how you've turned my life around."

"That's on you, Lori. You knew you deserved better."

"I hope that's true." Lori looked at her feet, stretching her toes. "We have moved awfully fast."

"Too fast?"

"Not really. It's weird how nothing seems rushed with you."

"Come here." Brandon shifted Lori onto his lap, and she curled against him. "That's because we never followed the rules."

Lori nodded into his torso.

"We found each other back when we were still honest." Lori traced her fingers around his chest as she listened to Brandon. "Impressionable enough to leave a mark, despite the tough exterior we went and put on to survive." She nestled further between Brandon's legs as he lifted her chin. "You're still soft where it matters, Lori, and when two people are very lucky...," Brandon added before their lips met in a lingering kiss. When he spoke again, their lips remained close enough for Lori to feel the heat in his words, "they find this amazing thing called chemistry..."

"That zips through the preliminaries." Lori finished his sentence before cuddling deeper into the comfort of his body. "Can I ask you something?" She asked after a long while.

"You're thinking your way right out of how nice this is, aren't you?"

"Not really," Lori protested. "I can't help wondering..." She paused to look up at Brandon with pained eyes. "Why didn't you break up with Sharon? Why did you keep following Jocelyn when we were so good together?"

Brandon stiffened and turned, forcing Lori to sit up. "Okay. We're doing regrets. I might need a drink."

"It's not a joke. I was so hurt and confused."

"You don't think I was crushed when your wedding invitation arrived in the mail?"

"Why didn't you stop me?"

"Because you and Peter seemed good. You had all those big plans."

"Forget Peter. Why didn't you leave Jocelyn? That was all I was waiting for."

"I don't know, loyalty, maybe, or fear."

Lori's face was a question mark.

"It's hard to explain," Brandon answered. "My parents would have fist fights and then passionate sex on the living room floor. I heard it all. Even after their divorce, they never seemed to stop getting off on their anger. It left me with twisted ideas about commitment, so I avoided it." Brandon was shaking his head. "And let's remember, Lori, you pushed me away as often as I ran back to Jocelyn."

"Yeah, sure, but they were preemptive strikes so I wouldn't get hurt." Lori gave a bitter laugh. "Like that ever worked."

"You weren't the only one protecting yourself. It was intimidating how sure you were about what you wanted. How could I keep up?" Brandon asked emphatically. "I ran rather than disappoint you."

"Are you serious?"

"Of course."

"I feared I could never live up to *your* expectations. You were going to change the world, no matter the cost..., and I wanted a family."

"I really do need that drink." Brandon returned with a bottle of whiskey and two glasses. They took a few sips. "I guess we should've had this conversation twenty years ago."

"You think?" Lori chuckled a bit harshly.

"We can feel terrible about that, or we can accept that you live and you learn. I've learned that it's really hard to change the world and that when a kid comes along, it breaks your heart wide open."

"You're still so damn smart, Agent McManus."

"And you're still so beautiful." Brandon looked at her intently.

"There's one more thing I'm curious about," Lori said finally.

"What?"

"Are you anxious about going to work tomorrow?"

Brandon chuckled. "Trying to keep up with your thoughts is giving me whiplash."

"Can't help myself."

"Touché." He smiled. "Why should I be anxious?"

"Because you'll see John!"

"So?"

"Won't it be awkward?"

"I don't think so."

"Really? I mean, after the other night... Won't it be, you know, a little uncomfortable?"

"Honestly, Lori, in our line of work, John and I have stumbled into way weirder situations."

"If people only knew." Lori shook her head. "At least promise me you guys won't gossip around the water cooler."

"I'm sure we'll save that for after hours. Over a drink."

"I don't think I'll ever understand men."

"We're pretty simple."

"So you say," Lori muttered, still shaking her head.

Chapter Fourteen

Back east, Lori's optimism was gone almost immediately. There was a large pile of dirty clothes sitting by the washing machine when she came through the basement door. Lori could hear her kids upstairs, already returned from school. Catherine waited about thirty seconds after saying hello before complaining about the lack of snack food. Lori surveyed the pantry, pointed out several healthy options, then realized there really was nothing for dinner. She logged on to her computer to order some takeout and suddenly remembered her conversation with Abby about the struggles of working mothers. Unexpectedly, an image popped into Lori's head. Abby's breasts, her nipples and barbells.

Catherine suddenly appeared, shoving a piece of paper in Lori's direction. "You have to sign this." Catherine added with a look of confusion, "Why are you smiling like that? It's a stupid form saying I showed you my math test."

"Nothing. Never mind." Lori quickly composed her mommy-face. "Wait! You didn't show me your math test."

"What?! I passed."

"Catherine?"

"Fine, I'll go get it," Catherine said, stomping out of the room.

Dinner, at least, lasted more than five minutes. Ben surprised Lori by asking about her weekend. He even asked after Brandon and Fiona before dropping his bombshell.

"Dad took us out to a fancy restaurant Saturday night," Ben said.

"That's nice. Where'd you go?"

"The food was weird," Catherine said.

"Did you find something to eat?"

"It was an Asian place. Downtown." Ben answered Lori's first question.

"Dad ate frog legs," Catherine piped in. "They were gross, and it made me sad. I mean, right there on the plate. They still looked like their little fat legs."

"I'm sorry, sweetie, but people eat chicken legs, you know. It's what you get used to."

"Yuck! I think I'm going to become a vegetarian."

"That's fine, as long as you make sure you're getting enough protein. We can..."

Ben interrupted. "Dad brought his girlfriend."

"Oh."

There was a long silence. A litany of questions went through Lori's head before she scratched through each as not appropriate to ask the children: How old is she? Does she look like me? Did they hold hands? Do you like her?

"How was that?"

"Weird," Catherine answered.

"That seems to be your new favorite word. Did you have fun?"

"It was fine. She's nice," Ben said.

"Okay." Lori stretched out the word.

"We probably shouldn't talk about it."

226

"Why not, Ben? It's an important milestone for you guys. I'm guessing that's why you told me."

"Dad doesn't like us to tell you about the stuff we do when we're with him," Catherine responded.

"That's silly." Lori feigned nonchalance. "We're still both your parents. It's not like you stop mattering to me when you go to your dad's."

"She's pretty," Catherine said, "but she wears too much perfume."

"Catherine!" Ben said sharply.

"What?! Mom's right."

"Ben, you certainly had no problem telling your dad about me and Brandon." Lori regretted saying the words before they left her mouth.

"You see," Ben said.

"I'm sorry. That was the wrong thing to say. I just care about what's going on in your life."

"Mom, let's not..."

Lori opened her mouth to respond.

"Look. I'm not trying to mean," Ben interrupted, his voice softened, "but you guys decided to get divorced. Now you get to deal with the consequences."

Lori was still absorbing that obvious truth when Ben excused himself.

"Don't go," Lori pleaded. "I've missed you guys."

"I've got a lot of homework tonight."

Lori and Catherine sat quietly for a moment. Lori struggled not to show Catherine how much Ben's comment stung. "Well, I hope you had fun, Lori said finally, forcing a smile, "apart from the poor frog. It's fun to go out to a nice restaurant."

"I had fun."

"You know you can always tell me what's on your mind. That's what moms are for."

"Thanks, Mom. I should probably do some homework too."

"Okay. I love you, sweetie."

"Love you too."

Lori remained at the table, a bit stunned. Things were good with her and the kids. Ben was taking on more responsibilities. He actually came home early a few times when a party got out of hand. Catherine, meanwhile, turned over her phone and password every few nights. Lori read through the texts and snap chats, sometimes in horror, but found ways to talk with Catherine about what was potentially calamitous without Catherine cutting her off or insisting on her privacy.

Their life with Peter, though. Huh. Lori was to be excluded; the door locked no matter how hard she tried to peek in before it slammed shut. Lori could not decide whether Ben wanted to protect her from the pain of hearing about places she was no longer invited, that would be a certain kindness, or whether he believed Lori deserved the punishment. Catherine would likely slip up and let Lori in on some news, but Catherine would figure it out eventually. If parents betray their children, loyalty was no longer required.

Was that the shape of her new life? Lori thought sadly as she absent-mindedly traced little squares on the table. Pieces of her world existing only in discrete boxes: life with her kids, her relationship with Brandon, his with Fiona, and her children's life with Peter. It felt so wrong, knocking up against a fundamental belief that she could bring together everything and everyone she loved. Had that been her first mistake? Lori was still wondering, feeling out of sorts the next morning, but the three got through their routine with habitual practice. Breakfast eaten, lunches made, plans confirmed for after school, and when exactly each kid would check in. Two days away from her desk at the foundation wreaked havoc. Lori returned to scheduled meetings, hundreds of emails to read, and a last-minute presentation to prepare. By lunchtime, any sadness was replaced with productive anxiety. She had a job to do. She wanted to do it well. It occurred to Lori that maybe that was another reason why people went to work.

The next few weeks were all work, chores, sleep, then repeat, like every other multi-tasking parent with a day job to boot. No wonder everyone was running around cranky, mistake-prone and sleep-deprived. That month Lori paid the same credit card bill twice but failed to pay her mortgage. Jeanette was put out that Lori didn't have time for lunch. It was not helping matters that Ben was anxiously waiting to hear from his first-choice colleges. He was accepted to his safety school, but that did not seem much consolation.

Lori felt a distinct sense of deja vu. She was rejected from the college she most wanted to attend and still remembered sobbing on the stoop of her house. Brandon was there and tried to console her, stating what, in retrospect, seemed obvious. Lori's other options would all be fine. Wherever she went, she would work hard and do well. What if Lori went to her college of choice, though? She would not have been standing in the quad of the college she *had* attended when Brandon showed up as a transfer student. They would have lost their first chance to reconnect. More strange to think about, what set of choices or coincidences had reunited Lori and Brandon after her years chasing the suburban dream? Lori watched the curlicue of steam rise from her coffee, thinking that what she really wanted to tell Ben was, please don't worry. What the fuck do any of us know when we make these big decisions? Lori also knew her advice would be worthless. Ben would have to learn the hard way.

~

I keep thinking about you kissing Abby.

Brandon's text caught Lori in a meeting. She hoped no one noticed her hot blush as she turned off her phone.

John keeps looking at me like he's
discovered the elixir of life.

That one reached Lori as she was whipping up some excuse for dinner and she felt a flutter of embarrassment which she let slide on by, followed by a different feeling. Lori flicked the paring knife around a tomato with an artful twist like she was suddenly a contestant on Top Chef.

I would love to watch you being taken by two men.

Wow. That text came late one evening and caused Lori to drop *Anna Karenina* down on the bed. The ambitiousness of Brandon's message caused her to panic. Lori tried to imagine what, exactly, that might look like.

You'd be one of them, right?

If that's what you'd like.

Would she like that? Lori wondered, and can two men do that if they aren't gay? Lori almost texted Brandon to ask, but thought it might ruin the fun. It was all just fun, right? She didn't ask him that either.

> I'll have to think about it.
> Need to get to bed. Big day tomorrow.

Okay baby. I'll let you off the hook... for now.

Thankfully, Lori was parked and waiting on Catherine to pick up something from the drug store when she saw Brandon's latest text.

Would you like to show off your squirting prowess
to a larger audience? You might enjoy it.

Lori could barely imagine that level of exposure. Had Brandon intuited some hidden sexual desire? No, Lori decided. It was a word game people play to keep the sex exciting.

> I'll need my toy.

Lori lobbed that one back, deciding sexting was a lot more fun than errands and traffic and the laundry piled up at home.

Of course. Would you let me dress you?

> Why not!

I'm thinking a strap-up leather bodice,
leather thong and a collar.

> Good thing Catherine's in CVS.
> She'd want to know why

I just made such a funny noise.

Maybe I should call you so we can discuss the details.

Don't you have work to do, Agent McManus?

Copy that.

Lori's life remained insanely busy, but she managed to squeeze in a quick lunch with Jeanette. They met at a local sandwich shop and ordered some to-go salads before finding a sidewalk table. The weather that morning turned unseasonably pleasant.

"Don't you love the first sneaky-warm day in the new year?" Lori asked. "It reminds you spring will return no matter how cold and dark the winter."

"It's lovely," Jeanette agreed, "but," she added, "I miss this."

"I do too!"

"Sometimes I wish I hadn't told you about the foundation." Jeanette made a mock frown.

"I have to thank you again," Lori said. "A million thanks. It's really the perfect job for me."

"I knew it would be. I shouldn't complain."

Lori squeezed Jeanette's hand. "We can meet more often, I promise. I've just about," Lori made a wishful squint, "stopped feeling like I'm drowning!"

"That's good to hear." Jeanette sat back in her chair. "So, what's it like?"

"Everyone's so nice, and the work is great. We're really helping kids. Plus, they've been super flexible about my schedule. That would never happen at a law firm."

"I'm sure they're thrilled to have you." Jeanette dug into her salad. "You're setting an example for stay-at-home moms everywhere who think about going back to work."

"Now," Lori paused her fork midair, "I need to learn how to say no. They seem to forget it's a part-time job. They keep giving me more responsibilities."

"I'm so proud of you."

"Thank you, Jeanette." They clinked their water bottles. "I'm proud of me too. I'd forgotten how nice it is to be appreciated for my training and education instead of as chief cook and bottle washer."

"How are the kiddies adjusting?" Jeanette asked with a grin.

"They're coming along nicely. I'm ready to believe that it's all for the good. Ben's willingly doing chores and learning skills he'll need when he's off to college."

"And Catherine?" Jeanette's tone evidenced genuine concern. "School can be so hard for her."

"Actually, Catherine's doing better than ever. She keeps a planner and we make a schedule every Sunday. She checks in with me after school and lets me know any new assignments." Lori stabbed another forkful of salad. "I was double-checking everything online with the school portal, but she seems on top of her work."

"Wow."

"Makes me wonder what would have happened if I didn't go back to work. I mean, I can't go to college with her, right?"

"I think my kids are hoping I will."

Lori laughed. "Maybe you should think about getting a job."

"Me? No." Jeanette waved her hand in a dismissive gesture.

"Why not?"

"I haven't worked since the kids were born, and, unlike you, I didn't have much of a career before then either."

"That's not true."

"Yes, it is. I was merely an executive assistant. A very good one, mind you, but everything's changed. I don't know any of those fancy computer programs. I cringe to think about it. And who would take care of the home front?"

"It does wreak havoc. I can't deny that. But you've got a husband. Richard can pick up the slack."

Jeanette made a strange sound. "Yeah, right."

"Just sayin..."

"Enough about me. How was your trip to Seattle?"

Lori paused for a moment, trying to imagine telling Jeanette about the adventure with John and Abby. "It was really interesting."

Jeanette gave her a look.

"We had dinner with one of Brandon's colleagues and his wife."

"That sounds nice and..." Jeanette made a questioning face, "what normal people do, right?"

"Yeah." Lori smiled. "They're a great couple." She took a bite of her food. "Brandon made lots of fires, and we took a beautiful hike. It was great to have the extra day."

"So you're really going to try to keep this up?" Jeanette stopped eating and was looking at Lori intently.

"Of course," Lori answered, waving her fork as it batted away an annoying fly. "That's why I insisted the foundation give me the long weekend each month."

Jeanette put down her utensils. "Sweetie, I'm not trying to tell you how to live your life..."

Lori felt herself bracing.

"Can you really keep up the relationship now that you're working?" Jeanette asked.

"It was definitely harder coming back last time." Lori opted for honesty. "There was so much to catch up on, but the good news," Lori punched the air with her fork, "Brandon and I are going to try to spend another weekend together each month."

Jeanette looked pained. "Isn't that kind of going in the wrong direction?"

"What do you mean?" Lori put down her fork.

"I'm sure it's been nice having Brandon in your life, what with the shock of the separation and that awful negotiating a divorce with Peter, plus your difficulties with Ben..."

"Ben was being a teenager." Lori waved her hand dismissively. "He's really matured these last few months."

"Okay, but it seems like, with the new job, your life is getting on more solid footing, and..."

"Jeanette," Lori interrupted, "Brandon wasn't someone to fill a temporary gap in my life."

"I know you want that to be true. But your life is even more tied to Maryland now. Will Brandon move here?"

"Now's not a good time." Lori looked down at her plate. "His daughter is looking at some new schools in Seattle."

"That's exactly my point." Jeanette paused until Lori looked up again. "I don't mean to sound harsh, Lori." Jeanette softened her tone. "Sometimes you find the perfect guy at exactly the wrong time."

"That's where you're wrong," Lori answered quickly. "I've made that mistake before, putting everyone's needs before my own." Lori was stabbing at her food on the plate. "Brandon is the man I'm meant to be with. Everything else will have to fit around that."

"Listen, sweetie." Jeanette looked at Lori like she was willing her to understand. "That's a very tall order given the circumstances."

Lori flashed to her last conversation with Brandon. The frustration..., and crazy hope. Maybe they'd have a child together. She pictured telling that to Jeanette. The thought made Lori shudder.

"Where'd you go?" Jeanette asked.

"Sorry, I spaced out for a minute."

"Please don't be angry with me. I don't want to see you get hurt again."

"I'm not mad." Lori tried to exhale some of the tension from her body. "Brandon is the one person in my life who will do everything in his power not to hurt me."

"He can't do the impossible, is all I'm saying. He's got a kid too. And you and I both know what sacrifice that entails."

"That's one of the reasons I love him. He's a great dad," Lori leaned in closer, "and, yes, that makes it complicated, but we can talk about the hard stuff. God, how I've missed that." Lori sat taller. "We've actually been able to make new decisions when the old ones stop working."

"You make it sound like you two could win the Nobel Prize for relationships." Jeanette pulled back. "All I'm saying is... You're in dangerous territory."

"You are absolutely right, Jeanette." Lori tried an encouraging smile. "Is that really such a bad thing?"

Chapter Fifteen

A few days later, Brandon texted, suggesting another change in the schedule. Lori had grabbed some lunch and was checking her phone. Brandon assured her it was a one-time request, but would she be willing to come out to Seattle again instead of his traveling to Maryland? Lori texted back.

> Sure, if I can make the schedule work.
> How come?

Where are you right now?

> Some salad place. It's lunch time here.

Oh right. We've been invited to something.

> How nice. Who's invited us and to what?

John and Abby are having a get together.

> Oh...

I would love to see your face!

I did experience about ten different
emotions at once! Unless I jumped to
conclusions and they're just having
a dinner party.

No. Your first guess was correct.

What exactly are we being invited to?

One of their things, where couples play.

OMG

We don't have to say yes. Just thought I'd ask.

I take it, you'd like to go?

Thinking about it.

What exactly happens at such a party?

LOL. You'd like an exact description?!

You know what I mean.

I've been assured there's no agenda.
They're never sure where things will go.

That is less than reassuring.

John swears we don't have to do

238

anything that makes us uncomfortable.

We could sit and watch?

I'm not sure that would be entirely comfortable.

You're right about that.

I think he means we could hang out
for a while. Slip out if we're not feeling it.

So we have permission to be party poopers.
Great…

We could sneak into the guest room.
Come out in the morning and
pretend we were in the mix.

Doubt we'd get away with that, but I like how
you're thinking.

Play with the idea.
No pun intended LOL and no pressure.
I leave it to you to decide.

I call bullshit on no pressure, but okay. I'll think about it.

Let me know if that makes you horny. We can FaceTime.

Brandon, I have to get back to work.

Lori was thankful for yet another benefit of being gainfully employed.

Lori arranged to have a drink with Jill after work that week. Meeting for coffee seemed entirely the wrong setting and beverage for the conversation Lori wanted to have. She even decided to use Uber so she could get inebriated and not have to drive home. They were trying a new place, a bit off the beaten path, at Jill's suggestion. Lori wondered if it was the spot Jill met her Tinder dates.

"Well, hello there." Jill already snagged a table and greeted Lori with an enthusiastic hug. "It's good to see you again."

"Thanks so much for meeting me."

"Of course. That's what divorced friends are for."

"So true," Lori said. "My married friends are never available for a drink on Friday night."

"They don't know what they're missing."

Lori laughed. "It's been a while. I have to catch you up."

"Do tell."

"For one thing, I got a job." Lori thought she'd talk about easier subjects until the drinks kicked in.

"Wow. Let's order something. I want to hear all about it."

They both ordered manhattans. Jill let Lori go on about her job and the improvement in her relationship with Ben. Jill filled Lori in on the goings-on with the other divorcées. Apparently, Susan went on a date with a man who had three daughters. They laughed, imagining the *Brady Bunch* implications if things worked out, and the show's totally unrealistic portrayal of an idyllic blending of two families. When they'd started on their second round, Jill took a stab.

"I'm assuming you didn't want to meet because you missed the other ladies."

Lori laughed. "Not exactly."

"Are you ready to try Tinder?"

"Not really."

"Okay, so maybe Match.com? E-Harmony's a little too 'traditional values' for you, I'm guessing, even if you're not ready for a hookup with a total stranger. We can work up to that."

"I tried Match a while back. It was a total disaster."

Jill scrunched her face, thinking. "Well, we can circle back to Tinder..."

"I've already, sort of, had sex with a stranger."

Jill's eyes shot open. "What?" You're only telling me that now."

"It wasn't exactly planned."

"This I have to hear." Jill leaned in. She didn't actually rub her hands together in excitement, though it felt to Lori as if Jill had.

Lori briefly described her evening with John and Abby. At the risk of disappointing Jill, Lori left out the intimate details.

"You haven't given me much to chew on, but it seems like you liked it."

"It does? I wasn't sure."

"Oh, you liked it. That's definitely the vibe I'm getting."

"Huh. Funny. Abby told me I gave off a sensual vibe. Right before she asked if I wanted to kiss her."

"I love it!" Jill clapped her hands.

When Lori looked embarrassed, Jill asked, "Did her invitation bother you?"

Lori made a weird, half-laughing sound. "For many reasons."

"Like what?"

"I've never thought I was attracted to women."

"Tush, tush, men, women, you don't strike me as having such a limited view of human sexuality."

"Apparently not. I kissed her and then went a little further."

"Wonderful! How did it feel?"

"Fine. Interesting. Everything about Abby is silky soft. I liked that."

"Okay."

"The guys really liked it. Watching us, that is."

"Of course. That's predictable. Anything to do with sex." Jill grinned.

"My boyfriend swears he enjoys seeing me be intimate with other men. Isn't that weird?"

"It all depends. Why do you think it should be?"

"I've been trying to figure that out. I mean, it certainly isn't cheating on my part if he wants me to do it."

"Agreed."

"I think it's... I don't know, embarrassment? I'm uptight? That sounds lame," Lori added quickly.

"Not at all. Women have been taught for a long time to be ashamed of our bodies and suspicious of our desires. You can blame Eve."

Lori laughed. "I was raised Catholic. That certainly can't help. I never thought of myself as particularly religious. I ignored the rules that didn't make sense. I even lost my virginity to an Irish-Catholic boy."

"Repression can be quite the aphrodisiac." Jill pursed her lips. "Underlying shame, though, that can be a tougher nut to crack."

"My ex and I embraced liberal positions on all social issues. But with intimacy, we were always conservative. I don't know why."

"So maybe it was your upbringing. Good girls are never supposed to stray far from what's normal." Jill raised her hand to her heart in mock horror. "We might get carried away."

"When I try to imagine telling my sister, or close friends, about what happened with John..."

242

"Well, that does sound like shame wrapped around identity. I'm betting you did everything your parents expected of you."

"How'd you guess? When I imagine telling them about my going to a sex party..."

"Why on earth would you tell your parents?!" Jill laughed, then paused dramatically. "Excuse me. Did you just mention a sex party?"

"That seems to be the next step. John and Abby kinda 'play,' that's what they call it, with other like-minded couples."

"I might have to move to Seattle."

"I'm sure it happens here. Or does it? I can't think of anyone who has a kinky sex life."

"No one?"

"Okay, maybe you, but..."

"So, are you going?"

"That's the thing. It's fun to joke about with Brandon. It's even kind of sexy. You should see the texts he sends."

"I'd love to."

"Ha ha." Lori took a sip of her drink to hide her blushing. "Intellectually," Lori said after a pause, "I get what you're saying. We've wrapped so much unnecessary baggage and rules around something that can be a fun adventure."

"So...?"

"How do I get out my head enough to actually do it?"

"A little booze always helps," Jill offered.

"That seems like another manifestation of the problem," Lori responded, shaking her head. "From all I've read, getting shit-faced is what girls do now so they can engage in hookups they have no real desire for so they can prove they're cool."

"We haven't progressed much, have we?"

"If I do this, I want to be fully awake for the experience, hopefully, enjoy it, and maybe even learn something about myself."

"I wouldn't load too much on, sweetie," Jill said, laughing. "It's just sex, after all."

"That's it, though." Lori sat back in her chair. "I don't think I've ever experienced sex as, well, just sex."

"Never?"

"Maybe, when I was a lot younger."

"You need to rediscover that part of Lori."

"It was always different with Brandon. Our sex was so intense. It was usually *forbidden*," Lori added with air quotes, "because we were dating other people."

"What does that tell you?"

"We get off on guilt."

"Could be."

Lori sat up, grinning. "Jill, are you a therapist in disguise?"

"I'm whatever you want me to be tonight."

It was Lori's turn to laugh. "That would be a great pickup line." Lori paused. "I think maybe I was afraid of what I felt with Brandon. That it held too much power over me," she said finally.

"But you were a partner in that intensity, and you've matured since then. You can harness that power. How awesome is that!"

"I knew there was a reason I met you." Lori lifted her glass in Jill's direction but grew serious. "I'm not sure I can do it..., the party."

"That's a requirement. You have to want to."

"I like that Brandon wants to try. I like that he seems to want it for me as much as for himself."

Jill nodded encouragingly.

"I'm guessing that we'd bring something back to our relationship, in a good way, something new about our own sexuality. I wouldn't do it if I didn't believe that."

"I think you might have your answer."

244

"Maybe as to the why, but not the how. How do I let go?"

"There's always meditation."

Lori laughed out loud.

"I'm quite serious," Jill said.

"I'm sorry. I'm laughing because, lately, it seems, meditation is the answer to everything: health, happiness, and, dare I say, world peace."

"Well, in this case, it makes perfect sense. You want a genuine experience, right? You want to give yourself permission to feel whatever it is you might feel, no judgment. Especially no self-judgment, right?"

"I guess."

"If you practice mediation, you learn to shut off that part of your brain. You let thoughts pass by like a momentary cloud floating across the blue sky." Jill waved a hand slowly to demonstrate. "You have to recognize that having a thought, no matter how real it feels, doesn't make it true."

"I need to think about that." Lori smiled at her attempted joke.

"Ha ha," Jill smirked. "What I'm saying is you focus on the sensations, in the moment, then what you see, hear, taste, and smell gets your full attention. You just have to practice."

"Let me guess. There's an app for that."

"Actually, there are several that give reminders and guide you."

"I've wanted to practice meditation for, like, forever," Lori said. "I beat myself up all the time for not doing it enough."

Jill opened her mouth to speak, but Lori interrupted.

"Believe me, I know that means I've missed the whole point." She laughed, adding, "Maybe a sex party is the motivation I need."

~

Lori finagled the Friday off the weekend of John and Abby's party. She suspected the foundation was being generous because Lori worked some serious, unpaid overtime preparing a position paper for the county council. Lori got on the plane, determined not to think about work, her kids, or, especially, the party. For fortification, she downloaded two movies and Tina Fey's *Bossypants*. For weeks, Lori's insides had been roiling with nerves and excitement. It was as if a first date, a public speaking obligation, and watching her kids perform were all going to happen at the same time. Lori occasionally harnessed the power of meditation to tame the butterflies, but it was getting harder the closer to the big night.

Brandon met her inside the airport despite that she texted she would meet him in the pick-up lane. "Why'd you come inside?" Lori asked when she met him beyond the security exit.

"I got here early and figured I'd park and come in."

She gave him a skeptical look. "Admit it. You were afraid I might turn around and get back on a plane."

"There might have been a little of that." Brandon smiled reassuringly. "May I remind you that we don't have to go?"

"And waste all my meditation practice?"

Brandon looked confused.

"Long story, but, really, I feel like Cinderella. I want to go to the ball."

His smile broadened, and he pulled her into a tight embrace. "We don't have to decide anything until tomorrow," he murmured in her ear, "until we're there, really."

"I get it," she said, pulling away, "but we have a whole day until then. What will we do?"

"Stay busy, I think. If I know you as well as I think I do."

Lori laughed. "You do."

"I was considering a good hike, not so much that you're

exhausted but enough to keep your thoughts otherwise occupied."

"Excellent plan."

Brandon grabbed Lori's bag, then her hand, and headed towards the exit. "I thought we could stop for a bite to eat," he said. "I haven't had time to shop for groceries."

"I totally get that now." Lori stopped him for a moment. "I genuinely apologize if I ever acted smug about the contents of your refrigerator."

They stopped at a neighborhood restaurant near Brandon's house. Lori ordered a hamburger with all kinds of toppings, and a small pomegranate cider, overwhelmed by the choice of beers offered. When their food arrived, she turned the plate so that her french fries were facing Brandon. "Please help yourself." She was busy removing the bun from her burger and digging into the burger with a knife and fork.

"I never knew you to be so fussy."

"I'm avoiding carbs. I don't want to look fat tomorrow."

Brandon shook his head. "How are the kids?"

"Ben got into the University of Maryland's honors program."

"That's great."

"And the University of Georgia," Lori added. "He's thrilled." She shrugged. "They're both so different from where I wanted to go to college. Fraternities, big sports teams, huge lecture halls. I'd hate it."

"That's probably why he chose them." Brandon was chuckling as he grabbed a few of Lori's fries.

"There's a big price difference depending on which he picks. I'll just have one," she added, reaching for the fries.

"We can hike an extra mile to make up for it."

"Ha ha. Anyway, Ben would be out-of-state at Georgia. I can guess which school Peter will encourage, not that he can't afford the higher tuition."

"I'm guessing, then, that Ben will pick Georgia."

Lori laughed in agreement. "It also has the benefit of being farther away. Ben probably worries I'd hover otherwise. As if I have time these days." Lori shook her head. "Getting good news does have its benefits." Lori took a sip of her cider. "Ben took out the garbage twice without needing a reminder."

Brandon raised his glass. "To small successes."

"Small?! It's taken me five years of nagging." She offered Brandon her cider to taste. "How is Fiona?"

"Great. She got into every school where she applied."

"Wow! She must feel good about that."

"Yes. I'm not sure she'll have a choice, though."

"What do you mean?"

"The best of the bunch offered help with tuition, to the tune of $10,000, but I don't think I can come up with the other $20,000."

"Ouch."

"I still have to save for college."

"Can't Jocelyn help with tuition?"

"I doubt she has the money, and anyway, it's not her priority."

"Really?" Lori scrunched her face in astonishment. "Her idea of parenthood never ceases to amaze me."

"You're preaching to the choir."

"Did Fiona get any more affordable offers?" What Lori really wanted to ask was whether Brandon looked at the information she'd sent about public schools in her county. Lori figured that was a conversation to have after the party.

"There's an excellent, independent catholic school that

248

accepted her. I would only need to come up with about $12,000 for each of the next two years. I think I can do that, though it will be a big stretch."

"You went to catholic school, didn't you?"

"Yes, before we moved out of the city." Brandon shuddered. "I endured the torture."

"Oh, come on, I'm sure the nuns gave up rapping knuckles with a ruler by the time you attended."

"You'd be surprised. It probably made me a better student, if not a very good catholic." Brandon laughed.

"Thank goddess for that."

"Anyway, I checked. There's only one nun left at the school. Fiona will be safe."

"I'm sure she'll ace school wherever she goes. What does Fiona think?"

"I'm guessing she's disappointed about not going to the top school in Seattle, but she's not complaining." Brandon moved some food around his plate. "Fiona actually went and bought a school sweatshirt. Her way of letting me know it's okay, I guess."

"She's a great kid."

Brandon was frowning. "I wish I could do more for her."

"You're a great father."

"Thanks for saying that, but..."

"Do you know how much she adores you? You probably can't see that; you're too close, but believe me, I see it."

"There are so many times I have to say no."

"Is that really such a bad thing?" Lori asked, helping herself to one last french fry.

~

By the time they got back to Brandon's house, Lori was yawning.

"Sorry to bore you," Brandon said, smiling.

"You never ever bore me. It's going on midnight, though, on east coast time. I haven't been sleeping well."

"Thinking about tomorrow?" He winked.

"Maybe a little."

"Well, let's get you to bed. You might not sleep a lot tomorrow night." He winked again as he held out his hand and led Lori to his bedroom. She took off her clothes and climbed into Brandon's cozy sheets, rubbing the warm flannel as she watched Brandon undress. He climbed in next to her, tucked Lori inside the crook of his shoulder, and wrapped his other arm around her.

"Get some sleep," Brandon said, closing his eyes.

Lori felt a sudden pang of disappointment. They'd never, even once, just gone to sleep their first night together. As tired as she was, Lori wanted to reconnect physically, to feel Brandon inside her. Two people but one body. She cupped his balls in her hand. Even as she felt Brandon's cock harden, she heard the shift in his breathing. Brandon was falling asleep. That was another kind of comfort, Lori thought, nestling tighter into his arms.

Lori and Brandon woke early, perhaps both roused by the earlier sunshine as the earth moved steadily towards the summer solstice. A bright, blue sky beckoned through the slats in the window shades. They discussed hiking options over coffee after making a big breakfast of eggs, bacon, and toast with marionberry jam. Brandon raised an eyebrow when Lori slathered on a big spoonful.

"What?" She shrugged. "I love this stuff, and you can't get it on the East Coast. I can work off the carbs on the hike."

"We better pick a vigorous one."

They settled on Summit Lake near Mount Rainier. It was more than an hour's drive and an ambitious five-mile circuit, but they were getting an early start and would still have time to get home, shower, and take a nap before they were due at John and Abby's. Brandon had been to the lake years before and promised breathtaking views.

"The only problem, if I'm remembering correctly," he added, "is that the road in to the trailhead is a bit rough. My car doesn't have great clearance."

"Should we pick a different hike?"

"Nah, we'll take it slow. Nothing ventured, nothing gained."

"I really hope that," Lori gave him a look as she paused from stuffing water and snacks into their backpacks, "not everything we do is going to be a metaphor for our sex life."

The dirt road they confronted indeed looked to be a tricky ride, with small boulders and large potholes scattered throughout the roadbed.

"Buckle up," Brandon said, "metaphorically," he added, grinning, though Lori had, in fact, reflexively tugged to check her seat belt.

Lori noted Brandon's child-like glee like he was revving up for a car race. "Take it easy there, Mario Andretti. Remember, you said we should take it slow."

"I got this."

It felt treacherous to Lori, bumping up and down in the seat as Brandon navigated around rocks and trenches in the road. Eventually, though, she started to enjoy the ride. It reminded Lori of a whitewater rafting trip many years ago. She was terrified and embarrassed when she bounced right out of the boat on the first set of rapids. If Lori was not so determined to save face, she would have refused to climb back in the raft. That, and the fact that finishing the rapids was the only way to get back to her car. Somehow, a few terrifying rapids later, Lori realized that all she needed to do was hunker into each oar stroke and relax with the movement of the raft.

"You're pretty good at this," Lori said.

"Like chasing the bad guys." Brandon glanced at Lori quickly before turning to grab the wheel hard to shift the car around another pothole, making a weird sound of exhilaration. "We're not there yet," he cautioned as the car rode up and seemed to leave the ground for a moment. "That was a big one."

"That's what she said."

They both laughed, but Brandon grew quiet as he continued to drive, squinting hard at the road before them. They could finally see the trailhead parking lot ahead.

"Phew." Lori exhaled before the back of the car seemed to drop out from behind them, and they came to a shuddering stop.

"Damn it!" Brandon hit the steering wheel, then quickly exited the car leaving the door hanging open and forlorn. Lori stayed put until Brandon came around and knocked on her window. She rolled it down. "The rear wheel is stuck in a hole," he said. "You need to get out and help me push."

Lori unbuckled awkwardly; her hand was shaking. She walked back with Brandon to inspect the damage. "That's in really deep. We can't push out of that."

"Let's try." Brandon showed Lori where to stand. "One, two, three, push," he said.

Lori gave it all her might, but it felt ridiculously meager, next to Brandon, his arm muscles bulging with exertion. The car barely moved.

"Are we stranded?" Lori asked. They had not seen another car on the road. "We'll never get back for the party on time." Lori wasn't sure if she felt regret or relief.

"Not so fast. I've got a few more tricks." Brandon popped open his trunk and rummaged around. He pulled out a jack. "I think if we lift up the middle," he said, surveying the road beside the car and then squatting to look under it, "and you give it a little gas, I can push us out."

"That sounds dangerous. What if the car falls back on you?"

Brandon walked around to where Lori was standing. He seemed to finally notice her trembling hands and took hold of them. "I'll be fine. I'll jump away if it starts to slip."

"What if I panic and press too hard or hit the break by accident."

Brandon laughed.

"I'm serious, Brandon. I freeze up in emergencies. I don't think I can do this." Lori looked down at her feet, waiting for Brandon to say something. She expected Brandon to be angry in response to her incompetence, mixed with his own anxiety. That was how Peter would behave.

"You can panic all you want," Brandon said gently, "but please, keep your foot on the gas." He squeezed her hand before releasing her.

Lori stood and watched as he set the jack and began pumping, the car lifting. Lori could see how it might work.

"Okay, Lori, climb in the car. Leave the door open. Press firm and even when I say so."

Lori gave Brandon a last questioning look.

"You've got this," he said before she slipped into the driver's seat.

Lori looked in the rearview mirror and rested her foot on the gas peddle when Brandon disappeared from view, glancing down to make sure it was in the right place.

"Go!" She heard Brandon and pushed on the gas. The car resisted and shimmied until Lori felt a sudden grab and release. She heard a bang on the bumper and intuited that she should push the peddle harder. The car was moving forward.

"Stop!" Brandon shouted. Lori slammed on the breaks. Her body bounced forward and then back into the seat, hands trembling on the steering wheel, when Brandon appeared beside her. She started to exit. "Wait! Put the car in park."

"Shit!" Lori finally noticed that the car was rolling a little.

When she got out, Brandon was already at the front of the car where the front wheel sat perilously close to another pothole with a rock stuck in its edge for good measure.

"We almost went from the frying pan into the fire." Brandon was laughing as he stood up.

Lori felt buoyed by his good spirits. She lifted her hand for a high five. "We did it."

"Yes, we did. The rest of the way should be manageable."

Lori glanced towards the parking lot. "I think I'll walk and meet you over there."

She could hear Brandon's belly laugh as he slipped into the car to navigate the last few yards alone.

Their hiking ascent started quickly with a series of switchbacks. Lori appreciated the steepness. The need to concentrate, her busy legs and pumping heart, cajoled her body to release the built-up tension from lingering images of disastrous what-ifs. They emerged eventually from a forested path, and Lori followed Brandon as he forked left when the trail split. They wandered into a meadow. A scattering of wildflowers heralded the blanketing of color to come. Beyond the meadow and lake sat the snowy bosom of Mount Rainier, which, along with gathering clouds, was reflected pristine and perfect in the dark water below.

"If we hike counter-clockwise, we can climb to a really fantastic view," Brandon said.

Lori was startled. It was the first words they spoke, and a human voice sounded out of place. "It's hard to imagine anything prettier."

"You'll see." Brandon began walking again.

A little past the halfway point, Lori and Brandon started climbing again on a woodsy trail up and away from the water. The summit came slowly, with brief sneak previews of mountain peaks. When they finally stepped out of the trees, Lori felt her breath snatched away. There was a sweeping view of the Cascade Range and the Olympic Mountains. Brandon pointed out Mount St. Helens and a building he said was downtown Seattle. Lori grinned widely and gave Brandon a vehement kiss.

"What was that for?" Brandon asked as he pulled her back against some rocks and sat them down. Lori could feel her legs humming with exertion. She zipped up her jacket against the chill and leaned against Brandon as she turned her face to the sun. Brandon handed her a protein bar.

"*Aaahhhh.*" Lori finally vocalized what she was feeling.

"It's incredible, right?"

"It's so beautiful."

A sudden memory came to Lori. Another rocky outcropping. Her first time making love to Brandon. They'd sat on their bottoms, shoulders brushing, just like on the mountain top, though it was small rock back then, a bump in the woods, and unlike the current view, that moon had shone on a perfectly ordinary scene. Still, Lori recalled the same feeling of wonder.

"I can tell you're thinking."

"No, a good memory." Lori touched her lips as if reliving something.

"Tell me."

"I bet you can guess."

Brandon looked confused, and then a smile spread across his face, crinkling the corners of his eyes.

"Remember when I said I felt like Cinderella?"

"Didn't understand that," Brandon chuckled.

"I want to do something bold."

Brandon smirked. "It seems like that's all we've been doing."

"The party is a big deal," said Lori. "At least for me."

"Me too, baby. I've never done anything like it before. You know that, right?"

She looked at him hard. "Good," Lori said, then looked down. "I'm glad it will be a first for us both." Lori lifted her eyes again. "What I'm talking about is doing something bold with our lives."

"I know what you meant, Lori, but you've been doing bold things since I met you."

Lori scrunched her face in doubt. "Maybe, once upon a time..." She turned to scan the outsized view. "Sometimes it feels like everyone's moving forward," Lori said finally. "Ben's going off to college. Fiona has her new school. Jocelyn gets her priorities." Lori snarled out the last word. "Even Peter has a girlfriend he's serious enough about that she met the kids."

"I didn't know that."

"Peter introduced them to frog legs and the girlfriend all on the same night."

Brandon laughed. "Brave man, or very stupid."

"Let's be both," Lori said emphatically. She turned to hold Brandon's gaze. "I don't want us left behind, to manage the drudgery alone while they all go off to the ball and dance into the sunset."

"Some mixed metaphors, there," Brandon avoided Lori's playful swat, "but I hear you." He took her hands in his own. "I understand."

"Good," Lori said, "but this definitely needs a longer conversation."

Brandon looked wary.

"Don't worry, not today, but soon."

The hike back seemed to pass in a blur; their legs propelled forward by the constant, downward slope until they reached the parking lot. Brandon's car sat waiting, dusted up but looking no worse for the wear. The drive out was quick, almost smooth. It hardly seemed possible that they got stuck on the way in.

"Like I promised," Brandon said, though his face mirrored Lori's own surprise that they were exiting the dirt road and onto smooth pavement again. "We'll have plenty of time to get home and rest before heading to John and Abby's."

"I've got a theory," Lori said. "Whenever my flight out here is bumpy, I'm sure to have a smooth ride home."

"Really?"

"So far, it's proven true, like some kind of karmic balance."

Chapter Sixteen

"What does one wear to a swingers party?" Lori was picking up pieces of clothing from her suitcase and then quickly throwing each aside.

"I don't think anyone says swingers anymore," Brandon answered as he rummaged through his dresser drawer.

"Great. I don't know what to wear, and I won't know what to say when we get there." Lori gave her shoulders an exaggerated shrug. "Where's my fairy godmother when I need her?"

"Don't sweat it, baby. Wear something sexy that feels comfortable."

"Oxymoron!" Lori slammed shut the top of her bag.

"You're not giving yourself enough credit." Brandon came behind her and squeezed her shoulders. "I got you something to wear. If you like it, that is."

Lori turned back to look at him. "Really?"

Brandon was holding a hanger with a dangling corset. Lori had occasionally glanced at them in Victoria's Secret. They always struck her as fussy and overdone; maybe appropriate for going to a costume party as a western frontier prostitute. Brandon's gift was simple and elegant. Dark black, unadorned except for laces up the front. Lori reached out to touch it. The leather was soft and supple.

"It's beautiful. Thank you."

"Why don't you try it on."

"Okay," Lori said tentatively, noticing what appeared to be two stiff stays inside the front of the corset as Brandon handed it to her.

"How do you put it on?"

"I'm guessing it will be a pain to re-lace the whole thing," Brandon said. "Let's see if we can loosen it up enough to slip over your head."

Lori worked at the cords, pulling them loose and expanding the front of the corset, bit by bit. "I think that's enough."

"Lift your arms," Brandon said, taking it back. The corset went over Lori's head easily enough but required some serious tugging to get past her breasts. Lori was still yanking and twisting as Brandon guided her towards a mirror. Lori immediately stopped fidgeting. The corset was incredibly flattering, Lori thought, as she turned left and right to assess herself. The bottom hit her waist without causing muffin tops. There were nice, wide straps and a low, squared neckline that skirted the top of her bosom, like the perfect tank top. The effect of the stays was to push her breasts above the top edge, almost athletically taut, yet round and ripe, a subtle invitation. It reminded Lori of the funny contradiction of Victorian dresses. Excessive amounts of fabric surrounded the body like a barricade, but plunging bodices revealed cleavage and bosom that stirred with each breath, just asking to be noticed. Lori suddenly realized that she wasn't breathing normally.

"I love it, Brandon," Lori's voice was a bit gasping, "but I think it's still too tight."

"We can fix that." Both of them were laughing as Lori worked to loosen the laces while Brandon stretched them, Lori gasping for breath. She was covered with a sheen of sweat by the time they got it fitted comfortably.

"You look even sexier."

"I do look kinda hot," Lori responded, hands on her hips, "but elegant, right? Not slutty?" She asked the question to the mirror, her own bemused smile gazing back before Brandon slipped into the scene behind her. He nuzzled her neck with kisses.

"You look perfect." Brandon slowly traced the top of the corset, grazing her plumped flesh with an electrifying touch, dipping his finger below the laces deep into her cleavage. There was hunger in Brandon's eyes, intensified through the reflected glass, it gave Lori goosebumps, but she shifted away.

"I still need to figure out the rest of my outfit."

Brandon slumped on the bed in mock defeat.

"Oh, stop!" Lori made a face. "It's all for your benefit," she added, surprised to see Brandon's skeptical grin.

A stranger greeted Lori and Brandon when they knocked at the door of the Bartlett's house, followed by a wave of voices and laughter as the door swung open and they stepped in. Abby immediately broke from a conversation and flew over to hug Lori warmly, then introduced Michael, the man who had opened the door. Michael shook Brandon's hand and slipped back into the room. When Abby gave Brandon a full-lipped kiss, Lori turned away to see the festivities in progress. It looked like five or six couples in the midst of an ordinary cocktail party. Guests chatted in small groups in the living and family rooms. A small bar was set with wine, vodka, and several pretty bottles of whiskey. Small plates of food and snacks were scattered on available tables. The men were all dressed casually, lots of jeans and quarter-zip sweaters. The women were a different story. They dressed with purpose. Short skirts, low-cut blouses, lots of heel, all tasteful, provocation implied.

Abby cleared her throat to get the group's attention and introduced Lori and Brandon. The chatter subsided; hellos and welcomes were directed their way before conversations quickly bubbled again. John walked in from the kitchen with a large container of ice.

"You made it." John gave Lori an awkward one-armed hug, balancing the bucket like a baby in his other arm. "You look fantastic," he whispered in her ear. Lori was sure she blushed; she definitely felt a flutter deep inside. Lori forgot how cute John was, thin and fit, with those sharp, fresh-faced, almost feminine features. "Let me put the ice down. Can I get you a drink?" He asked Lori. "I'm assuming you can take care of yourself," John added, winking at Brandon.

"Sure," Lori answered. "A whiskey." She planned to have one strong drink and leave it at that. Might as well get started, she thought.

John took Lori's hand and led her to the bar. He poured a rather large amount of golden liquor over some ice and handed it to her. "Let me walk you around so you can meet everyone," John offered, remaining at Lori's side as he shifted her from group to group. There were lots of questions, particularly about how Lori managed a cross-country relationship while raising teenagers. Lori noticed that conversations seemed to flow effortlessly when John was around. Lori periodically gauged her libido, checking to see if any guests aroused the chemical shift in her brain towards shameless desire and sex with a stranger. Nothing to speak of.

At one point, John excused himself to change the music selection. It must have been his sexy playlist, Lori thought. As if by magic, the mood of the room shifted. Couples started dancing. Lori hadn't yet sorted out who went with whom, so she wasn't sure if spouses were dancing with each other or whether swapping rituals had begun. Lori looked around for Brandon. With enough alcohol in her belly to loosen her hips, Lori felt like dancing. It was hard to resist the sultry, grind-inducing sounds that poured from the speakers, and Lori finally slipped off the jacket she was wearing over the corset. Brandon caught Lori's glance and came towards her, slipping around entangled bodies while keeping his eyes on Lori. It felt like a movie… A high school dance, one boy locking eyes with that one girl, and, suddenly, they were the only people in the room.

"Care to dance, miss?" Brandon asked as if he was propositioning a stranger.

"I would love to."

Brandon slipped an arm around Lori's waist, and they began to dance, his hand moving towards her ass.

"Come here often?" Lori went along with the game, moving in closer.

"First time. And you?"

"Mine too." Lori rubbed her hips slowly against Brandon's crotch.

"Do you like what you see?" Brandon asked.

Lori looked around; their bodies in motion dancing gradually shifted her view. A few couples had broken away, settling on club chairs scattered in the room. Women were nestled in men's laps, and there was kissing, some obvious tongue action. One couple was on the couch, bodies grinding, legs flexed taut to the floor. Early adopters, Lori thought, smiling at her own joke, but they had her attention. She slowed her steps, dancing in place so she could watch. Things were moving fast. Locked in a lustful kiss, the man was clutching at the woman's breast while pushing up her short, leather skirt with his other hand. He shifted to his knees on the floor, working the skirt slowly and steadily up her thighs. Lori noticed that the woman wasn't helping but offered no resistance. The man continued his efforts, up and past her hips. The woman wasn't wearing panties! Her small, neat triangle of pubic hair was suddenly unveiled. Lori constrained a small gasp as the woman's legs slipped partially open, and she held the man's head above her knees, an almost goofy, libidinous smile on her face. He gently spread her legs, and though Lori couldn't see the man's face, his reverent pause made clear that he was lingering on the view. As were other men in the room, some still in conversation, but their eyes pulled towards the couch, as if by an invisible string, drawn to the center of the dark, inverted V that was the woman's legs.

Lori tried to imagine changing places. It caused her to shudder in both horror and a sudden thrill. Lori simply could not picture herself acting with such confidence, but she could imagine the woman's itchy desire. Having allowed things to get that far, not shutting her eyes on the subtle stares of an appreciative audience, the woman must have been yearning for her reward. Brandon seemed to sense the shift in the room's attention, and he turned and twirled Lori so that both were facing the couch with Lori's back tucked against him. He put his hands on top of hers below her navel, and they swayed. The man suddenly dropped his head between the woman's legs. As the woman groaned, Lori strangled some sound of her own.

"Do you like that?"

Lori tilted her head and whispered back, "I'm a little shocked, honestly."

Brandon quickly turned her to face him. His eyes were all concern. "Do you want to leave?"

"I also can't stop looking," Lori answered.

A smile spread over Brandon's face. He twirled Lori again

to face the couch. The man carried on, pleasuring the woman with slow and more ostentatious finesse. The woman continued to moan and writhe, her eyes finally closed, seemingly unaware of anyone else in the room. Brandon buried his face in Lori's neck, covering her with wet, open-mouth kisses while he guided her hands around her belly and over her breasts. Lori closed her eyes, trying to feel only his hands on her body and not the other eyes in the room.

"We already know you guys are into each other."

Lori opened her eyes, startled to see John at their side. She separated herself from Brandon.

"I wasn't saying you should stop," John added, grinning.

"So I take it those two didn't come to the party together?" Lori lifted her head in the direction of the couple on the couch.

"Nope, their first hookup."

The three of them stood in a line observing. Lori felt strangely like a gaggle of sports commentators. It took the edge off her libido.

"Do you know the sexual history of everyone in the room?" Lori asked, glancing at John.

"Pretty much."

"I bet you place wagers on who gets together."

"I would never do that." John feigned insult.

"So, who am I going to end up with?" Lori brazenly lifted her chin.

"There are several interested takers."

Lori's expression shifted quickly to doubt.

"Lori," John gently touched a wisp of hair around her face. "You are the most interesting and beautiful woman in the room."

"I don't think I'm ready," Lori said in a rushed voice.

John turned her to face the others. He leaned down and crooned softly. "No pressure. I'm just wondering..." He slipped an arm around Lori's waist. "Is there anyone here that gets your juices flowing?"

Lori shot him a look. "You haven't told anyone, have you?"

"Ouch." John pulled away. "It's a common expression. I promise I have not revealed your special talent."

Lori relaxed and pursed her lips. "You are a troublemaker, Mr. Bartlett."

"So I've been told." His grin widened. "Look around."

"There's only one man here that gets my juices flowing," Lori said, throwing Brandon a smile.

"I guess two would be more accurate," she added quickly, shifting her gaze to John.

John seemed to consider her remark. "We can work with that."

John whispered something to Brandon. Before Lori could decide if that made her angry or turned on, John took her hand. "Let's go someplace private." He pulled her towards the bar and swiped a bottle of whiskey and three glasses before leading her out of the room and down the hall. Brandon followed. They walked past the guest room. The door was open, and Lori spied a couple, half-naked, on the bed. She tensed as John flashed a smile and used his hip to nudge open the door to a room at the end of the hall. It was obviously the master bedroom. With a glance, Lori could tell it was cleaned up for the party. Bed made, dirty clothes spirited away, but the telltale clutter of lived lives remained on the tops of dressers and bedside tables. Lori entered the room, drawn towards a framed family photo on one dresser surrounded by warmly glowing candles. "I like to set a mood," John said.

"And here I was thinking that Abby was responsible." Lori

threw him a flirtatious smile, though she tipped down the photograph as if to shield John and Abby's daughters from what might transpire. John came towards her and set the glasses down. He poured three short drinks, handing one to Lori and then to Brandon, who had joined them to make a small circle.

"To fun and exploration." John lifted his glass. Lori and Brandon followed suit; each gulped the bracing shot of whiskey. John put his glass down with a resounding clang. He brought his hand to Lori's face, traced his finger down her cheek, across her lips and chin, then down her neck and further until he dipped into her cleavage, tugging down at the bow of the laces.

"Leather suits you." He leaned in to whisper in Lori's ear before his mouth found hers. It was a smoldering kiss, the mingled burn of whiskey, and his tongue exploring. Lori broke away, worried that Brandon would feel excluded, perhaps threatened. She turned her face towards him and saw a loving smile and eyes filled with encouragement.

"The corset is a nice touch." John touched her cheek to draw back her attention. "Very sexy and as elegant as you are."

"You can thank Brandon for that." Lori glanced again in Brandon's direction.

"It does wonders for your bosom." John drew his finger across the swollen flesh atop the corset as Brandon had done earlier in the day.

"I guess that's why they invented these things. It's certainly not for comfort."

"Let's take it off then, and make you comfortable." John cocked his head at Brandon as if inviting him into some kind of disrobing ceremony.

"But we worked so hard to get it on." Lori was laughing weakly, perhaps stalling, she wondered.

"Then we won't rush taking it off." John began pulling, ever so gently, to untie the top bow. He laced one string through his fingers and pulled it slowly out through the first hole. Brandon joined them. He took up the other string and pulled it as slowly through the hole on the other side. John and Brandon continued with deliberate, matched gestures. Lori's breasts filled the expanding gap created by the loosening corset until the ties were gone. She heard tiny plops as each let the laces drop to the ground. John slowly took hold of the flapping edges of the leather and folded them back as if opening a special package. Lori instinctively drew her hand to cover her breasts, conscious that they no longer stood so firm and plump as when bound and supported by the corset's boning. John gently pulled her arm away.

"Your breasts are lovely, Lori; don't hide them." He drew his finger down her cleavage and then traced her breast in a slow, tightened circle. The room hushed but for Lori's small, sharp breaths as John finally brushed her hardening nipple. He bent his head to meet her other erect nipple with a sharp flicker of his tongue, and Lori wobbled a bit from the pin-point intensity. Brandon was suddenly behind her and took hold of her shoulders. He turned her and drew her in tight. "You're beautiful," he whispered before kissing her with open lips. Lori felt a certain relief, knowing so well his taste and touch, and she clung to the comfort of Brandon's arms, rubbing her hand against the textured cotton of his shirt. It was tactile reassurance while she caught up with the strange thrill; two different mouths exploring hers so close in time, undressed and appraised by two sets of hungry eyes.

From behind, John had taken hold of Lori's arm and was slipping off the corset. Lori felt John's open mouth on her back, wet kisses planted on her skin covered in goosebumps. John moved in closer, holding Lori's arms against her side. She could feel the flesh of his torso, smooth and hairless, brush against her back. John must have taken off his sweater. He shifted his hands, thumbs hooked into the waistband of her skirt, pushing down optimistically. Brandon seemed to be struggling with where to place his hands. There was little he could do without also touching John. Was that forbidden? Lori wondered, before thinking to unbutton Brandon's shirt, intent on equalizing the nakedness and creating some distance from her unexpected sandwiching, provoked and prickling, both front, and back. Lori stared at Brandon as she worked, finally peeling his shirt back over his shoulders. She kissed Brandon's chest, conscious of John's body more tightly against her back, his mouth tucked into her neck, hips wrapped against her ass, swaying Lori gently. She could feel John's erection. She let herself enjoy the moment, so many parts of her body experiencing the spiky electricity of touch. John was pushing at her skirt again. She lifted her eyes to Brandon and waited for his nod before she let John wiggle off her skirt, panties captured in the motion. John bent to slip them past her feet, kissing the backs of her legs, finally grabbing her hips as he pulled himself upright.

"You have a very fine ass," John said, leading her towards the bed, but Lori took back her hand. She returned to the dresser to pour another shot of whiskey. After a few moments, she turned again to face the bed. She walked over and sat down on the edge. John sat down next to her. He kissed her neck and whispered, "Relax, Lori, we can stop at any time."

Lori gave him a doubtful smile but allowed him to take her hands and guide her down, stretching her arms above her head as he climbed over her. Lori wondered briefly if Brandon was simply going to watch, but she was quickly distracted by the fervency of John's mouth on her breast, his tongue a sinuous, wet squall against her hardened nipple. Her body's greediness surprised Lori. She arched off the bed to meet John's tongue as he traced it firmly down her belly, through her navel, finally letting go of her hands so he could shift off the bed and onto his knees. He grabbed her thighs and spread her legs with a hungry, methodical look. Lori thought briefly of the woman on the couch but then succumbed to the riot of sensation as John's deft tongue glided through her pussy and danced against her clit. Lori's moans came loud and unstoppable, her frenzied eyes locked on Brandon still watching, though at a closer distance. John's mouth and tongue continued to devour her while he moved his finger inside. He aimed purposefully, seeming intent to hook a particular spot, harnessing some power there. Lori came with a howl, her pussy rocked with clenching spasms, and an ejaculation poured from her like a flood.

"What the hell did you do to me?" Lori exclaimed, sitting up and spying a puddle on the floor.

"I'll explain later." John was pulling to disengage his belt buckle. She felt that odd ambivalence, the motion registering as both threat and erotically charged, the latter causing a jolt of magnetism that must have been felt in the room. John pulled his pants off swiftly, his fully erect cock bounding from his pants like an unleashed puppy. It was skinny, though, like the rest of him. "Come join us, Bran," John said, turning to Brandon. "I'm always willing to share."

"So I've heard," Brandon said with a small smile, "and Lori really likes something in her mouth."

"Well, okay then." John's expression caused him to look like the puppy was being offered a bone. Lori got up and looked back at the bed. Now that she had cum, she felt unsure of what, if anything, she wanted to happen next. Brandon came up behind her and brushed his lips through her hair. "That was beautiful, baby." He whispered in her ear. "I could watch you all day."

Lori turned, ready to make a joke, but saw that Brandon was undressed. He looked serious, his cock fully aroused, thickly

270

swollen, perpendicular to the floor. She gulped instead of speaking. "Do you want my cock in your mouth," he asked with a deep and steady voice.

"Yes." Lori's eyes locked on Brandon's.

Still holding her hand, he climbed on the bed and lay back against the pillows. Lori followed the direction of his eyes and, on her knees, crawled between his legs. "I wish you could see yourself," Brandon said. "You look as powerful as a tigress hunting."

How to answer that? Lori thought before taking him deep in her mouth. The fullness of his cock, Brandon's instantaneous groans, caused her mouth to water unabashed, dripping onto his balls. Lori moved faster, but Brandon took her head in his hand and guided her in slow, extended movements over his member. Remembering, she paused to lick her middle finger, then returned her mouth to his cock while her finger fondled his asshole, making a small then deeper incursion when she sensed his pleasure spike.

Lori had almost forgotten about John until she sensed him behind her as a rush of movement in the air, over her backside, then the pressure of his hands stroking the length of her back like a deep massage. It felt automatic, her back curving into his elongating touch, preordained that her body would open to the power of bequeathing one man pleasure while accepting another man's gaze and caresses. Lori dropped her head further into the triangle between Brandon's legs, sucking his balls wildly, as John fondled Lori's ass.

"That is a sight to behold." John's voice seemed an octave deeper.

"It is." Brandon's answer was an exhalation of pleasure.

Before Lori could picture the scene, John spread her legs from behind and was quickly inside her. With one hand pressing the small of her back, John cupped her pussy. He must have been holding a small vibrator. Suddenly, Lori's clit was locked in an assault of penetrating vibrations, her wetness dripping down her thighs while John thrust powerfully. Lori's head lifted, mouth opened in a greedy search for Brandon's cock. She nearly swallowed him as it hit the back of Lori's throat. Each push and pull of her lips over Brandon's swollen trunk coincided with John's drives inside her. Her clit quaked, perilously close to the precipice. An assault of erotic feedback came at Lori from all sides, top and bottom, front and back, building, in a rushed trio of sensations, to an orgasm that erupted from Lori in a garbled moan caught up with Brandon's cum filling her mouth. John thrust once more and stilled. Lori heard John's hard breathing and felt the galloping of Brandon's heart beneath where she finally laid her head on his chest. After a few moments, Lori rolled over to lay next to Brandon. She spied John waiting at the end of the bed. He looked a bit forlorn, so she motioned for him to join them. John bounced onto the bed and sidled next to Lori.

"I love this part," John said, "like a pile of puppies that rumbled until they crashed."

Lori felt something different. Sandwiched again between them, she felt gratitude and a certain honor. Tears began to fall down her cheeks. Both men moved to brush them away.

"Are you okay?" John asked, looking more confused than concerned. "You seemed to be enjoying yourself."

"I'm perfect." Lori gave him a questioning smile. "So perfect that it all feels a little overwhelming. Does that make any sense?"

"Play can be pretty emotional, especially the first time. That surprises most people," John answered.

"It's just... to feel so desired. I've never..." Lori's voice trailed off. She took each of their hands and looked up at the ceiling, happy not to find words for what she was feeling.

272

John must have slipped away at some point during the night. When Lori woke to daylight, her first thought was to feel bad that they commandeered the master bed. She wondered where Abby spent the night... and with whom. She nudged Brandon.

"Should we get up and give Abby and John their room back?"

"Let me hold you for a few more minutes."

Lori snuggled tighter against him, her hand on his belly.

"How are you feeling?" Brandon asked tentatively. Lori didn't answer immediately, and Brandon shifted quickly so he could see her face. "Are you okay?"

"Fine. Don't worry. I'm struggling to find words."

Brandon rested his head back on the pillow. "You're not usually at a loss for words."

Lori chuckled. "New experiences demand a new response."

Brandon laughed then. Lori could feel the muscles quacking in his belly, his mirth seeping into Lori's hands.

"I still like myself this morning," she said finally.

"That's a good start."

"Did you enjoy yourself?"

"I thought it was amazing, baby. You were beautiful."

"Thanks." Lori was absentmindedly drawing circles around Brandon's belly button. "It was something, that's for sure. You two spoiled me."

"You deserve everything that happened."

"I'm guessing it will be hard to go back to the missionary position."

Lori was rewarded again with the sound and feel of Brandon's deep laughter. She couldn't help but join in, the two of them shaking the covers until they heard a soft knock on the door.

"Yes," Brandon said while Lori wiped away her happy tears.

John poked his head inside the door. "We've got coffee and some breakfast treats. Come join us. Clothing optional."

"We'll be right out," Brandon answered, and John slipped back out, leaving the door slightly ajar.

"I'm not going out there naked."

"Don't worry." Brandon said, "I know when not to push my luck."

Only a few couples spent the night. Everyone was at least partially clothed with thrown-on coverups, like they were at a pool party, not inside a kitchen in the earliest days of spring. Lori feared there would be Monday morning quarterbacking of the night's events, but the kitchen had the vibe of friends at brunch, light conversation, mimosas, and laughter. Still, the belated exhaustion from jet lag, hiking, the bumpy road to the lake, not to mention the threesome, suddenly caught up with Lori. Brandon made excuses for them to leave. Lori interrupted Abby's topping off mimosa glasses to say thanks, mumbling apologies for stealing her bed. Abby barely responded, seeming distracted with hosting.

Brandon and Lori headed for the door with John accompanying them. He brought Lori in for a long, tight hug, then held her at arm's length with a searching gaze.

"What?" Lori asked.

"I want to see if you look different."

"Do I?"

"Yes. You're more beautiful in the light of day."

"Mr. Bartlett, you are an incorrigible flirt."

"Guilty as charged." John turned to Brandon. "You get his lovely lady home before she collapses."

Brandon took her arm to guide her to the car, but Lori turned back.

"You're sure that Abby's okay with everything?" Lori asked John.

"Of course. She was in her element, as, I think, were you."

It was a quiet ride home, followed by a quiet afternoon. They lounged, read a little, and hardly spoke about the party, as if understanding that what happened needed more time to simmer before it could be dissected. Brandon glanced at Lori occasionally, asking with his eyes if she was okay.

"I'm fine, really, better than that." Lori felt as if she was digesting a decadent meal. She sensed a strange power coalescing, but no words came to mind. It seemed no time at all before she had to get ready to leave. "Are you still able to come to Maryland in two weeks?"

"I'll make sure of it. I realize you've done all the traveling lately."

"I don't mind."

"Don't say that. You've got a job. That makes things a lot harder."

"You're right, and I shouldn't be so quick to dismiss what it takes to get here." Lori sat up taller on the couch. "Listen, Brandon."

He sat up as well. "This sounds serious."

"It is, but... It's not a conversation we should start now." Lori paused, unsure of what to say next.

"Is this about Abby? I think you may be overthinking..."

"It's not," Lori answered, "though I have an intuition about that."

Brandon raised an eyebrow.

"It's about us, of course." Lori looked sharply at Brandon. "Please don't roll your eyes."

"I've told you, we're good," Brandon said. "We have enough. For now. Hell, think how many people have told us that they're envious of our romantic, bicoastal weekends."

"That's what people say," Lori waved her hand dismissively, "because it would be rude to tell us that we're crazy."

"That's not true..."

"We need to talk about real possibilities," Lori interrupted. "I'm tired of daydreaming."

"Okay." Brandon drew out the word slowly.

"Not right now," Lori offered in an apologetic rush, "but when you come to Maryland in a few weeks. It could be the perfect time to make big changes, with Ben leaving for college and before Fiona starts a new school year."

"Wow, okay." Brandon skewed his eyes and mouth into an expression Lori couldn't decipher. "I'm sorry," he added quickly. "This conversation wasn't on my radar."

"All I'm asking is for you to start thinking about it, and let's talk in a few weeks."

"I can do that."

Chapter Seventeen

Lori was a bit surprised at how little she and Brandon communicated before their next weekend together. No phone calls, a few inconsequential texts. Work remained busy and Ben offered Lori more distraction as she listened to him debate which college offer to accept. All of it made the waiting, if not easier, a bit faster. Lori was trying very hard in the pre-dawn hours not to create an imagined PowerPoint: The Indisputably Persuasive Grand Plan. She wanted a discussion, not a mental chess game. She played that so often with Peter; Lori too many moves behind to see that Peter had already determined the outcome. Why would she do that to Brandon?

What was so scary, Lori realized, was that if Brandon was honest, and she believed he would be, and if she had the courage to say what she wanted, they might reach an impasse; the outcome however sensibly and mutually arrived at might be the end of their relationship. When Lori got to that point in her thinking, she raced from her bed feeling she might throw up. God, how she wanted Brandon. Lori crept back under the covers to test the pain. Could she survive a breakup? Was she strong enough, finally, after navigating a divorce, a new job,

Ben's rebellion? Hell, she had sex with two men. Lori never felt as powerful as during her encounter with Brandon and John. She was beginning to fully recognize that strength involved risk-taking. It was better to live with the consequences than remain afraid to ask for what she needed.

Lori picked Brandon up from the airport as usual. On the ride to her house, they caught up on the past two weeks. There was more small talk before they opened a bottle of wine and took sides on her living room couch to face each other. Lori felt like she had set up an epic... what? Confrontation? Negotiation? With Brandon there, Lori was no longer sure she wanted to start *The Conversation*, but how could she not. It was starting to feel awkward.

"So..." they both said at the same moment, then laughed until Brandon offered Lori a foot rub.

"You seem a little tense," Brandon said.

"And you seem awfully relaxed."

"It's nice to get away from the job, the kid, the gutters in desperate need of cleaning." He took Lori's foot into his lap. "To see you." He squeezed her foot and then started in with deeper pressure.

"I'm glad I didn't scare you off." Lori sank into the couch and extended her other foot to Brandon.

"Takes more than the threat of conversation to scare me off."

"Well now, I can't talk. My feet feel too good for me to concentrate."

Brandon smiled but remained silent. He kept rubbing her feet. Lori closed her eyes, stretched her toes against Brandon's kneading, rolled her neck against the back of the couch, inhaled, and exhaled luxuriously and the words just slipped out. "I want you to move east."

Brandon's hand stopped, and Lori sat up abruptly. "I'm sorry," she added quickly. "That just came out. It's not how I wanted to start."

"How did you?" Brandon asked.

"You know, with a bit of introduction, talk about the possibilities, pros, and cons."

"I see, counselor."

"We could backtrack," Lori offered sheepishly.

"Why bother. Tell me more."

"Okay. If you're sure."

"I want to hear."

Lori fidgeted to sit back against the sidearm. She pushed her hair behind her ears and cleared her throat. "I know we just started to try two weekends a month, but I can already feel that it's gonna kill us both."

Brandon laughed. "I won't deny it was a small miracle to get here. I used up a lot of chits to get Jocelyn to keep Fiona the same weekend that I didn't get pulled on to an investigation."

"You see! Something's got to give, and it seems to make more sense if you guys move here. Not forever," Lori added quickly. "I would love to move to Seattle when Catherine graduates. Or someplace entirely new. There are so many possibilities."

"But for now, Fiona should leave her home."

"That makes it sound awful." Lori squirmed again, searching for the right words. "Fiona is going to change schools anyway, so new friends and everything, and we've got great public schools around here. She would be safe, and it wouldn't cost you anything."

"It would cost me."

"You know what I mean, not tuition at least. And it seems

clear to me... if we still want to be together, not just a few weekends a month, but two years from now when Fiona graduates, or three years from now when Catherine does..."

"Someone's got to move."

"Yes, well, if that's what you want, for us to be together for the long haul." Lori stopped and looked at Brandon a bit fearfully. "I guess I should have started with that."

"Come here." Brandon scooped Lori into his lap. "Of course, I want us to be together. Remember, I started us down this road."

Lori felt a sudden relief. She wasn't crazy. Brandon wanted the same thing! Lori lifted her face to kiss Brandon. It felt like their first real kiss since he got in her car at the airport.

"Of course, the devil's in the details," Brandon said, finally breaking from her lips. "More precisely, in all the moving teenagers."

"And I was thinking that everything else was mere technicalities ..." Lori's abashed smile acknowledged that she might have declared victory too soon. "How about we tackle the rest in the light of day?"

They moved from the couch, and Lori switched off the downstairs lights. Brandon checked that Lori's doors were locked, and they headed upstairs. It was beginning to feel so normal, shutting down the house, brushing teeth side by side, undressing, then climbing into bed, the end of another day. Yet it still made Lori's heart leap to feel Brandon's bare skin, to note that the first thing he did after switching off the nightstand light was to pull Lori in tightly.

"Are you tired?" Lori asked

"A bit. Long day of travel. How about you?"

"A little. Hard day at the office." They smiled at each other; it seemed at the mundanity.

"Too tired?" Lori asked.

"Maybe."

"We can go to sleep." Lori tucked her head tighter to Brandon. With a light touch, Lori drew circles on his chest. Brandon rubbed her arm. Lori looked up to find Brandon's eyes were wide open. He pulled her face close and gently kissed her eyes, cheeks, and nose as if collecting treasured objects. Brandon suddenly shifted over Lori, arms in a pushup, staring intently. Lori stared back and began to move under him. Brandon settled, lowered his body, and joined in the motion, rocking his cock back and forth against her clit. On the precipice of an orgasm, Lori opened her legs. Brandon slid inside her, moving faster, their eyes unwavering even as they both came. Then Brandon silently rolled to Lori's side, tucked her back into his arms, and they both quickly fell asleep.

They decided to go out for brunch the next morning, perhaps intuiting that the conversation would be easier with a table between them and strangers around. It wasn't until they were seated and served mugs of coffee that Brandon asked, "Can we take a step back?"

"Sure."

"What about you moving to Seattle?" He looked around them. "You've never seemed to like, what do you call it, the 'judgy' vibe around here."

"It's true. I would love a new start somewhere else, but ..."

"Let's hear the buts." Brandon sat up taller as if to brace himself.

"Well…, it was no small feat that I got my job, what with my long absence from the workplace."

"You might be selling yourself short."

"Maybe, but I have to assume it would be easier to get a job in Seattle when I have some experience on my resume."

"But you might find one, and I could support you while you look."

Lori nodded. "I guess it's only fair that you get some 'buts' in the argument."

"It's not an argument, but," Brandon laughed, "strike that. If Fiona and I move east, I'd have to find a job."

Lori sat back with her hands wrapped tightly around her mug. "Didn't you say you could transfer to another field office? It might only be temporary if we move back to Seattle."

"I work for a federal agency." Brandon gave Lori a small smile. "I may have made transferring sound easier than it is."

"Okay… What about a full-time training job at Quantico?"

"That's a possibility. What else is in your plan? I'm sure you have one."

Lori smiled in acknowledgment. "Well… if I want to move west with Catherine, we'll have a full-on court battle."

"We can handle that."

Lori put her hands on Brandon's lying tight against the table. "I really love to hear you say that, and if we do this, whatever 'this' is, I'll need your help to stand up to Peter. Litigation, though…, it's invasive, exhausting, and expensive." Lori sat back, shaking her head slowly. "Catherine might have to testify; I wouldn't put that past Peter. It doesn't seem like you'd face the same magnitude of issues with Jocelyn."

"Perhaps not with Jocelyn, but Fiona might want to kill me."

Lori nodded. "That's a harder nut to crack." She breathed in and exhaled audibly as if readying to command the troops.

"Fiona's starting a new school, no matter what," Lori continued. "She's already making a big change. If she really likes the idea of a private school without the nuns, we could look into that. There are some great schools around here. If we combine our resources, there would be money for tuition."

"Sounds like a bribe."

"No! Just leveling the playing field. So it's not all burden for her." Lori's face softened with curiosity. "Am I crazy to think Catherine and Fiona might enjoy being sort of sisters? I love having a sister."

Brandon gave a surprised laugh. "You have a very optimistic way of looking at things. Our kids will likely hate all of it."

"I know I can be starry-eyed," Lori said. "I believe more is better when it comes to family."

Brandon practically guffawed.

"Okay, I get it. Let's agree to disagree. It's not really my point."

"Which is?"

"You and me. There's always been crazy chemistry, but we would flirt with commitment and run." Lori's shoulders slumped. "Maybe only I ran. I know I was intimidated by you, but I'm not sure why I was so willing to give in to the competition. Now we've got Abby and John."

"I wondered when we'd get to Abby."

Lori sat back up. "This is not about Abby. Though I'd make a bet she's not as cool with everything as you boys think."

"How so?"

"I don't know... Maybe it's about me being with John at the party and her not being with you. I sensed she felt threatened."

"Hmmmm."

"Okay, maybe I'm projecting that I feel threatened. Let's be honest, if we review our history, I always lost out in our love triangles, first to Sharon, then Jocelyn."

"That's not entirely accurate."

"It felt that way." Lori reached for Brandon's hands again. "I believe this time is different," Lori slumped back in her chair, "even if my friends warn me that's not likely." Lori gave Brandon a small smile. "Look, what happened at John and Abby's party was amazing. I think it's made us better. My point is that I don't want to risk our relationship *again* with a new complication, especially since we've already got some tricky triangles to navigate."

"We do?"

"Our kids."

Brandon gave a pained laugh. "They're not love triangles, Lori. They're our biggest responsibility."

"I understand that." Lori paused a moment, debating what to say next. "You and Fiona have built a world of your own. It's beautiful," she added quickly. "The kind of father you are to Fiona is one of the many reasons I love you." Lori paused again and played with the remnants of a sugar packet before looking back up at Brandon. "I guess what I'm asking... Is there a place for me to come first?"

"Is there for me when it comes to you and your kids?" Brandon sounded defensive.

"That is what I want us to figure out." Lori slowed down her words hoping to diffuse some of the tension. "We could keep things the way they are. Only a few more years of prioritizing the kids at the expense of our own dreams. I don't love that idea, and it's not because I'm impatient, or hear my biological clock ticking." Lori smiled, trying to lighten the mood but there was no getting past her final point, that straddling the awkward middle, sticking with the seemingly safe compromise, had its own

284

dangers. "I'm afraid the struggle will undo us. Maybe beyond repair."

Brandon grew quiet. In the empty space, Lori almost laughed aloud. It was as if, after all the time she'd spent discounting their arguments, Lori suddenly understood that everything Emily and Jeanette were saying might be true. Some complications were insurmountable, regardless of a compelling love story, or how hard you wished it to be otherwise.

"Want to take a walk?" Lori asked.

Brandon motioned for the check, and they headed out of the restaurant. It was a beautiful day with a touch of chill, and they kept on walking. It must have been almost two miles before they circled back to the parked car having barely spoken. Lori drove them back to her house, offered to make some tea, and they sat at the kitchen table.

"I've pushed too far," Lori said finally.

"Not necessarily. Tell me more about how it would work? Where would we live?"

"Maybe we should talk about the weather."

"Lori..."

"I don't see the point in discussing the details when you clearly don't like the big picture."

"I didn't say that. I want us to be together, you have to know that, but I have to sell this to Fiona."

"Well...," Lori began reluctantly, "with Ben going to college, there's room for you and Fiona to move in with us."

"Okay..." Brandon stretched out the word, digesting the concept.

"I can see that might be asking too much of the girls, too fast." Lori's statement sounded more like a question. "And there's a risk that Peter will try to stop paying alimony because we're living together."

"I see."

"But screw Peter." Lori's voice grew animated. "I'm working again, and we can make the life we want with what we earn. However much that is, it will be enough." Lori stopped abruptly, hoping, unsuccessfully, to get a read on Brandon. "You think I've been spoiled by Peter's wealth."

"I never said that."

"You think I've had it easy not having to worry about money." Lori paused. "It's probably true, and losing that might be harder than I imagine. The funny thing is, however nice it might seem, I mostly felt sad. I love being a mom, but what I really wanted was to create a family. I tried so hard to work around Peter's conflicting priorities, but it was…," Lori paused for a long moment, "incredibly lonely."

Brandon took her hand. "I'm sorry, Lori."

Lori looked down and drew her shoulders in protectively.

"Are you okay?" Brandon asked.

Lori looked up again finally. "Are you sorry," she asked with pain in her eyes, "because you're saying no to my proposal?"

"I'm sorry that you felt that pain."

Lori nodded, calibrating, her head low again as she spoke to the table. "I've been suggesting a lot of big changes at once. You and Fiona could rent a place instead. We could wait for a more," Lori searched for the right word, "*strategic* time to move in together. Like that Navy SEAL manual you talk about. Take manageable steps." Lori looked up again, searching Brandon's eyes.

"I don't know if I can ask Fiona to do this," Brandon said after a seemingly endless moment.

"I know." Lori pulled back her hand to grab hold of her mug.

They both sipped their tea, silent again. Lori excused herself to use the bathroom. She really just needed to get away and regroup. When she returned, Lori stopped at the doorway to the kitchen. "Brandon," she said, and he turned to meet her gaze. "There will always be times when our children come first. They *are* our primary responsibility. Believe me; I've thought a lot about this."

Brandon shot her a knowing smile.

"I can give you all kinds of reasons why the timing works," Lori continued, not returning his smile. "I can lay out how we make the logistics work, how the finances could be better for us both. What I cannot promise is that our kids will agree. I also recognize that you will be making yourself vulnerable."

Brandon nodded several times.

"That's sacrilege in your line of work, right?" Lori smiled but grew serious again. "I'm still asking you to move in with us."

"You've given me a lot to think about, Lori."

Lori just nodded. There was so much more she could say—that she loved him. How much she believed her proposal was the right step. That there would be difficult moments, but no more than the wonderful things that would come of it and how hard she would work to make those things happen, but she wouldn't talk him into her plan. It suddenly occurred to Lori what she was asking of Brandon: *Please risk everything for me.* It was a hell of a lot, but she wasn't going to take any of it back. Brandon didn't seem to have anything more to say, so Lori retreated to the living room. Brandon joined her eventually on the couch. She suggested they watch a movie. At some point, they ordered some takeout. They went to bed early, having somehow made it through the awkward hours without addressing the elephant in the room. Lying on their backs, side by side and staring at the ceiling, Lori cautiously reached for Brandon's hand. He held hers in return, their only contact through the night.

Over coffee the next morning, Brandon explained that he rebooked on an earlier flight. "Please don't read anything into this, Lori. I just need some space to process the ramifications." Lori sat staring into her mug. She felt like she was sleepwalking. Lori doubted she slept a wink the night before. "Please say something," Brandon said.

"I've run out of things to say."

"Lori, it's not that I didn't hear you. What you're proposing is *not* crazy."

Lori responded with a bitter laugh.

"Don't do that," Brandon said. "I just need some time."

They left for the airport early; Lori couldn't decide which of them was more anxious for the weekend to end. She did the autopilot thing she reserved for her kids. As they sat in her car in the departure lane, Brandon touched her check and turned her to look at him. He winced, as if finally noticing her dead expression. "I love you, Lori. We'll figure out the right thing to do. I promise." Lori nodded and turned back to look for the exit signs.

She only made it a few yards before pulling over, unable to see the road through her tears. Lori was shocked by their sudden appearance, unsure if they sprung from the chance to finally cry alone…, or the gut-wrenching emptiness of the car. It felt like swimming through mud as she heaved and sobbed and tried to figure out what the hell just happened. Lori knew she was taking a huge risk, one with the distinct possibility of failure. Hadn't she decided that the *new* Lori could accept the consequences? Instead, she sat there in despair. Her budding confidence lead to the same old place—feeling rejected and alone.

When Lori finally could take a normal breath, she roughly wiped the tears from her cheeks with the back of her hand. She put the car in drive and made her way, zombie-like, home. Lori made it through the rest of Sunday with the help of whiskey and ice cream, the couch and a blanket, a stream of rom-coms. Perhaps she hoped watching other people's improbable but happy endings would cause her own defeat to grow into a boil she could lance and be done with, leaving only a small scar. Lori talked herself out of calling in sick on Monday, recognizing work as a kind of balm. She got lost in emails and meetings, though at times, it seemed like hours had gone by, and Lori had no idea what she was looking at on the computer screen.

Lori's kids returned Tuesday and life went on in a strange simulacrum of the time after Peter left. They both seemed oblivious to Lori's coma-like state: a numb, hollow trance as if Lori's brain flipped a switch so that emotions would not overload the circuitry. When panic broke through Lori told herself, over and over again like a mantra, that she had been there before and survived. In a strange way it felt better this time, proper, not pathetic, even if it hurt so much more, because she *was* heartbroken. Lori had been truly, deeply loved, and that made her a better person. Lori could answer the questions she had posed to herself: She *was*, in fact, strong enough to push for an honest reckoning. She *did* have a good enough life to fall back on, a home, a job, secure finances, more-independent kids, and new friends. She truly enjoyed sex again. Lori worried that the latter was singularly tied up with her feelings for Brandon. Would she ever feel that passion again? That fear could stop Lori cold in her tracks, but as the day approached when it would have been her turn to travel to Seattle, and Lori heard nothing from Brandon, she canceled her flight. She did so at the office so she would not have time to wallow.

Chapter Eighteen

Lori had taken to walking to work. The weather was growing more consistently spring-like, and walking, a shuffling at first that mirrored her strangled mood, seemed to wake her up, bit by bit. Lori's strides lengthened each day. She started to notice the plucky little daffodils, then tulips started to push out of the soil. When Lori left the office on Friday night, having stayed a bit late since it was the kids' weekend with Peter, she was immediately struck by the lingering warmth. The sun was high enough in the sky that Lori turned her face towards it and stood for a moment, eyes closed, hand to her belly, breathing to feel it expand and contract again. She walked toward home thinking it was high time to start planning a graduation party for Ben. By the time Lori turned the corner of her block, she had decided to use her weekend alone to make improvements to the uninspired landscaping left by the previous owners. Lori stopped at her front walk to assess the ugly hedge she was determined to replace. When she looked up, Brandon was standing on her front steps holding a large bouquet of roses.

Lori froze to the spot. She had been determined to spin an uplifting tale around her heartbreak, but to actually see Brandon... She could taste anger in her throat, but something else was tickling her gut, a wave-like sense of reprieve, however temporary, and delighted butterflies. Lori did not know which emotion trumped, and in her confusion, she simply walked past Brandon, fumbled with her keys, and walked through the front door. She got all the way to the kitchen before she dropped her briefcase, thought to get a glass of water, anything to calm her racing heart. It took a few moments for Brandon to follow her inside. She heard the thump of his duffle bag hitting the floor.

"Lori," he said after a few moments. She didn't turn from the sink. "I'm sorry if I surprised you."

"That's what you're sorry about." Lori finally turned to face him. Brandon stood in the doorway to the kitchen, looking as tall and strong as ever, but his usual self-assurance was missing, replaced by a look of regret as he shifted his gaze uncertainly from Lori to the cluster of flowers in his hands. Was he sorry he came to break her heart in person? Lori wondered. "Why are you here?" Lori asked, her voice strained by anger mixed with that stupid hope she always clung to whenever Brandon came around.

"So we can talk."

"You didn't tell me you were coming." It suddenly occurred to Lori that without communicating, they could have crossed paths in the sky. "I might have been landing in Seattle right now."

"I knew you weren't coming. I got a notification from the airlines that you canceled."

"Oh," Lori said, "one mystery solved."

"I wasn't sure what to do," Brandon responded. "I was so sure you would come to Seattle so we could talk."

Lori formed a mean retort about what he should have done but held her tongue. She learned well enough from conversations with Ben that sarcasm was mostly a worthless habit.

"So, um, I made up a family emergency and headed to the airport, you know, to catch the red-eye," Brandon continued, seeming confounded by her silence. "I didn't get off the standby list, so I slept in the waiting area and caught the first flight this morning."

"Oh…," Lori managed to say as she digested what it must have cost Brandon to get there, and not just the plane ticket.

"Can we sit down?" Brandon asked finally. He moved towards her kitchen table and motioned towards the other chair. He sheepishly lay the flowers between them and sat across from her. "I'm sorry I've been so quiet. I wasn't avoiding you. I was — I just needed time to think and to talk with Fiona."

"It felt, no, it feels, like you abandoned me."

Brandon tightened his lips and closed his eyes for a moment as if swallowing a huge portion of second-guessing. "That was my mistake," he offered. "I should have called. I'm suddenly remembering your habit of thinking for the both of us."

"This isn't funny," Lori said. "You ran away when I asked you to be vulnerable. It's what you do, and I finally get it. It's what you will always do."

"Lori, I asked for some time to consider the risks, and, yes," he paused, "it's what I do. You jump to conclusions." Brandon laughed lightly, but when Lori frowned, he added, "But I know you, and I should have been more careful about checking in."

"Are you here to make sure I'm still standing? Because I'm okay." Lori's determined voice softened from her own bit of second-guessing. "Honestly, Brandon. I understood the risk I was taking." She dropped her eyes and breathed deeply as if absorbing, one more time, the *impossible* weight of what she had asked of him. "You didn't need to fly three thousand miles to cushion the blow."

"Lori, I didn't run away." Brandon paused until she looked up at him again. "I'm here, right now, to give you my answer."

When Lori half-rolled her eyes, Brandon added, "And not the one, I'm sure excellently written, that you drafted on my behalf."

Lori couldn't help but smile. Despite everything, it was nice to be reminded of how well they knew each other, and that Brandon could be complimentary even when chiding her.

"I'm pretty sure I got it right," Lori said, clasping her hands on the table to listen politely. "Since you came all this way, though, the least I can do is hear you say it."

"So, I guess it will *not* surprise you that I have an interview at Quantico?"

Lori's hands flew to her mouth. "What?" It came out as barely a squeak.

"It's mostly a formality."

"I don't understand," Lori replied.

"Yes, you do, and now," Brandon shoved aside the flowers to lean in closer, "so do I."

"You're moving east?" Lori asked, her eyes still registering confusion.

"We're moving in."

"How..? When..? Fiona..?" Lori stuttered out small bits of her bigger questions.

"Fiona took the bribe." Brandon gave her a broad smile which Lori met with a hesitant one of her own. "That wasn't the deciding factor, but it certainly made things easier," Brandon said, reaching for her hands. He surrounded them with his own looking at her with a frightening intensity. "Lori, you were right. It's now or never for our relationship. As hard as it might be for Fiona, I can't lose you."

Lori stared, still dumbfounded and a bit chagrined.

"Fiona and I are *not* going to rent a place," he said, squeezing her hands even harder. "If we do this, I'm all in. I'm

294

not letting your ex, or my kid, or our mothers dictate the terms. You and me. We're in charge. That's the way we roll."

"Brandon, I don't know what to say."

"That's a first."

Lori ignored his smirk and frowned, as if still not believing what she was hearing. "Are you sure?" She asked finally.

"Are you withdrawing your offer?"

"God no," Lori answered in a rush. "If we're going to pull it off, though, we have to be certain."

"I'm in no way certain about the *hows*, but I am about us. You are my future, Lori. We've messed around long enough."

Lori still sat rigid. "Thank you," were the only words Lori could articulate as tears began to stream down her cheeks. Brandon abruptly pushed back his chair to stand. Lori rose and tipped her head in time to meet Brandon's lips. He kissed her deeply, ignoring her tears slipping between their lips, until Lori turned her face so she could hug him tightly. She felt her body realign, absorbing Brandon's words of strength to replace the scaffolding of false bravado Lori erected to make it through the day. She finally looked up at Brandon.

"I was so sure…, you know, that things would end… just like every time before." Lori's tears spilled again as her brain processed what her body had already accepted. "I mean, I *thought* we had finally learned something, after all we've been through…but then, I figured, people don't really change." She snuffled up her tears as Brandon wiped her cheeks tenderly with his thumbs. "You fought for us…" Lori was slowly nodding her head. "You took a stand."

They kissed more passionately than Lori had every felt with Brandon. When she pulled away, surprised that such a thing was possible, a broad smile crossed Lori's face before she said, "You know how much I like it when you're in charge."

The weekend passed in a blur. Lori could not recall having felt so buoyant since she first became a mother. Her feet never quite touched the ground, and her thoughts percolated without trepidation as she and Brandon talked through plans and details. Their conversations only made it more obvious that none of it would be easy, but they were no longer skirting around obstacles—Lori darting ahead, fingers crossed, while Brandon withdrew to scan the scene for a safer option. What a difference to be in sync and to agree that where they failed, they would fall together.

They made plans for Lori's house and how to make it home for all of them. It would be cramped during the summer before Ben left for college.

"Catherine and Fiona will have to share a room for a few months, but then it might feel like a luxury when Fiona gets her own room," Lori suggested. Brandon raised an eyebrow. "We can test my theory that more family is better," Lori offered with a hopeful tone. When Brandon laughed out loud, Lori decided that actions might be better than words, and she took Brandon for a drive past several of the nearby private schools. He was a bit shocked by the opulent grounds.

"It's an abundance of riches, especially since our public schools are great too."

"Fiona is going to feel like she won the lottery," Brandon said.

"She's not the only one."

Lori expanded her tour to the surrounding neighborhood, and they stopped for an early dinner at a cozy restaurant she had been to only once, years before when Lori and Peter first bought their house. Nothing about the place had changed, Lori noted, as they sat down at a corner table. She did a gut check.

Did it feel wrong to be there with Brandon? Too much like revenge? No. Just a lovely meal with her partner and best friend.

Lori was exhausted by the time they returned home, and she curled up on the couch while Brandon called to check in on Fiona.

"How's she doing?" Lori asked when Brandon came back and flopped on the couch.

"Good. She's already emailed a few admissions offices."

Lori laughed. "What was it that Jocelyn said? You definitely want Fiona on your side..."

"In the zombie apocalypse. Yes," Brandon finished her sentence laughing.

"Well, I can survive anything as long as you're massaging my feet." Lori snuggled them deep into Brandon's lap. He started with her toes, stretching out each one between his thumb and index finger before flattening his palm on Lori's arch. The pressure was a bit painful until Brandon's handiwork smoothed away any tension. Lori had nearly fallen asleep when she felt Brandon shift and lay down behind her on the couch, tucking her in his arms and cupping her breasts. Lori breathed deeply, aware that as she expanded her chest, her breasts filled Brandon's hands. He rocked her gently. Lori nearly purred as their hips seesawed in tandem. At some point, they stripped off their bottoms so efficiently that they barely broke the rhythm. Brandon took Lori's hand and brought it to her pussy.

"Play with yourself," he whispered while he kept his hand on top of hers, fingers aligned, his following along as Lori played with her clit, her ass thrust back against Brandon, her entire body tightening to a crescendo.

"Make love to me," Lori whispered back.

Brandon turned Lori in an instant onto her knees, his hand never shifting. His other hand grabbed hold of her hip, entering her commandingly from behind. Lori dropped her head, her back bent concave to meet his thrusts. Their fingers remained joined to play with Lori's clit. She groaned, orgasmed, tightened her pussy around Brandon's climax, and fell flat on the couch with Brandon on top of her, it seemed all at once.

No amount of sex, however, could keep Sunday night from arriving. They drove to the airport in near silence, spent. When they reached the drop-off lane, Lori pulled over and turned to Brandon, summoning the courage to try on one more possibility. "I'm thinking about throwing away my birth control pills."

Brandon's eyes grew wide. Lori waited, searching his face, until she saw the small nod she had come to rely on.

Epilogue

It had been a chaotic few days. Too many trips to the airport even though Lori and Brandon divvied up shuttle service duties. Emily and Thomas flew to Seattle from New York. It was their first time celebrating Christmas away from home. Lori hoped to offer a worthy consolation prize after Emily and Thomas realized that all their combined children planned to spend the holidays with the families of boyfriends and fiancées. Fiona arrived soon after from Boston. She had stayed on campus after the semester ended to work on a research project for her English lit professor. Catherine had been home for a week, arriving under her own steam in an Uber from the UW campus and earning her keep by putting up all the Christmas decorations and occupying her baby brother, Declan, so Lori could prep the holiday meals. Ben was the last to arrive on Christmas Eve. He took a short flight from Portland, where he had started a new job. Lori was in the kitchen, covered in flour when she heard a commotion at the front door. She looked out to see that Brandon had returned with Ben from Paine Field.

"Decster monster," Ben shouted, barely inside the front door. He dropped his bag and flung his arms wide. Declan was drawing with Catherine on the coffee table but threw his crayons to the ground and ran as fast as his three-year-old legs would take him into the arms of his big brother.

"Ben Ben, I missed you," Declan declared before wriggling away from Ben's tickling. "Soooooopit."

"Declan's right. You better stop it." Lori pulled Ben in for a tight hug. "He's learning some moves to fight back, aren't you, Declan?"

Declan raised his little hands in a karate chop that barely grazed Ben's thigh while Ben, in return, mussed Declan's hair, then headed to the couch where he flopped down next to Catherine, causing her to bounce.

"We don't all have to act like three-year-olds," Catherine said before giving Ben a hug.

"What's the fun in that, Sis." Ben returned the hug as he slipped Catherine a brown paper bag. "I brought you something from Coquine's. It's the best chocolate chip cookie you'll ever eat."

"Dinner in fifteen minutes," Lori announced. "Catherine, do you know where Fiona is?"

"I think she's in our bedroom reading."

"Ben, can you give Fiona a ten-minute warning when you bring your bags upstairs."

"Sure, Mom. And you might want to do something about your hair. You look like you've gone gray."

Lori laughed and brushed away some flour. "You're sleeping with Declan, by the way."

"Yay." Declan was doing a little dance with his stuffed dog. He reached out for Ben's hand. "I want to show my new twain twacks."

"Okay, sport, let's go." Everyone else in the room shared a smile at Declan's mispronunciations.

"Aunt Em and Uncle Thomas are staying in your room. Can

you let them know, too?" Lori asked Ben as he and Declan headed up the stairs.

Lori paused then, startled at the sudden quiet. It felt so strange after all the commotion. She drifted back towards the kitchen, dropping first into the dining room for a last-minute check on place settings and serving accessories. Catherine's table decorations were lovely, and the dining room glowed with candlelight. Lori took a moment to take it in. The dining room was large and held the fireplace in Lori and Brandon's otherwise modest, quirky home in Madrona. They were able to purchase it with the combined proceeds from their previously-owned houses, particularly Brandon's, the value of which had gone up quite a bit during the three years he rented it out while they lived in Maryland. The house's strange configuration accommodated four small bedrooms, allowing temporary re-shuffling of bedroom assignments to accommodate current room-sharing preferences and everyone being home at the same time. It was only a few blocks' walk to Madrona Park with its little beach along Lake Washington. Lori went there nearly every day, rain or shine, for its beauty and to let Declan burn off some steam. She forgot how much steam a three-year-old needs to burn.

The quiet did not last. Brandon returned with some wood and was busy starting a fire. Declan barreled into the dining room, followed by other bodies, streaming in more gently, seemingly from everywhere at once. Emily helped Lori bring in platters of food. Thomas poured the wine. Ben helped Declan get seated on top of a pile of books on his chair. Lori finally sat down and smiled, deeply content to see almost everyone she loved at their table.

"Welcome to our home." Brandon lifted his wine glass and tipped it towards Emily and Thomas.

"There's no place else we'd rather be," Emily said.

Lori met Emily's eyes to show appreciation for Emmy's bit of a white lie.

"Kids, it's great to have you all home," Brandon said as he made eye contact with each of the three older children. "What do you think about all this?" Brandon asked Declan sitting to his right.

"I wuv it." Declan wiggled forward on his stack of books to reach his sippy cup. He waved it in the air.

"Here, here," everyone responded, clinking glasses.

After an uproarious dinner, Fiona offered to give Declan his bath before she went to the U-District with Catherine to meet some of Catherine's college friends. Ben said he would read Declan his bedtime story. Lori and Emily found themselves at the kitchen sink.

"As much as things change," Emily laughed, "somehow you and I always wind up with kitchen patrol."

"I wouldn't have it any other way," Lori chuckled before they made short work of the pile of dirty dishes. When they were done, they found Brandon and Thomas still at the table, the fire stoked to a bright flame, enjoying more wine.

"Come join us," the men said in tandem. Thomas filled up Lori and Emily's wine glasses while the ladies sat down.

"We haven't done this in a while," Lori said.

"Not since two Christmases ago before you moved to Seattle."

"Next year, we promise to come to east," Brandon said. "Joanne is counting on it."

"It's hard to believe how much has changed, Brandon," Emily said, "since that first time you and Fiona came for Christmas dinner." Emily twirled her wine glass wistfully. "You certainly ignored my advice to keep things simple."

They all laughed, though Thomas was shaking his head.

"As if you didn't already have enough on your plate, how's the new venture going?"

"Surprisingly well," Brandon answered. "The school will be open a year in January, and we're turning a profit."

"Wow. What are you offering?"

"Several types of martial arts, depending on participants. We've got programs for both kids and adults. More of the latter than I'd expected," Brandon added. "Word's gone round the law enforcement network."

"And I've apparently got street cred with the moms. It must be my mature age." Lori laughed. "We've added more classes for women."

"Who knew you could run a business, Sis."

"I know, right? It's amazing the skills you pick up raising kids. Ben's been fantastic helping with the social media stuff, and what we don't know, we google, mostly late at night after Declan's finally fallen asleep." Lori shared a smile with Brandon. "Regular bedtime is on the agenda for the New Year."

"Lori's law degree doesn't hurt," Brandon said. "She's saved us from some rookie mistakes up against more seasoned business folks like our landlord."

"That's true, contract law comes in handy, but I'm surprised at how much I'm enjoying the rest. Maybe it's because we're doing it ourselves or because we're doing it together. I love watching Brandon with the kids." Lori grinned in his direction. "You can see their little self-esteem blossom." Lori shook her head. "I can just imagine my friends back in Maryland... They would be rolling their eyes to see me sitting behind a counter, with QuickBooks open, ordering gis and belts."

"What's a gi?" Emily asked, adding with a smirk, "And do you care what those stuffy ladies think?"

"It's the name of the uniform students wear, and no."

"That's what I thought."

"Congratulations," Thomas added. "Really, I mean it. You two have pulled off quite a feat."

~

It was certainly different having a toddler again on Christmas morning, Lori thought, groggily setting up the coffee machine. Ben kindly played with Declan in his room, but apparently, they'd been up since five-thirty. Lori moved on to making breakfast. She figured they didn't have much time before Declan insisted on opening his presents. Fiona and Catherine came downstairs soon after, pausing from their whispered secrets to fill coffee mugs in the kitchen.

"Morning, miladies." Brandon had come in from the garage and hugged each one.

"Hi, Dad."

"Morning, Brandon. Why are you so chipper?" Catherine asked.

"Do I need a reason? Brandon winked at Lori to let her know he had finished assembling Declan's new tricycle. Just then, Declan raced into the room and grabbed Brandon's legs.

"Daddy, come! Santa bwought presents."

There were so many presents to go around, thoughtful gifts for everyone, but there seemed an unspoken understanding that Christmas was for children, and all eyes were on Declan as he ripped through the wrapping paper on too many boxes. It reminded Lori of the many, many changes caused by Declan's arrival. Despite his feverish energy, and the exhaustion it wrought for the adults in his orbit, Declan brought a powerful solace to their new family. No exes to consult on parenting decisions. Ben got a brother to balance out, if still a bit lopsidedly, Fiona and Catherine's sisterhood, and all three kids shared equal status with Declan as his biological sibling and most beloved friend in the world. Most significantly to Lori's eyes, Declan seemed to draw from them all—or gift to them like a sprinkling of magic—playfulness, a certain lightness of being, joy.

Once the tricycle was revealed, after an increasingly creative array of explanations for why Santa left that present in the garage, Declan was determined that he take it for a ride. They all got dressed to head to the park. Lori was sure the older kids would want to stay in, maybe go back to sleep, but each insisted that they wanted to see Declan's first try on his new bike. Emily hung back to walk with Lori so they could talk.

"Sooooo... How are you?" Emily asked.

"Exhausted."

"You don't look exhausted."

"I keep waiting to crash," Lori said. "Having a baby at my age, moving across the country with a toddler, starting the school with Brandon, the adrenaline has got to run out at some point."

Emily laughed. "Let me know when that happens, and I'll come out to give you a hand. I can't get enough of Declan."

"He's something, isn't he?"

Emily put out her hand and stopped them. "Do you miss it at all? Your old life?"

Lori paused only for a second. "Not at all," she said. "Things had already changed irretrievably after Peter left, but my friends thought it was incredibly impulsive to have Brandon and Fiona move in. When I got pregnant, I think most of them thought I was certifiable. Poor Catherine got the brunt of it because her classmates were sharing their mothers' gossip."

"I always wondered how you could stand all that *keeping up with the Joneses*."

"I'm making new friends here, mostly other moms, a hell of

a lot younger, but no one knows the history, and no one seems to care."

Emily pulled Lori in for a hug. "I'm so proud of you, Lori."

"Back at you, Emmy." Lori was tearing up. There was so much more to say, but the rest of the gang was moving away fast. Lori grabbed Emily's hand, and they ran to catch up.

The End

About the Author

Lisa Battalia is an attorney in the field of gender equity and a writer. She is the mother of two newly launched, young adults; a lifelong east-coaster who recently launched her own new life on Whidbey Island, WA. Her other novels and short stories can be discovered at www.lisabattalia.com

Made in the USA
Middletown, DE
29 October 2023

41444209R00187